JUDGING A BOOK BY ITS COVER

Judging a Book by Its Cover
Fans, Publishers, Designers, and the Marketing of Fiction

Edited by
NICOLE MATTHEWS
Macquarie University, Australia
and
NICKIANNE MOODY
Liverpool John Moores University, UK

ASHGATE

Published by
Ashgate Publishing Limited
Gower House
Croft Road
Aldershot
Hampshire GU11 3HR
England

Ashgate Publishing Company
Suite 420
101 Cherry Street
Burlington, VT 05401-4405
USA

Ashgate website: http://www.ashgate.com

British Library Cataloguing in Publication Data
Judging a book by its cover: fans, publishers, designers, and the marketing of fiction
   1. Fiction – Marketing 2. Book covers
   I. Matthews, Nicole II. Moody, Nickianne
   381.4'5002

Library of Congress Cataloging-in-Publication Data
Judging a book by its cover: fans, publishers, designers, and the marketing of fiction/edited by Nicole Matthews and Nickianne Moody.
       p. cm.
   Includes bibliographical references and index.
   ISBN 978-0-7546-5731-6 (alk. paper)
   1. Book covers. 2. Books—Marketing. 3. Paperbacks—Marketing. 4. Literature publishing. 5. Popular literature—Publishing. 6. Authors and readers. 7. Books and reading. 8. Book industries and trade. I. Matthews, Nicole. II. Moody, Nickianne.

   Z278.J84 2007
   002.068'8—dc22

                                                                                        2007007169

ISBN 978-0-7546-5731-6

Printed and bound in Great Britain by MPG Books Ltd, Bodmin, Cornwall.

Contents

Notes on Contributors

Nicole Matthews is Lecturer in Media, Critical and Cultural Studies at Macquarie University in Sydney. Her book *Comic Politics: Gender in Hollywood Comedy after the New Right* was published by Manchester University Press in 2000, and she has also published on autobiographical television, comedy and crime genres on television and in print fiction and pedagogical issues in higher education.

Alistair McCleery is Professor of Literature and Culture at Napier University in Edinburgh; he is co-author of *An Introduction to Book History* (Routledge, 2005) and co-editor of *The Book History Reader* (rev. edn, Routledge, 2006) and *The History of the Book in Scotland* 1880–2000 (Edinburgh University Press, 2007); he also co-edits *The Bibliotheck* and has published widely on Scottish and Irish literature, particularly Neil Gunn and James Joyce.

Angus Phillips is Director of the Oxford International Centre for Publishing Studies and Head of the Publishing Department at Oxford Brookes University. He is the author, with Giles Clark, of *Inside Book Publishing* (forthcoming) and the editor, with Bill Cope, of *The Future of the Book in the Digital Age* (2006).

Val Williamson is Senior Lecturer in Media and Culture at Edge Hill University, Liverpool, and visiting lecturer in Media and Cultural Studies at Liverpool John Moores University. She researches the production and consumption of popular fiction narratives, and has contributed several chapters to edited collections. She gained her PhD with a thesis about the Liverpool saga novels and novelists between 1974 and 1997.

Nickianne Moody is the Head of Media and Cultural Studies at Liverpool John Moores University. She has edited several collections of essays including *Gendering Library History* (2000) and *Spanish Popular Fiction* (2004) and is currently writing a book on popular narrative fiction for the University of Liverpool Press.

Elizabeth Webby is Professor of Australian Literature at the University of Sydney. She was a member of the judging panel for Australia's major literary award, the Miles Franklin Prize, from 1999 to 2004.

Claire Squires is MA Programme Leader at the Oxford International Centre for Publishing Studies at Oxford Brookes University. Her books include *Marketing Literature: The Making of Contemporary Writing in Britain* (Palgrave, 2007) and *Philip Pullman, Master Storyteller* (Continuum, 2006). Previously, she worked as a publisher at Hodder Headline in London, and she continues to work for a variety of publishing companies as a freelance editorial consultant.

Susan Pickford teaches at the Centre for Book Trade Studies at the University of Paris X Nanterre and is a lecturer in Translation at the University of Paris XIII.

Gerry Carlin is Senior Lecturer in English at the University of Wolverhampton. He has published on British modernism and aspects of critical theory. With Dr Mark Jones he is currently researching 1960s popular culture.

Mark Jones is Senior Lecturer in English at the University of Wolverhampton. He has published on J.G. Ballard, horror films, popular music and pornography.

Rebecca N. Mitchell is an assistant professor of English at the University of Texas, Pan-American. She has published articles and reviews on topics ranging from composition pedagogy to Dorothy Parker, but her primary interest is nineteenth-century realism. Her current project focuses on intersubjectivity in Victorian fiction and visual arts.

Alexis Weedon is Professor of Publishing Studies at the University of Bedfordshire. She is the author of *Victorian Publishing: The Economics of Book Publishing for the Mass Market 1836–1916* (2003), with Michael Bott *British Book Trade Archives 1830–1939: A Location Register* (1996) and has been co-editor of *Convergence: the Journal of Research into New Media Technologies* since 1995. She is currently working on cross-media cooperation in Britain in the 1920s and 1930s an Arts and Humanities Research Council (AHRC) funded project.

Melissa Sky is an English instructor at Appleby College, Ontario. She has recently completed her doctoral dissertation on lesbian pulp fiction and remains an avid collector of the books.

Chris Richards is the author of *Teen Spirits: Music and Identity in Media Education* (UCL Press, 1998). He is currently writing a book about 'young adult fictions' for publication by Peter Lang (New York). He teaches in the Department of Education at London Metropolitan University.

Pamela Pears is Assistant Professor of French at Washington College in Chestertown, Maryland. She is particularly interested in Francophone women writers; her book, *Remnants of Empire in Algeria and Vietnam: Women, Words, and War*, was published by Lexington Books in 2004.

List of Figures

Introduction

Nicole Matthews
Macquarie University

This collection argues that book covers – the wrapping of image, typography and puff prose that surrounds the written contents of a book – really matter. They matter because, despite the turn of phrase that admonishes us not to do it, as readers, we do indeed judge books by their covers. Citing Borges, Gérard Genette in his pathbreaking book *Paratexts*, refers to the cover, among other elements that make texts into books, as comprising a 'vestibule' or 'threshold' 'that offers the world at large the possibility of either stepping inside or turning back' (1997, 2). Book jackets are a key conduit through which negotiations take place between authors, the book trade and readers. Each of the chapters in this book takes on and extends this idea that the material form of texts is key to understanding the way they work as part of cultural practices of reading.

Since the nineteenth century, book covers have become an essential part of the marketing of books, in different ways, for different audiences, at different times. In the early part of the nineteenth century, the beautiful covers of expensive cloth-bound volumes made them visual objects of pleasure and desirable gifts for middle-class book buyers. Later, they came to provide an entry point to the text for browsers in bookshops and (sometimes) in libraries. Perhaps more importantly, increasingly they have helped to make sure that books reach their ultimate destination with interested readers.

Since at least the middle of the twentieth century, a glimpse of the cover of a forthcoming book has played an important role in the work of publishers' travellers as they tell retailers about their house's new books. As several chapters in this collection will highlight, book covers also play a central part in defining where in a bookshop that text will be located – as science fiction or fantasy, for instance, or as children's or adults' novels. They help readers make sense of the kind of book they are about to read, giving an impression of its genre, its tone and the kind of audience it seeks. From the cheerful collection sitting on the railway bookstall, they have signalled the cultural value that should be placed on each book. Is it a serious literary tome or a paperback to be read on holiday? Has the book been nominated for or won a literary award, or been reviewed or praised by an eminent writer or a popular newspaper? Covers often relate a book to others in the same series, by the same author, set in a similar place or time, or to film and television versions of the same work. In all these ways, the materiality of the book's cover – its fonts, illustrations and layout – generates a great deal of meaning.

Clearly and definitively demarcating the material dimension of the book from the more frequently studied 'text' – reached through the 'vestibule' of the cover – would be a difficult and not necessarily fruitful task. In its focus on the materiality of books, this volume does not seek to turn away from exploring the way books come to have meanings to their browsers, buyers and readers. Rather, the chapters collected here emphasise the way narratives are understood in relation to paratextual elements of books, and especially book covers. If we are to understand how books are read, borrowed, sold, become or fail to become popular, we contend, book covers are an essential part of that process.

Why Book Covers?

Each of the chapters in this collection makes an argument for the centrality of the covers of books in shaping the response of readers, markets and booksellers to the texts within them. This connection between covers and marketing is a longstanding one. As the work of Jeffrey Groves, for example, points out, in the nineteenth century and before, the style of bindings, the fonts and cover illustration were significant in allocation of cultural value to particularly literary works and the popularity of those texts (Groves 1996; McAleer 1992, 85). From the 1820s, with the use of cloth binding, both cheaper and more easily decorated than leather, covers came to be of greater significance in book sales. Covers, even at this early stage, were sometimes used for advertising purposes (Schmoller 1974, 288; Tanselle 1971). Some dust jackets, for example, originally conceived of as entirely disposable and minimally decorated protective devices, were also used for advertising, although this is not done consistently until the 1890s (Tanselle 1971, 102–3). Importantly, where earlier styles of bindings had often resulted in the book's decoration and labelling being undertaken by readers or booksellers, case binding and the cloth cover definitively linked together book cover and publisher (Hobson cited in Mansfield 2003).

If jackets and covers had a role to play in the marketing of books during the nineteenth century, they came to have new forms of significance in the twentieth. Undoubtedly one of the critical shifts in the marketing of books in the twentieth century was the development of the paperback. As Alistair McCleery will demonstrate in the opening chapter of this collection, all of the 'defining characteristics of the twentieth-century paperback can be traced ... back to the nineteenth century and before'. Paper-covered imprints like the pioneering European publisher Tauchnitz, and its successor Albatross, were produced cheaply, with long print runs, were portable and to some extent viewed as disposable. John Mansfield has also noted the existence of precursors to the full coloured, image laden US 'pulp' paperbacks in A.C. Rowlandson's Bookstall series, produced in Australia in the first decades of the twentieth century. Nonetheless, the 'paperback revolution' as it is more generally understood originated in the 1930s, with the launch of Penguin Books in the UK in 1935 and Pocket Books in the US in 1939, coming to full cultural and economic importance by the 1960s. As Gerry Carlin and Mark Jones document in their chapter in this collection, paperbacks offered not only innovations in pricing, format, portability and audience, but also in the way in book covers linked to other cultural industries, including music and the world of visual art.

Many of the elements now central to the way in which we understand book covers to work emerge with the paperback. The now ubiquitous use of cover colour, style and image to distinguish different genres of books was comparatively slow to develop, for example, appearing, among other places, on the colour-coded, typographic covers of Albatross and then Penguin Books in the 1930s (Schmoller 1974, 293).

With the consolidation of new media industries, connections were also forged between book covers and, for example, the film industry, with star images from film versions of books appearing on the covers of 1940s paperbacks (for example McAleer 1991, 87–8). Such covers are early examples of what has come to be described in later decades as synergies.

Research with the publishing industry's trade magazines and publishers' correspondence indicates that, since at least the 1950s, covers have played a privileged role in the wider strategies for marketing books. Trade magazines, for example, feature book covers heavily. Trade publications, such as *Publishers Weekly* in the US and *The Bookseller* in the UK, and the illustrations they include, were often used by retailers to select books to stock. This was especially true of those US and Australian retailers who were remote from bigger cities and rarely met publishers' travelling salespeople. Similarly, book reviews in both the trade and the popular press, particularly in the United States, frequently use either book covers themselves or photographs or images inspired by the covers for illustration. Thus, whether or not books were even available to be bought or borrowed by readers has been dependent on publicity drawing on book covers.

At the point of sale, too, showcards, posters and streamers used in bookshops very frequently use the same images and texts as those featured on front covers. As early as the 1940s, correspondence with authors illustrates that publishers were concerned about the impact of massed displays of front covers in retailing outlets. By the 1950s bookshops were changing their displays such that the front covers, rather than simply book spines, were visible to the browser. Publishers laboured to encourage booksellers to display their publications with the appealing front covers clearly visible (Aynsley 1985, 120), and devoted significant portions of their promotion budget to shelving which would enable arresting displays of the front covers of their own publications. Competitions and other incentives were used to encourage retailers to draw on the themes of front covers for window displays at the point of sale. In the 1960s, for example, with the increasingly large number of Europeans able to travel to newly affordable holiday destinations, publishers and retailers connected the exotic destinations pictured on the covers of their books to competitions and holidays (Matthews 2006; see also Hyde 1977). Writers on blockbuster films have described this use of a central image and graphic as 'high concept' and date its use in the marketing of movies from the 1970s (Wyatt 1994). However, research drawing on publishers' archives and trade papers has indicated the centrality of the iconography of book jackets well before this time, at least in the publicity of commercially oriented book publishers.

There is a compelling argument, then, to examine in detail the covers of popular twentieth- and twenty-first century books. A consideration of popular texts, in particular, would be incomplete without a look at the covers of these widely read books and the marketing campaigns tied into them. Close scrutiny of book covers in the context of marketing of leisure reading in the twentieth century becomes all the more critical when we consider the very significant changes in publishing and bookselling during the past 50 years. The title of Laura Miller's (2006) book *Reluctant Capitalists*, like Alison Baverstock's (1993) *Are Books Different?*, points towards the anxieties over the commercial dimensions to publishing and bookselling articulated by many in the book industry in the earlier part of the twentieth century. Trade magazines in the UK, US and Australia during the 1960s, for example, frequently called for shifts to a more systematic approach to distribution, identification of demand and marketing (Coser *et al.* cited in Moran 1997, 442). While it is important not to neglect the interest of publishing companies in an earlier era in promoting and marketing their books, as I have already argued (see also Matthews 2006), in the period since the 1960s, key shifts in the publishing and bookselling industries have dramatically changed the manner in which books are marketed and promoted.

During this period, independent publishing houses have been bought up by major publishers, while particularly since the 1980s, large transnational media organisations have come to control these larger publishing groups (Moran 1997, 443; Lacy 1997, 6–7; Compaine and Gomery 2000). At the same time, bookselling in the English-speaking world has moved from an industry based around independent bookshops to one dominated by a small number of large chain stores, and increasingly, since the 1990s, chains of out-of-town superstores such as Barnes & Noble and Borders (Miller 2006).

The dominance of publishing and bookselling by multinational corporations has posed the question of whether the industry is now global in new ways, an issue which is of some significance for our concern with book covers. Many recent trends in the book industry have indeed stretched across national borders. The dominance of chain bookstores since the 1970s has been noted, for example, not just in the United States, but also in Britain and Australia (Borchardt and Kirsop 1988; Feather 1993, 178). As with an emphasis on marketing within the book industry, this globalisation of the book trade has often been understood outside the United States as American led and there is some support for this proposition (Feather 1993). Lists of bestsellers, for example, were published in the US from the late nineteenth century, but only systematically produced the UK in the late 1970s (Sutherland 1981; Feather and Reid 1995, 58). The US book clubs, which developed innovative mass marketing techniques from their inception in the 1920s, were directly emulated by Britain's WHSmith by the 1960s (Sutherland 1981, 28; Radway 1997). More recently, the collapse of the UK's Net Book Agreement in 1997 has brought Britain's bookselling environment more closely into line with that of the United States (Moody 2006). Where mass market paperbacks have long been sold in a range of non-bookshop spaces in the US and indeed in Australia, this has been much slower to develop in the UK, with the notable exception of the longstanding existence of WHSmith's railway bookstalls.

The 'Americanisation' thesis has limitations, however, in accounting for the publishing industry as indeed it has in understanding other media industries (for example Katz and Liebes 1993). For example, more recent waves of multinational takeovers have been by companies that are not necessarily based in the US (Miller 2006; Lacy 1997). As Compaine and Gomery point out, in 1999, the two companies who sold most books in the US were Bertelsmann AG, based in Germany, and Pearson plc, based in the UK (2000, 80). Not only are book publishing enterprises with a reach around the globe not all American, neither are they entirely new. British publishers, as many writers have noted, have long invested heavily in overseas markets, with significant implications for their commissioning and marketing of books (Johanson 2000; Lyons 2001; Matthews 2006).

While global processes in publishing and bookselling may not be new, it is certainly the case that concentration of ownership has allowed greater homogenization and centralisation of marketing of books, as well as an increase in spending on the marketing of books (Radway 1984, 30). Laura Miller, in her recent analysis of contemporary bookselling, notes:

> In sharp contrast to a time when booksellers had little knowledge of the universe of published books or the tastes of the book-buying public, rationalized methods, from the collection of data on books and customers to the utilization of carefully planned marketing campaigns, were now being employed by chain retailers in an attempt to make the bookselling process more predictable (Miller 2006, 53).

While the development of online bookselling seemed to promise the possibility of enhancing independent booksellers, the dominance of a few companies, particularly Amazon.com, has pushed book marketing still further in the direction of centralization (Miller 2006).

It has been argued that corporate takeovers have led to an increased emphasis by paperback houses on category or genre fiction (Radway 1984, 36), while many commentators have suggested that shifts in the industry since the 1970s have led to greater emphasis on commissioning and maximising marketing for bestsellers (for example Sutherland 1981; Feather and Reid 1995; Coser *et al.* 1982). Some have argued that the decline of independent bookshops with their emphasis on personal service has placed more emphasis on book covers, alongside shop design, in promoting sales (Mansfield 2003).

The impact of changes in the book industry on the marketing of popular fiction is explored in detail in a number of the chapters brought together here, including the work of Angus Phillips and Nickianne Moody. As Richard Todd has suggested (1996), and Claire Squires and Elizabeth Webby explore in detail in this collection, such shifts in the industry have also had a major impact on the marketing and promotion of literary and prizewinning fiction. While book sales over the internet still form only a small part of book sales and internet booksellers have not been as profitable as many may have expected in the late 1990s, they have had a significant impact on bookselling and their use of book covers needs to be discussed alongside the sales strategies used by the chains and superstores, as Alexis Weedon does in her work here. Although the much anticipated synergies between the various media investments of multinationals have proven to be less profitable than many industry figures may have expected (Sutherland 1981; Moran 1997; Miller 2006; Lacy 1997), such synergies have nonetheless had an impact on the shape of book covers and book marketing more generally, as Rebecca Mitchell considers in her work in this volume on film versions of classic books (see also Compaine and Gomery 2000).

The fact that many of the largest publishing houses and bookselling chains now operate within the context of transnational media organisations provides us with yet another reason to consider book covers not as a mere adjunct to literature, but as media. The relationship between book covers, film and television, for example, is not just important when a jacket pronounces 'Now a major motion picture'. Rather this collection will consider book jackets as closely tied to a range of media and cultural forms – from youth culture to the tourist industry, from film to the marketing of popular music. If anything, new multimedia contexts for the book highlight the visual dimensions of the book still further. If we are to make sense of new developments in the marketing of books, it is imperative that we begin to consider the book and its marketing in a visual context.

Approaches to the Book Covers: Between the History of the Book and Media Studies

The chapters in this book bring a range of new disciplinary perspectives to bear on the book cover. Part 1 of this volume, in particular, demonstrates how quantitative methods from publishing studies, case studies drawn from book history, interviews with authors and publishers, and participant observation within bookshops – these last strategies drawn from media and cultural studies – can all be used to illuminate the reception of book covers. Underlying all of the chapters in this collection, regardless of their disciplinary perspective, however, is the notion that we need to consider books not just as literary texts but as material objects, and most especially material objects with a visual dimension.

This focus on the book as a material object is a commonplace amongst scholars exploring the history of the book, such as Michelle Moylan and Lane Stiles (1996). Historians of print have not focused on fine editions or rare books (Darnton 1990, 109). Instead, they have been concerned to place books alongside other printed texts like maps, pamphlets, chapbooks and posters, many of which incorporate illustration as an integral part of their make-up. Book historians have often taken careful scrutiny of the smallest details of not simply the text contained within a book but the physical details of the paper, type, binding and notations on the book. Robert Darnton has mapped out the way in which the multifarious concerns of historians of the book might be understood as a collective enterprise. Book historians are not just interested in the economic, intellectual and cultural context of reading and the creative production of authors, but also the activities of publishers, printers, shippers, booksellers, binders and readers. Scholars of print history have thus grounded their work in discussions not of the disembodied text but of physical books, which are printed, bound, moved around and sold. Despite their different disciplinary origins, each of the chapters in *Judging a Book by Its Cover* shares these concerns with the materiality of books.

Dorothy Collin sketches out the significance of this enterprise in the context of nineteenth-century books, citing Robert Darnton's comments that 'one could learn a great deal about attitudes towards books by studying the way they are presented' (Collin 1998, 61) Similarly, contributors to Michelle Moylan and Lane Stiles's important collection on the material book have explored a range of dimensions to the physical book – including annotations, translations, types of binding and illustration. In doing so, these authors engage with the task of bringing the materiality of the book, so much a part of book history, to literary studies of the text. Gerard Curtis

(2002) in his discussion of illustration in the nineteenth-century book, *Visual Words*, has similarly placed books in the context of the graphic arts.

These innovative interventions move a material account of books into the nineteenth century. Our aim here is to extend these concerns still further – not only to popular fictions but into the twentieth and twenty-first centuries. Like Genette's book, the work of Curtis, Moylan and Stiles is centrally concerned with literary fiction, and often the canonised literary fiction of the nineteenth century. Robert Darnton has emphasised the historically specific way books are used and understood (1990, 131). Drawing on this insight and borrowing from book history's interest in neglected, popular print forms, this volume focuses on the twentieth and twenty-first centuries and on popular as well as literary fiction.

The importance of covers to the marketing of twentieth-century books is signalled by the proliferation of coffee-table books about the colourful and often controversial covers of early 'pulp' paperbacks. These book jackets, especially those of the pulp fiction of the 1930s, 40s and 50s, have drawn the eye of collectors and design historians (for example Schreuders 1981; Heller and Chwast 1995; Powers, 2001; Johnson-Woods 2004). Much of this work on book covers has been evaluative in nature. Authors like Powers have asked 'What makes a great front cover?', picking out innovators in typography and graphic design for consideration (see also Drew and Sternberger 2005). While it is very useful for marketers and designers to know what makes for a good book cover, the questions we are asking here are a little different. Rather than looking for excellence in design, one of our key concerns here is the influence book covers have on their audiences. This interest in the role of covers in shaping the distribution, reception and use of books turns us away from a central focus on books valued either for their literary greatness or covers singled out for their innovative design.

Popular fiction has often been neglected in accounts of the history of book production and reading. Nile and Walker (2001), for example, have argued that the contours of national book industries would be transformed if such books were reincorporated into the story of reading. This gap in the literature is certainly detectable in work on book covers. It is perhaps unsurprising that among monographs on book covers, the jackets of more up-market or literary publishing houses have taken centre stage. The covers of Penguin paperbacks, for instance, have been subject to some consideration, including a recent exhibition at London's Design Museum, as indeed have the covers of Faber and Faber's books (Baines, 2005; Aynsley, 1985; Faber and Faber, 1983; Wilson, 1967). Some chapters in *Judging a Book by Its Cover* do consider canonical literary texts – such as the prizewinning novels of Peter Carey and Yann Martel discussed by Elisabeth Webby and Claire Squires respectively. However, rather than selecting their case studies on the basis of the aesthetic merit of the works or covers in hand, Squires and Webby use their case studies to frame the ways in which the critical evaluation of books, and indeed their authors, are in part structured by the design and production methods used to pull together book jackets.

Our focus here is on books selected for leisure reading. This very loose definition of popular fiction serves less to definitively identify a separate group of books than as a useful corrective to the emphasis in existing published work on book covers on quality design and literary publishing houses. By paying close attention to popular fiction, this collection thus takes as a starting point not the interests of the critic or the design historian but the perspective of the reader and the book trade.

The role of the book as visual medium in the marketing, selection and digestion of contemporary popular texts is often little better understood than the meanings of the physical book to previous generations of readers. This is despite the fact that, in trying to make sense of the marketing and consumption of contemporary books, a range of research methods, including interviews and participant observation, are available that simply aren't at hand for those investigating, for instance, the Victorian novel. One challenge in trying to understand the impact of the marketing of books is the difficulty of obtaining even quite recent marketing material. Publicity materials and advertising – especially ephemera such as showcards and streamers for booksellers' windows and shelves, posters appearing on buses, radio and television advertisements – are often inadequately archived and indexed, even within collections of publishers' correspondence and business records. The marketing of books as a topic falls awkwardly between advertising, the history of the book and literary studies, and as such is poorly documented in archives and collections concerned with each of these themes.

This invisibility of book promotion can be partly attributed to the perception of the book trade as less commercial than other industries. Joe Moran describes this view as 'the survival within many houses of the genteel image of the 'gentleman-publisher' supposedly working for love of literature rather than mere financial gain' (1997, 442). As Moran comments, this perspective was linked to an implicit hierarchy that considers the most prestigious parts of publishing as those most apparently separate from commerce. Perhaps as a consequence of this view, publishers' archives, for instance, often have extensive documentation of author correspondence but little record of the campaigns used to promote and sell books. As Robert Darnton has trenchantly observed 'unfortunately ... publishers usually treat their archives as garbage. Although they save the occasional letter from a famous author, they throw away the account books and commercial correspondence' (1990, 127; see also Schreuders 1981, 3). Book jackets, too, have often been seen as ephemeral marketing devices, to be discarded when a hardcover was placed in a library. Indeed, as Randy Silverman (1999) has argued, the collections policy of many libraries even now frequently involves discarding the covers of books, at great loss to the collections concerned. Despite these collection policies, book covers are often one of the few accessible artefacts available to document the marketing of books after the event.

The (inter)disciplines of media, communication and cultural studies are most germane in taking a sustained examination of the mass-circulation book covers of this period. Contemporary and popular forms have been central to its concerns. However, media, communication and cultural studies have been inclined to neglect books, seeing them not as media forms but as literary texts, and thus the province of other disciplines. Despite the existing work on individual publishers within the field of book history, Lorimer and Scannell commented in 1993 that 'publishing is perhaps the most neglected area of English language communication studies' (1993 163; see also Luey 1997) and little has changed within the disciplines of media and communication studies since that time.

We will argue here that books should be considered not just as literary texts but as visual media, to be considered alongside television and film as well as other forms of advertising. However, this visual element of the book has rarely been discussed in relation to twentieth-century publishing. Even Genette, who in *Paratexts* considers a number of aspects of the materiality of the book – prefaces, introductions, colophons and even covers – gives much less attention to the elements of the paratext which draw on the visual. Illustrations, covers and frontispieces, he comments, 'exceed … the means of a plain "literary person"' (1997, 406). Taking Genette's hint here, many chapters in this book will bring the tools and ideas of disciplines like media studies to bear on this crucial entry point to the book.

Arguments and Issues: An Outline of the Book

All of the chapters in this collection share a focus on popular twentieth-century fiction and a concern with the material and visual dimensions to book jackets. In addition, however, a number of shared themes, each central to contemporary debates around books, media and marketing, bring together the chapters collected here. Much of the work here addresses the interaction between culture and commerce. A number of chapters consider the meanings of genre and the ways in which book covers help form and reflect those genres. Many of the chapters of this book also address the way that book marketing is shaped by and plays out cultural practices around individual and national identities. However, I would like to focus here on four thematic clusters around which the book itself has been organised.

The first part of the book will introduce a range of methods for exploring book covers and, more broadly, book marketing. This section demonstrates the value of a range of sources in understanding the origins and meanings of book covers, including insights from editors, marketers, designers, bookshop staff, authors and fans. Chapters within the section map the way in which the characteristic methods and research questions of different disciplines – including book history, communications, design, literary and media studies – can be used to understand book covers and book marketing. Alistair McCleery demonstrates the contribution of historical methods and context to an understanding of twentieth-century book covers through an exploration of the influence of Tauschnitz and Albatross imprints on the emergence of the famous Penguin paperbacks. Angus Phillips, in contrast, uses the tools of marketing and publishing studies to investigate the way in which covers reflect the marketing strategy behind each book's publications. Val Williamson brings together accounts by publishers, authors and fans in her examination of the covers of saga fiction. Nickianne Moody, also working from within media and cultural studies, uses participant observation as a strategy to analyse the shifting location of genre fiction within the bookshop. Each of these chapters shows how particular research methods can be used to make sense of the meanings of book jackets to their various producers and users.

The second section of the collection returns to the central concerns of existing writing on books covers, with a twist. While the chapters in this collection set aside questions of the design excellence or otherwise of book jackets, notions of cultural value are in fact central to the way in which readers select and consume popular literature, as our title suggests. Book jackets impact on the overall sales of books, but also on the way in which they and their authors are valued. Elizabeth Webby analyses the way book packaging shapes the views of cultural gate keepers and opinion formers, in her insider's discussion of whether the quality of presentation or production values in the making of books affect the judges of literary prizes. Such opinion formers are important, as Claire Squires goes on to show, because of the way these markers of literary value shape readers and directly affect book sales. Squires investigates the relationship between cultural value, book jackets and book awards by exploring the way that the awarding of book prizes comes to situate books' authors in hierarchies of cultural value – via the book cover. Susan Pickford provides a detailed case study of that underexplored textual dimension to books, the blurb. Her focus, not on the more conventional use of positive write-ups but on the negative blurb, tests the limits of the ways that cultural value can be generated.

These accounts of the evolution of cultural worth of books consider the relation between book covers themselves and surrounding media forms, especially the press. However the chapters in the third section of the book take a more sustained look at the relationship between book marketing and surrounding cultural industries. Gerry Carlin and Mark Jones begin by tracing the way paperback covers of the 1960s forged a close connection between book marketing and popular music. Rebecca Mitchell similarly explores intertextuality in the promotion of books, this time by focussing on the way cover art from film adaptations of novels shapes the responses of readers. Finally Alexis Weedon explores the crossover in the use of the book cover image from the dust jacket to the online bookstore. She explores the way in which front cover images might work as a key marketing device as part of internet browsing.

In some senses, a test of the importance of the jacket to the marketing of books is the way in which the repackaging of books impacts on the kinds of readers they reach and the way in which they are valued. Genette notes the particular centrality of the paratext to this process. He comments 'Being immutable, the text itself is incapable of adapting to change in its public in space and over time. The paratext – more flexible, more versatile … is, as it were, an instrument of adaptation' (1997, 408). In the final section of this volume, contributing authors consider four different ways in which fictions have been adapted or 'translated' for different audiences – audiences varying along the lines of age, sexuality, nationality, gender and taste.

Melissa Sky's chapter on lesbian pulp fiction considers the way in which these pulps were transformed through reissues by different publishing houses during a period of over 40 years. These books were originally published as sexploitation novels for heterosexual men, but were also read by a small but loyal lesbian audience. Sky traces the shifts in the way the books were packaged into the 1980s Naiad reprints and their reflection of second-wave feminist ideology, and finally to the Cleis reprints, holding the status of postmodernist camp. Chris Richards's work on Francesca Lia Block considers the way in which this popular author's Weetzie Bat novels, originally published for 'young adults', were then reissued in a new way, referencing youth culture as lifestyle. In the final essay in the collection, Pamela Pears considers the way in which images of Algerian women have been used to market books by such authors, considering in particular the contradictions between the images selected for front and back covers and the self-representations of Algerian female writers themselves.

Judging a Book by Its Cover, then, demonstrates the way in which some of the key debates within contemporary marketing, literary, publishing and media studies can be opened up through a sustained examination of the materiality of the popular book. Questions of reception, of cultural value, of synergy and globalisation; questions about the way identity categories such as sexuality and ethnicity inflect meaning; about para-, epi- and intertextuality; about the relationship between industry, audience and text – each of these debates is articulated across the surface of the book jacket. The apparent ephemerality of book covers offers a new dimension to the analysis of media and another way of exploring the materiality of the book.

PART 1
Approaches to the Book Cover

Chapter 1

The Paperback Evolution:
Tauchnitz, Albatross and Penguin

Alistair McCleery
Napier University

If you really like it you can have the rights,
It could make a million for you overnight.
If you must return it, you can send it here
But I need a break and I want to be a paperback writer
Lennon and McCartney, 'Paperback Writer', *Revolver* (1966).

When the Beatles sang these words from 'Paperback Writer' (and John Lennon was, indeed, published by Penguin), this aspiration caught the mood of a period in the 1960s when the paperback was both a key vehicle for cultural transmission and an aesthetic object in itself. In hindsight, the paperback may then have been at the height of both its influence and its popularity. 'When *Paperbacks in Print* was first published in May 1960, as a "reference catalogue" of paperbacks on sale in Britain, it listed as many as 5,866 titles; and by June 1962 this total had risen to 9,578 – an increase of 65 per cent' (Findlater 1966, 12). This recapitulated an earlier period of expansion in the USA where 3 million paperbacks had been produced in 1939 but 214 million in 1950 (Pryce-Jones 1952, 18). The UK and the USA had both seen the scope and range of paperback publishing extend: in the former case, beyond reprints to original work in both fiction and non-fiction and, in the latter, beyond genre fiction to literary fiction and non-fiction. This convergence between the two largest English-language publishing countries was apparent also in paperback design. The UK production of paperbacks began in a European tradition of typographical covers, showing restraint and austerity in their functionality, while the US production of paperbacks, faced with competition from magazines for the same retail space in drugstores and markets, adopted the vivid colours and illustrations on the covers of these rivals to create a more flamboyant and exuberant tradition. This essay follows in detail the development of the European tradition through Tauchnitz and Albatross to Penguin. In the UK in the 1960s the Europeans assimilated the US tradition, rather slavishly in its initial use by Pan and other paperback houses, and rather tentatively by Penguin in the early years of the decade. From that imitation and hesitation emerged a creative and innovative flowering of UK paperback cover design, particularly in Penguin books from 1965 through to the end of the decade.

All of the defining characteristics of the twentieth-century paperback can be traced, however, back to the nineteenth century and before: the binding and cover material, the convenient size and the long print run. In Europe the development of the form had been closely linked to function. If books were to be rebound by their owners to create a more permanent and uniform library, then the publishers need only issue them in inexpensive covers. If books were regarded by their owners as relatively disposable upon reading, after whiling away the time on a railway journey or on holiday, for example, then the publishers need only issue them in inexpensive covers. If books were to be carried around a great deal, on a train or to the salon of a spa hotel, then publishers needed to produce them in conveniently portable sizes and weights. If publishers regarded their mission as the democratisation of knowledge through provision of good books at low prices, then they could reduce costs by reprinting, in long runs and in uniform formats, titles that had already proven themselves in the marketplace or critical cockpit. Such books, moreover, would sell through that pre-existing reputation (of title or author) rather than the visual appeal of the cover. Mass-market consumption did not demand self-advertisement of the individual title but it did require recognition of and confidence in the publisher as brand.

The 'Universal-Bibliothek' of Reclam in Germany, for example, comprises a large series of reprints of well-known authors at low prices that began with a liberalisation of German copyright law in 1867. The small format paperbacks (152 × 95.25 mm), produced using stereotypes, were sold initially for 20 pfennigs in a standard art nouveau paper cover in red with a rose logo. In the 1920s the cover design became more self-consciously typographic while the immediate post World War II volumes adopted calligraphic covers with the occasional line drawing. The more familiar undecorated, yellow covers were introduced in 1970. The standardisation of the Universal-Bibliothek lent itself in 1912 to the introduction of book-vending slot machines of which there were 2,000 by 1917, chiefly at railway stations, mainline and branch, as Reclam exploited a hunger for self-education and a renewed cultural nationalism.

That same market was sought by 'Die Insel-Bücherei', founded in 1912 by Insel Verlag in Leipzig. Insel, however, introduced higher production values, in design, typography and materials, to its books than Reclam. Consequently, its hardcover titles, though produced in print runs of 10,000 to 30,000, sold initially at 50 pfennigs, more than double the price of rivals in the Universal-Bibliothek. That margin permitted the use of illustrations within the books. Boccaccio's *Decameron*, published in 1912, contained seven contemporary woodcuts while the *Bilder des Todes* of 1917 was a vehicle for Holbein's illustrations – although it retained a typographical cover enhanced only by the use of rules. The standard Insel-Bücherei covers (until 1961) are decorative, consisting of abstract or semi-figurative patterns (resembling wallpaper) with a label, stuck on or printed, that gives author, title and series data in the same Gothic typeface in which the text of all the books is printed. These patterns, a concept later copied by Penguin for its Penguin Poets (from 1941), King Penguin (from 1943) and Penguin Scores (from 1949) series, generally bear no relation to the nature of the title they distinguish: an edition of Beethoven's letters is covered in a faux-Japanese design of a twig falling into a stream and a row of grass or bamboo set in alternate squares, while the woodcuts of Jost Amman are covered by a repeated flower design set against a tweed rug. What is important is that the cover pattern, no matter its precise nature, makes these volumes instantly identifiable as belonging to the Insel-Bücherei. However, the Insel books were not paperbacks. Only the exigencies of wartime restrictions in 1941 led to the adoption of paper covers; and the familiar board covers were reintroduced in 1951 by the

Figure 1.1 *Das Ständebuch, 114 Holzschnitte von Jost Amman mit Reimen von Hans Sachs* Insel-Bücherei Nr. 133 (nd)

West German Insel Verlag in Frankfurt (an East German Insel Verlag survived in Leipzig). Despite their low price, the numbered volumes of the Insel-Bücherei were intended to be collected and retained by their owners; the attractive covers with their patterned papers promoted not the individual book but the brand.

Tauchnitz Editions in Leipzig was another such brand and, because it published in English, it became more influential in the development of the paperback and its design in the UK. Tauchnitz had established in the mid-nineteenth century a confident reputation for its reprints of British and American authors in an English-language paperback series not for sale in the UK for copyright reasons. From 1841 to 1937 it issued some 5,000 titles, selling some 60 million copies in total, becoming 'the cherished companion of English-speaking travellers in central Europe and the royal road for foreign students to the treasures of English and American literature' (Steinberg 1955, 354). All the great figures of English literature, particularly its Victorian novelists, were to be found in its easily recognisable but undistinguished format. Hans Schmoller remarked: 'Up to about 1930 there was nothing to commend the books typographically: they were squat volumes, rather too wide for the coat pocket, and set in small type with too many words per line to make for easy reading. The covers were white and almost identical with feeble title-pages' (Schmoller 1953, 37). The fortunes of the company had begun to decline in the decade before 1930. That Tauchnitz had not earlier collapsed altogether during World War I and its immediate aftermath was due to the endeavours of its then Director, Curt Otto. However, its bare survival, without the necessary major restructuring in response to wartime conditions, specifically the closure of markets and lack of materials, particularly paper, left it in a weakened state to face the problems of hyperinflation that seized Germany until the introduction of the Reichsmark in 1924. The decision of the Society of Authors, initiated by John Galsworthy, to recommend to British writers (and agents) a change in contractual practice from concurrent UK and Tauchnitz publication to a delay of one year between former and latter compounded the problems of the publisher from 1926 onwards. Curt Otto died in July 1929 and achieved on his demise an apotheosis in the eyes of the Board of Directors. Tauchnitz Editions was reorganised, in that November, as a private limited company with all the shares held exclusively by the direct descendants of the first Baron Tauchnitz. Dr Hans Otto, brother of Curt, became the Chairman of the Board. Max Christian Wegner, formerly at Insel-Verlag, was appointed as 'Geschäftsführer', or manager-in-chief, with day-to-day responsibilities for the ailing firm but answering to a conservative Board very conscious of the company's traditions and glorious past. His appointment accounts for Schmoller's design 'watershed' of 1930, as Wegner set out to modernise Tauchnitz and place it upon a more secure footing.

Herbert Kästner characterised the mission of Wegner's training ground, Insel, as the provision of quality books in volume at relatively low prices (Kästner 1987, v). This goal emanated from the democratic ideals of its founder, Anton Kippenberg; Wegner was Kippenberg's nephew and shared those ideals. He wrote an afterword to Aurbacher's *Die Abenteuer von den sieben Schwaben* published by Insel in 1919; in 1924 he was one of a number of translators of the novels of Balzac's *La Comédie Humaine* issued by Insel in ten volumes; and in that same year he was responsible for the production of a catalogue of all Insel's titles since 1899. Wegner was a man of learning and cultural refinement; the high production values and aesthetic appeal of the Insel volumes reflected his own preferences. Wegner was 'Prokurist', or a company officer with statutory authority, at Insel before leaving to take over at Tauchnitz; he would have been acutely aware of the commercial need to integrate those production values with effective marketing of the brand. The decisions he began to implement at Tauchnitz from late 1929 until his departure in 1931 stemmed from that need, those preferences and those ideals.

Wegner introduced a coloured band to the Tauchnitz volumes to distinguish genres. 'A paper band, coloured to express the various types of works published, encircles each book; bearing a short description of the contents, it serves as an aid to booksellers and purchasers' (*Tauchnitz Edition* 1932, 13). He indicated the breadth of the Tauchnitz library by changing the half-title to 'Collection of British and American Authors'. However, it was not so much the design changes Wegner brought about as those he made to the company's publishing operation that led to his rupture with Tauchnitz. The odds were stacked against him: the nature of the literary market and of publishing practice, not least the delay initiated by the Society of Authors and the increasing role of literary agents, had changed since the company's heyday without the Board fully comprehending it. Where Wegner did attempt to rejuvenate the Tauchnitz list, he was frustrated by the Board. As Peter Mayer was to do when he took over the cultural icon of Penguin Books in 1978, Wegner set out to restore the financial health of Tauchnitz by cutting back on the size of the backlist kept in print. The general economic climate in 1929 militated against the tying up of company assets as stock in its warehouse. Wegner also took what would now appear to publishers the sensible step of divorcing the editorial and marketing aspects of Tauchnitz books from their production by employing two other Leipzig printers (and a third when necessary in Budapest) in order to secure the best price – eventually, one of these, Brandstetter, was to predominate to the point of monopoly. No doubt, if he had continued at Tauchnitz, Wegner would have pursued further reforms including the modernisation of the cover design and typography. It was not to be – at least, for the time being. Wegner's surgery, however necessary, proved anathema to the Board and he was forced out of the company by mid-1931. Tauchnitz lost its dynamic Geschäftsführer.

Wegner's ideas, experience and drive were put to new use in the creation of the Albatross Press with John Holroyd Reece in Paris. Curtis Brown, the literary agent, claimed the role of matchmaker.

> [Wegner] told me he would like to start a rival to Tauchnitz, which he believed had held a monopoly of Continental publishing in English cheap editions quite long enough, and that he was looking for someone to back him. Not long afterwards, that urbane and picturesque international, John Holroyd Reece turned up in my office, with the same sort of scheme Wegner had… I brought Reece and Wegner together, and they clicked at once. Through our Paris manager, who was a friend of both, they were brought into touch with a famous British financier, who put up the money, although he preferred to keep in the background (Brown 1935, 178).

The financier was Sir Edmund Davis, the Jewish 'Randlord' (and his ethnicity is not incidental), who shared with Holroyd Reece a longstanding interest in the collection of art and antiques. Where the millionaire was able to indulge this through the purchase of a large number of artworks, the publisher had channelled his enthusiasm through the establishment of Les Editions du Pégase/the Pegasus Press in 1927, with the support of the American typographer Frederick Warde. Holroyd Reece had begun his career in publishing with Ernest Benn, through which he had made a wide range of contacts, and in 1928 he had undertaken the Paris publication of Radclyffe Hall's *The Well of Loneliness* on behalf of Jonathan Cape. Under the imprint of the Pegasus Press, however, Holroyd Reece chiefly published expensively produced fine art books and material on typography and graphic design in small print runs. Through Warde, he met Stanley Morison, the noted typographer and designer, and then Hans Mardersteig, who played the major role in designing the modern paperback that Wegner had been frustrated in developing at Tauchnitz. Albatross Verlag was registered at the Leipzig 'Handelsregister' (register of businesses) on 26 November 1931, with Wegner named as 'Geschäftsführer'; he began signing contracts on behalf of Albatross that very month. The Board of Directors of Albatross included William and Ian Collins; its Chairman was Arnoldo Mondadori. Albatross was owned by the 'Publishing Holding Company', registered in Luxembourg and wholly owned by Davis.

These cast members interacted to create the template of the modern European paperback and to base its typographical design on printing practice rather than illustration. The leading actor was Hans Mardersteig, himself a typographer and printer. Mardersteig had begun his career working for Kurt Wolff in Leipzig from 1917, but left for health reasons when the latter enterprise moved to Munich in 1919. Mardersteig set up his own hand press, the Officina Bodoni, at Montagnola di Lugano in Switzerland in 1922, where he produced three books for the Pegasus Press in 1927, 1928 and 1930 that were edited or co-authored by Stanley Morison. Mardersteig printed a limited edition in 1926 of an Italian translation, *Dell'Arte della Stampa*, of Charles Ricketts's 'A Defence of the Revival of Printing' (1899). (Ricketts, in turn, was the principal adviser to Sir Edmund Davis in his acquisition of the large art collection housed until the late 1930s at his home, Chilham Castle in Kent; this collection, including some 170 oils, 100 drawings and 30 sculptures, reflected Ricketts's taste as much as that of Davis and his wife in its focus upon modern artists and prints).

In 1926 Arnoldo Mondadori encouraged Mardersteig to enter an Italian national competition to produce the collected works of d'Annunzio; Mardersteig won and moved the Officina Bodoni to Verona within the Mondadori printing works. This was necessary to fulfil the conditions of the competition: not only was a limited hand-set and printed edition of 209 copies of each of 49 volumes on Imperial Japanese *velina* to be produced but a further 2,501 copies of each volume were to be machine-printed on hand-made Fabriano paper. (The Italian state spared no expense for its national poet). Through publication of these volumes from 1927 to 1936, Mardersteig demonstrated the successful marriage of high craftsmanship in typography and graphic design with modern production methods. Indeed, he was invited by Collins to Glasgow in 1934, at the suggestion of John Holroyd Reece, to inspect and provide recommendations for the improvement of the design and production of its titles. The Crime Club and Mystery Club titles published by Collins in the UK represented a key component of the Albatross list and Mardersteig was able to make direct, unfavourable comparisons with the typography and printing of other Albatross titles produced in Leipzig. (Early Albatross titles had been printed by Mondadori in Verona.) Mardersteig also had a hand in the production in the immediate post-World War II period of the Biblioteca Moderna Mondadori of Italian reprints.

Much of Mardersteig's authority in undertaking this later work derived from his design for the Albatross Modern Continental Library in 1931. He chose for the Albatross books the more attractive (than Reclam or Tauchnitz) size of 181 × 112 mm that matches the 'Golden Mean' of 1.62 and offers a good line length in terms both of reading and of the compactness of the book. The cover was typographical, adorned only by the black and white logo of the albatross with its long wings outstretched in an embodiment of the elegance of the whole design. The cover also contained the standard title, author and publisher details supplemented by the copyright notice – 'not to be introduced into the British Empire or the USA' – and surrounded by 'The Albatross Modern Continental Library: Paris: Hamburg: Milano' stressing its pan-European ambitions. 'To this day it forms perhaps, from the point of view of design, the pinnacle among paper-covered books' (Schmoller 1953, 38). Where Tauchnitz had introduced, under Wegner's management, a coloured band to indicate genre, Albatross, under Wegner's management, used the colour-coding of its covers: red for stories of adventure and crime; blue for love stories; green for stories of travel and foreign peoples; purple for biographies and historical novels; yellow for psychological novels and essays; and orange for tales and short stories, humorous and satirical works. (Silver was later used for volumes of special merit or length, such as *The Albatross Book of Living Verse*, issued in 1933). The commercial success of Albatross books from 1932 onwards was in no small part due to the freshness and modernity of their appearance. Its visual restraint underlined the seriousness and quality of their contents. Both aspects – appearance and contents – placed Albatross ahead of its major commercial rival in the marketplace, Tauchnitz. Wyndham Lewis, for example, wrote to Stuart Gilbert in 1934 after he had visited Berlin:'The *Albatross* editions I saw everywhere' (Lewis to Gilbert 19 June 1934).

From Wegner's departure in 1931, the condition of Tauchnitz had continued to decline, not least because of this competition from the energetic and youthful-seeming Albatross, until in mid-1934 it was put up for sale. Karl Pressler recounts, via Wolfgang Brockhaus of the august and eponymous German publishing house, the rumour circulating in Leipzig at that time that Tauchnitz was to be bought by a English publishing house, that is, Albatross, owned by a Jewish tycoon, that is, Sir Edmund Davis (Pressler 1985, A5). Pressler also paraphrases the question on many people's lips: was the old German company of Baron Tauchnitz to fall into the hands of a Jew – in only the second year of National Socialist government? From 1933 Nazi policy had been directed towards control of the media; publishing and the book trade were a priority for reorganisation. The Börsenverein lost its independence and purpose; the German book trade was controlled by the Reichsschrifttumskammer and its subsidiary the Gruppe Buchhandel; and a process of Aryanisation was implemented in Jewish-owned or managed businesses. Whether the takeover by Brandstetter, the printing company producing by then most of the Tauchnitz titles, represented an attempt to avoid Jewish ownership or forestall Nazi intervention or both, it was clear that Tauchnitz needed a more assured editorial management than its new owners could provide. Wegner had maintained his links with Brandstetter, the company he had first brought in to print Tauchnitz and then also Albatross; he, in association with Holroyd Reece, had the range of contacts and experience necessary if the dying Tauchnitz were to be at all resuscitated.

On 1 September 1934, Max Christian Wegner resumed vicarious responsibility for the company he had attempted to save, if not for the intransigence of its then Board of Directors, four years previously. He did this through the agency of Albatross, itself both a rival to Tauchnitz and a model of what a modernised firm could do. Albatross assumed editorial control of Tauchnitz while Brandstetter oversaw production. Wegner was now free to continue the process of modernisation he had been thwarted in previously. During the five years of stewardship by Albatross, the number of Tauchnitz titles published mounted steadily – 37 in 1934/35, 39 in 1935/36, 42 in 1936/37, 46 in 1937/38 – until 1938/39 when only 29 were issued in a worsening German (and international) situation.

By 1936 other, more overt, positive benefits from the Albatross stewardship of Tauchnitz could be remarked: the original, rather squat format of the Tauchnitz editions, 164 × 118 mm, was replaced by the more elegant Albatross; the books were made more comfortable to read by a change to Monotype fonts – Garamond, Baskerville, Poliphilus and Bembo; the shorter line length resulting from both new format and typeface facilitated legibility; and a coloured cover, derived also from the Albatross precedent and using the same coding, enabled easy identification by the reader in a rush. The paper band was abandoned. The short description of the book originally printed on the band now appeared in three languages – English, French and German – on the cover. The appearance of the two paperback series was harmonised, with resultant economies of scale in production, distribution and display, the only distinguishing device being the monogram 'T' for the Tauchnitz titles (designed by the eminent British engraver and typographer, Reynolds Stone, at Holroyd Reece's request) instead of Mardersteig's bird logo for the Albatross. The harmony and success were not to last: World War II changed Europe forever and the conditions pre-war could not be recreated. In particular, an aggressive UK paperback house, in the benign form of a penguin, enhanced by its successes during the war, began to dominate the English-language market on the Continent.

Allen Lane in 1935 introduced this paperback imprint that was to overshadow all these predecessors, Penguin Books. The inspirations for this were both sociological, the quest for a new constituency of readers, and commercial, the successful precedent provided by Albatross since 1932. In September 1934, Allen Lane was a participant in a weekend conference on 'The New Reading Public' held at Ripon Hall, Oxford, attended by some fifty publishers and booksellers, and initiated by the then presidents of the Publishers' Association and the Associated Booksellers. The conference was itself prompted by an article by Philip Unwin in *The Bookseller*. Unwin draws an analogy with the creation of a new newspaper reading public at the end of the nineteenth century and asks where the equivalent of Northcliffe and his papers are in the booktrade. 'Another new reading public has arisen, but the Book Trade has not yet been able to secure its support as did newspaper proprietors a generation ago' (Unwin 1934, 184). He highlights the growth of public libraries and in their use, the buoyancy of the market for non-fiction material made accessible to non-specialist readers, and the large audience for 'talks' on the BBC (radio). The potential of this market was not being exploited by publishers. Unwin argues that 'there is nothing wrong with either the quality or price of the product which the book trade offers to the wide public' and illustrates this with the examples of Everyman's Library and the Home University Library (184). For Unwin, the fault lay with booksellers who had not made their shops sufficiently attractive or indeed made much effort to attract 'the new reading public'. A general awareness of the existence of a reading public at the cheaper end of the market was articulated at the resulting conference, but few, if any, conclusions were drawn as to the best methods of reaching that market.

Others had tried. In fact, the market was full of rival sets of cheap reprints and the struggle for dominance was intense. 'The sixpenny paper-covered book is at least three-quarters of a century old', wrote Harold Raymond (1938, 23). Collins had entered the field at the beginning of April 1934 with the announcement of a new series of reprints priced at sevenpence per volume. The titles included Somerset Maugham's *The Painted Veil* (about to be released as a film starring Greta Garbo), several detective novels by Agatha Christie, Edgar Wallace, Freeman Wills Croft and Philip Macdonald, and Rose Macauley's *Staying with Relations*. Collins was followed by Hutchinson in May 1934 but the latter quickly withdrew when faced with hostility from booksellers concerned about shrinking margins on low-priced titles and declining sales of higher-priced editions. This hostility, based on the book trade's innate conservatism, re-emerged on the issue of the first Penguins. Harold Raymond crystallised the doubts and fears of the book trade related to Penguin in particular and cheap reprints in general. The detractors of Penguins are characterised as 'open-minded critics who are anxiously wondering whether the booktrade can afford to cut its profits to the fine point which a sixpenny novel nowadays involves' (Raymond 1938, 24).

> Many booksellers report that the sales of three-and-sixpenny, half-crown and florin reprints have shown a disastrous decrease during the last few years. Can the sale of Penguins at a gross profit of twopence a copy possibly replace that sale? The question also arises to what extent Penguins are finding an extra market … In other words, is the converted public spending more or less on books as a result of Penguins? (24)

Raymond concluded his jeremiad:

> These prognostications may appear to be unduly alarmist, but to any one who feels that the stability of our trade and a reasonable remuneration for author, publisher, and bookseller can only be preserved by maintaining a fairly high initial price for general literature and avoiding too rapid and too steep a reduction in price in a subsequent cheap edition, the advent of the Penguins must appear to be a veritable bomb-shell (27).

The Collins and Hutchinson sevenpenny editions were cloth-bound, but sixpenny novels in paper covers already existed in editions of genre fiction and the (non-copyright) classics. Pearson was selling in July 1936, one year after the first Penguins, a sixpenny series, in striking orange and black covers, of genre novels including detective, western, romance and adventure by less well-known authors such as Harold Ward, Victoria Cross and Ernest Goodwin. Newnes was also advertising sixpenny phrasebooks in the 'What You Want to Say and How to Say It' series in a similar format. The Martyn sixpenny library for children, 'beautifully printed on good paper complete with three colour jacket', offered reliable titles such as *The Coral Island*, *Black Beauty*, *Little Women* and *The Water Babies*. Collins persisted in the battle and by February 1935 was advertising 19 titles in its sevenpenny library, including 12 available in a box or case for seven shillings, 'less than the price of one 7/6 Novel' as the advertising copy read. The promotional material was aimed at both booksellers and private, often twopenny, libraries, 'Both Lend and Sell!' At the same time, Collins was also selling over 140 titles, with jackets and full-cloth bindings, in its one-shilling novel series. This latter reprint venture included all of the authors, and some of the titles, issued in the sevenpenny format.

The real commercial inspiration for Lane's venture was to be found in the success of Albatross books. By the time the first Penguins appeared, the Albatross Modern Continental Library had reached volume 272 (Sinclair Lewis, *Elmer Gantry*). Allen Lane entered into discussions with John Holroyd Reece in 1934 about a collaboration between Albatross and the Bodley Head, of which Lane was then managing director (confidential memo, 1934). These discussions included the setting up of what was

Figure 1.2 Sinclair Lewis, *Mantrap*, The Albatross Modern Continental Library no. 3 (1932); and André Maurois, *Ariel*, Penguin Books no.1 (1935)

to be called the 'Modern Library' in the UK on Albatross lines, co-publishing with Albatross which would continue to handle continental sales from sheets supplied by Lane. This is the system that was later used for the issuing of Collins Crime and Mystery Club novels as Albatross paperbacks, although, in that case, the binding was also carried out in Glasgow. Albatross was also to advise Lane on the production details necessary to obtain the optimum economies of scale within such an operation. The key to the low prices of paperbacks lay not in the nature of the binding but in the cost reduction obtained through the economies of scale of a long print run across which fixed costs could be spread. From this proposed use of common printed sheets, as well as the later Collins initiative, it is clear that the planned UK Modern Library would have adopted the same format as the Albatross Modern Continental Library and there is every reason to believe, given the part that the freshness of the cover design had played in the latter's success, that a similar typographical cover would have been adopted. In other words, this would have been a British Albatross with perhaps a different avian imprint and logo.

That the arrangement with Albatross did not come to commercial fruition was a result of difficulties in copyright licensing and of the precarious finances of the Bodley Head. The existing licences held by Albatross were, of course, solely for the continent of Europe; its books were not to be sold or circulated in the UK or USA as other publishers held the English-language rights there. It will be clear from discussion below that these publishers were very reluctant to cede any of those rights. Moreover, in 1934 the Bodley Head was in a poor financial state of health and in no state to enter into a collaborative agreement with Albatross. By the end of June of that year, the firm was carrying a cumulative deficit on its Profit and Loss Account of £42,367.18.5; by the end of June 1935, a further loss for the year of £4,968.18.11 had to be added to that.

This is the context out of which the Albatross collaboration came to nought. This is the context out of which his fellow directors refused Allen Lane the authority to go ahead, independently of Albatross, to create Penguin Books as an imprint of the Bodley Head, regarding it as a 'make-or-break' enterprise more likely to shatter the already fragile company. This is the context out of which Allen Lane, his confidence buoyed by the Albatross precedent, went ahead anyway to found Penguin Books as a separate company – although the first 80 Penguin titles also carried the Bodley Head imprint on their covers – launched on his personal security and those of his two brothers. None of them were at that time wealthy, and what they owned they stood to lose if Penguin failed. It was an outstanding success. Twelve months after its first publications, Penguin was making as much as the Bodley Head was losing. The latter's deficit had increased to £8,700 by the end of June 1936. Penguin, on the other hand, had made a net profit of £4,500 in its first nine months of operation in addition to the £1,000 Allen Lane had drawn for himself. The Bodley Head went into receivership – partly to avoid its losses killing Penguin. The latter remained an independent entity wholly owned by Lane and his two brothers; it had become a private limited company in early 1936. It had a nominal share capital of £100 and its initial operations were underpinned by a bank overdraft of just over £7,000 secured on the personal assets of the three Lane brothers.

The planning for the launch of Penguins, and the need to focus upon the marketing of the brand, through bookshops and other retail outlets, must have been underpinned by a short news item on the front page of *The Bookseller* of 17 April 1935. Using information taken from the US-based *Publishers Weekly*, the article confirmed, and highlighted in its subhead, that reprint publishers in the USA reached 60 per cent of the total population, 'a far greater percentage than that reached by the publishers of original editions', and were therefore both creating a new reading public as well as servicing the existing one. Moreover, 'the sale of reprints [was] to a large extent left to the department and drug stores', who did not necessarily know what the books contained but did know how to sell them in an attractive and non-threatening setting. While *The Bookseller*, organ of the establishment, may have concluded by emphasising the parasitic nature of the reprint trade upon 'new-book' business, Allen Lane drew other conclusions from the North American experience.

Lane had absorbed the lessons of the Albatross, of the US experience and of Unwin's warning about the booksellers. He realised that marketing and distribution of the brand across a range of outlets were the keys to making Penguin a success. The tale of the origin of the penguin device has been repeated through most accounts of Penguin's history, although few acknowledge that this was in direct emulation of Albatross's clean and balanced covers. Edward Young, the original artist, tells it in his reminiscence of the early days of the company: editorial discussions covering the entire bestiary had reached a stalemate when a secretary suggested a penguin;

Young was dispatched to London Zoo to find this substitute for the albatross and 'the following morning produced, at first shot, the absurdly simple cover design which was soon to become such a familiar sight on the bookstalls' (Young 1952, 210). Of course, the absurdly simple cover design owed much more to Mardersteig's original in 1931 with Young surely deserving credit only for the penguin icon replacing the previous albatross. When Beatrice Warde, wife of Frederic and herself a more eminent typographer and educator, wrote that 'the typographic planning of these early Penguins was an exercise in discipline, good manners, and economic realism which would have reflected credit on the most mature designer', she was recognising the work of just such a 'mature designer', namely Hans Mardersteig (Lamb 1952, 40).

Lane wished to sell his brand of books to the reading public where it went, Woolworths and other chain stores, and in those places where it feared to enter, the bookshops. The key element was the brand rather than the individual title.

> In making what amounted to the first serious attempt at introducing 'branded goods' to the book trade, we realized the cumulative publicity value of, first, a consistent and easily recognizable cover design, and, secondly, a good trade-mark that would be easy to say and easy to remember (Lane 1938, 42).

The cover and the logo were very successful. The company provided shops with huge quantities of brand-oriented display materials, centring on that logo and extending the characterisation of the Penguins. In April 1936, Hudson's bookshop in Birmingham won a company-sponsored prize for the best window display of Penguin(s), while in May the whole of the front page of the *Bookseller* was given over to an advertisement for Penguin's 'Great Summer Sales Drive' and a sales promotion competition offering cash prizes to booksellers at seaside resorts and holiday towns for the most effective and original selling displays of Penguin books. Showcards were available in two colours; streamers in three colours; penguin cut-outs 15 inches high; and long window strips – all advertising the brand, not specific titles.

Not that the choice of titles was unimportant. On the contrary, to sell the brand entailed convincing the public of the rightness and reliability of the Penguin selected titles. Penguin had a limited choice of titles from hardback publishers other than the Bodley Head itself. Jonathan Cape only released some of his titles to Penguin because he felt that the company would not survive and, in the meantime, he might as well take its money. Harold Raymond of Chatto and Windus later reluctantly conceded that Lane 'is obviously getting away with the series and there seems to be little point in individual publishers or individual authors trying to hold out against the scheme' (Raymond to Ralph Pinker – of the family firm of literary agents J.B. Pinker – 8 October 1935). The titles licensed to Penguin possessed proven track records; their imprint pages indicate prior continual republication and appearances in other reprint series. The initial ten issued were a judicious mix of detective fiction, such as Collins was producing in its sixpenny Crime Club series, of the 'naughty but nice' autobiography of Beverly Nichols, of the light, deft humour of Eric Linklater and of the accessible seriousness of *Ariel*, the biography of Shelley by André Maurois. Allen Lane's 'genius' lay in the selection of titles to build the brand image, a selection partially based on his own taste: 'in choosing these first ten titles, the test which I applied to each book was to ask myself: Is this a book which, had I not read it and should I have seen it on sale at 6d., would make me say, "That is a book I have always meant to read; I will get it now"?' (Lane 1935, 497). The standard typographical nature of the cover reflected and communicated the respectability and dependability of the brand. The use of an illustrated cover, as in the US tradition, would have vitiated that brand image being so carefully built by Lane.

However, the use of the word 'tradition' in this context misleads if it implies that paperback publishing itself had been of long standing in the USA. The illustrated cover was the chief selling aid of magazines, including the pulps, that jostled for space and attention in the wide range of retail outlets *Publishers Weekly* had identified for reprints. (Hardback reprint series in the USA such as the Modern Library, that introduced pictorial dust jackets in 1928, had always targeted a more sophisticated market and shown appropriate moderation in their design.) The first major US paperback house, Pocket Books, was founded in 1939 based on the Penguin model (eschewing the class of birds and choosing a kangaroo as its logo) after several ventures, including that of the Boni brothers, had failed in the preceding two decades. Its first ten titles were as conservative as those of Penguin four years earlier: a judicious mix of detective fiction, including Agatha Christie's *The Murder of Roger Ackroyd*, the classic, Shakespeare and Emily Brontë, the contemporary, Dorothy Parker and Thornton Wilder, and the title that defies categorisation, Felix Salten's *Bambi*. Nevertheless, in order to compete for readers, each title had its own distinctive cover ranging from the semi-surrealist to the semi-photographic. Avon Books was founded in 1941; it was almost immediately sued by Pocket Books for plagiarism of format; Pocket Books lost – little wonder given its own debt to Penguin and the latter's to Albatross and Tauchnitz in the evolutionary chain of paperbacks. Avon's covers were even more striking than those of its rival; they ranged from the semi-photographic to the semi-pornographic. Title competed with title lacking the emphasis on both brand and decorum characteristic of the European tradition.

The restraint of the Penguin covers proved a difficulty, however, when placed in competition with these US rivals in the 'open market' of Canada. In 1944 the Book Publishers' Branch of the Board of Trade of the City of Toronto produced a report on the Canadian book trade on the occasion of a visit by the Canadians to the Publishers' Association in the UK. The focus, therefore, was clearly placed on the effectiveness of British publishers in servicing the Canadian market. One of the key recommendations referred to jackets and covers. 'Even within the library walls, almost against the librarian's will, American books are given further advertisement, because the dust-jackets with their bright colour, good design, and story suggestion lend themselves so readily to displays and poster-board decoration. British jackets tend to be dull in colour and to give no information, often, beyond author and title' (*Report on the Canadian Book Trade* 1944, 28). The appeal of illustrated covers had become clearer in the period during World War II when Penguin USA began from 1942 to originate its own titles both to compensate for the actual or potential loss of imported books – every time a merchant ship was torpedoed, some 50,000 Penguins might sink with it – and to take advantage of commercial opportunities, such as its collaboration with the *Infantry Journal* from 1943. In order to compete within its home market against Pocket, Avon and their successors, Penguin USA had to adopt pictures, often by the artist Robert Jonas, for its covers rather than lettering as in the typographic covers of its UK parent.

In the UK itself, new competitors arose less in thrall to the typographic tradition. In particular, Pan Books, founded in 1944 and issuing its first mass-market paperbacks in 1947, seemed to represent a less staid, more 'American' approach to cover design with its use of full-colour illustrations. The most significant titles on its list from the 1950s onwards, Ian Fleming's series of James Bond books, relied on dramatic covers both to reflect the 'snobbery with violence' of the contents and to reinforce its appeal to readers. Corgi, founded in 1951, followed suit in emulating American rather than European models. UK readers increasingly surrounded by vivid advertising illustration were also becoming more attuned to the visual.

The response of Penguin was to consolidate rather than change. Jan Tschichold was appointed in 1947 to take charge of typography and production at Penguin – a role similar to that performed by Mardersteig for Collins in 1934. This move represented a perpetuation of the typographic cover. Tschichold had started his career in Leipzig working for Insel on covers and binding and for Poeschel and Trepte, printers of Insel books, on typography and print production. His hostility to the Nazis led to his departure in 1933 for Basle in Switzerland, which remained his base thereafter. In other words, he was steeped in the European tradition of typographic covers and the reforms he introduced were chiefly to the standards expected from the many printers who serviced Penguin. He did tinker with the cover's horizontal colour bars in a manner that allowed for the occasional discreet line drawing or engraving. The continuity of the brand image, and the concomitant values of sensibleness and quality, were retained. This stemmed partly from the personal taste of Allen Lane, who despised the flashiness of American 'breastsellers', and partly from the fear of altering a successful formula.

Hans Schmoller, Tschichold's successor in 1949, when the latter returned to Switzerland, appeared cut from the same cloth, having also served his time in the German printing and book trade. However, during his long period at Penguin – he retired in 1976 – he oversaw change, at first gradual, then accelerated as Allen Lane lost his grip on the company, towards the use of illustrations for covers. He developed Tschichold's concept of a vertical grid to replace the horizontal that had been used since 1935 and, in this way, opened up the covers to further decorous illustration. However, an experiment in 1957 and 1958 to determine the effect of introducing full-colour illustrated covers resulted in the loss of brand image – 'some of the public did not believe they were Penguins at all' – and an additional cost that was not justified by sales figures (Baines 2005, 87).

Tony Godwin's rise from his appointment as editorial adviser in 1960 to the position of chief editor within a relatively short time signalled a recognition of the need for fresh thinking within Penguin, despite the conservatism of Allen Lane. The designer Germano Facetti began from 1961 to build on the traditional Penguin colour-coded series such as Penguin Crime to introduce elements of collage, illustration and photography in keeping with the nature of the brand and the individual title. This was not as radical a makeover as the failed experiment of 1957–58 but the impact of these new covers was such that Facetti began to transform other series such as the Penguin Classics. Godwin revamped the Penguin Specials, relatively dormant since World War II, to handle the issues of the 1960s such as education, drugs and the trade unions; this overhaul included the revision of the traditional red covers to make each title more striking and more contemporary. The key to this evolutionary change, Phil Baines argues, was the development of graphic design education within UK art colleges and the consequent ability to find and hire innovative designers capable of divorcing cover illustration and design from typography and page layout (Baines 2005, 6). It must also be seen as a response to the increasingly visual culture of the time. This becomes particularly clear in Godwin's appointment of Alan Aldridge as art director in 1965. Aldridge paid little attention to continuity of brand image, treating each cover as a poster advertising that particular title. The result was a sudden flowering of colour and of witty and dramatic covers on Penguin books that owed little or nothing to the hitherto predominant European typographic tradition. The covers are as redolent of the 1960s as the Beatles' *Yellow Submarine*.

On Godwin's fall from grace in 1967, however, and Aldridge's leaving with him, Penguin falteringly returned to the typographic tradition; the company's lack of confidence originated perhaps in an inner realisation that the traditional cover's time had past and only the presence of Allen Lane in charge was providing it with life-support. James Joyce's *Ulysses*, Penguin 3000 issued in 1969 to celebrate Lane's 50 years in publishing, provided an instance of typographical design at its most stark and funereal (McCleery 2008). On Lane's death in 1970, the company was taken over by Pearson and in 1978 Peter Mayer, an American, became its managing director with the remit to 'modernise' the imprint and make it more profitable. He abandoned the continuity with the past; each title was promoted on its own merits rather than as part of a Penguin brand; the cover became a rather conventional expression of that promotion; and only the spine indicated any link to the older tradition. The Mardersteig, Albatross, Tschichold inheritance had disappeared, to resurface occasionally in a deliberate homage to the history of Penguin or one of its series. As *1066 and All That* (published by Penguin) had concluded: 'America was thus clearly top nation, and History came to a .'

Postscript

Steve Hare and Neil Harris read and commented on this essay and I am grateful for their pointing out my callow judgements and adding to my knowledge. Any errors that remain are of course my responsibility alone.

Chapter 2

How Books Are Positioned in the Market: Reading the Cover

Angus Phillips
Oxford Brookes University

The traditional view of the publishing industry is that it is product led, rather than focused on the needs of its markets. Editors bring out the titles that they want to publish, with little awareness of their customers. Continuing evidence for this is the high number of new titles entering the market and the low average sale per title. Most commercial publishers would argue, however, that practices have changed in the industry, with the development of marketing departments and a greater awareness of the needs of the markets into which they publish.

The cover or jacket of a book conveys a message about the contents of the volume, influencing both the retailer who stocks the book and the potential purchaser in the shop. The importance of the cover to a book's sales is reflected in the growth of the approval process for new designs, which may take into account the opinions of key retailers as well as the views of the publisher's editorial, sales and marketing staff. The aim of this chapter is to examine the cover in adult fiction and what it can reveal about the marketing of a book. Key concepts from marketing theory will be used to illuminate our understanding of how books are packaged. Can covers be 'read' to reveal the assumptions – conscious or otherwise – that publishers make about the markets they are targeting? How do covers position the book in the minds of their purchasers? How are new authors positioned, and do established authors have to be repositioned over time?

The chapter draws on contemporary perspectives, including those of designers, editors and marketers. The case studies, taken from the United Kingdom, include the bestselling author Agatha Christie. When sales of her books started to weaken, attention turned to the reasons for this decline. The mystery of the missing sales was solved by examining the covers of her books and what they said to potential readers.

The cover of a novel may echo the book's plot or characters; it may evoke a feeling in the reader, with a suggestion of danger, passion or mystery. Novels provide, as John Mullan says, 'an especially rich field for book cover design. This is partly because fiction so dominates the marketplace. Novels press forward, seeking to allure the passing browser. They also challenge and liberate the designer to suggest through the cover not merely what the contents of the book might be, but also what might be its special qualities, its singular imaginative space' (Mullan 2003).

To determine how publishers can view the markets into which they publish fiction, it is necessary to look in detail at how marketing strategy is developed. I will focus on three parts of the process: segmentation, targeting and positioning.

If readers are not all the same, publishers need to separate out different groups of customers and then aim their marketing activities at some or all of these groups. How in turn does this impact on book covers and their design?

Market Segmentation

Publishers are faced with choices when marketing their books to consumers. Do they target the whole consumer market, or do they break that market down into smaller segments? The costs of marketing to a broad audience are high – TV ads for books, for example, are rare – and it is more efficient to target promotions at particular groups of readers. The principles of market segmentation can be applied to book consumers. Kotler *et al.* (2004) outline four broad categories of segmentation: geographic, demographic, psychographic and behavioural.

Geographic segmentation involves breaking down the market by country, region or city, and examining any differences in the characteristics of consumers. Within the UK, we know there are variations in purchasing by region, but the application of this to book covers is not immediately obvious. We also know, however, that the UK and US markets have different tastes in covers, and for many consumer titles publishers will consider different designs – 'books are culturally sensitive things: imagery that might have a subtle resonance in one country can appear meaningless gunk in another; the one-size-fits-all approach, common in global design, just doesn't seem to wash when it comes to book covers' (Shaughnessy 2004, 18).

Through *demographic* segmentation the market can be broken down by age, gender and socio-economic groupings. The evidence is that reading increases with age, income and level of education: 'reading books is most popular among those aged 55 to 64, the retired, social group AB, people who are still in education, and those whose terminal education age was 19 or above' (Bury 2005a, 12). When it comes to reading fiction, patterns of reading are similar amongst different age groups, but the evidence is that women read more novels than men. The Orange Prize survey on reading habits suggested that 57 per cent of women are readers of fiction, compared to only 36 per cent of men (Hartley 2003, 27).

With *psychographic* segmentation, consumers are classified by their interests, aspirations and feelings. There is little research available for book consumers, and these variables have to be treated with caution. There is reason to think, however, that such characteristics are highly relevant to books, since they can often be an aspirational purchase:

> People have the mistaken notion that the thing you do with books is read them. Wrong … People buy books for what the purchase says about them – their taste, their cultivation, their trendiness. Their aim … is to connect themselves, or those to whom they give the books as gifts, with all the other refined owners (Riggio, cited in Kotler and Armstrong 2001, 183).

Books have become accessories to be shown off, as explained by Jennifer Richards, a designer at Time Warner Books:

Sex and the City has had a huge impact on the design of women's fiction. It is whole accessory things … The show made women want to look cool and sophisticated, and we should make books look appealing in the same way. Women should feel proud when they sit on the Tube reading a book because it has a great cover (Kean 2005b, 22).

This influence can be seen, for example, in chick-lit and romantic fiction, with the covers becoming bolder and more sophisticated. The market for chick-lit has also broadened, with greater room for different strands, from supermarket titles to a smarter, upmarket feel.

Behavioural variables include product usage, occasion and benefit segmentation, and brand loyalty. These all have relevance to books and their marketing. Firstly, the market can be divided up by how frequently consumers purchase books. A dilemma for the industry is whether to concentrate on those consumers who buy books, or try to expand the market to non-book buyers – one-third of adults questioned for a survey published in 2005 had not bought a single book in the previous year (Bury 2005a). By comparison 22 per cent of the survey could be classified as heavy buyers, purchasing more than 10 books a year. Women are more likely to be heavy buyers of books, purchasing for their children, gifts or themselves (Mintel 2005). It is tempting for publishers to focus their efforts on existing book buyers, since heavy users are likely to account for the bulk of sales (Cook and Mindak 1984), but there are titles that reach a very broad market, such as the Harry Potter books and Dan Brown's *The Da Vinci Code*.

Purchases can be classified by occasion – when the book will be read – and benefits – what the book offers to the reader. Covers can suggest a light read for the beach, an air of mystery or a mood of passion. In general, hardback novels have more elegant and restrained jackets, and literary titles in hardback may become collectable. Whilst hardback buying increases amongst the ABC1 socio-economic groups, fiction aimed at younger readers may go straight into paperback, since that market is less comfortable with the hardback format.

Serpent's Tail has published all its new fiction in paperback since it was established in 1986. Pete Ayrton says its 'young, urban' audience tends to prefer paperback originals. 'We see people putting their book in their pocket, carrying it round and reading it' (Bury 2005b, 27).

Brand loyalty is increasingly important in a crowded book market, when promotional costs are high for launching a new author, and the evidence is that readers would prefer to follow an author they like. When readers were asked to rank the factors influencing their choice of book, familiarity with the author came out as the highest factor above price and reviews (Bury 2005a, 6). The cover also proved to be an important factor.

Another common method of segmentation in publishing is based around the different retail channels. Publishers mostly sell to booksellers, rather than direct to consumers, and a book's sales prospects can be determined by whether it is widely stocked and prominently displayed in bookshops. The market can be broken up by the different types of bookshops and their customer profiles. For example, in the UK, Waterstone's has a large audience amongst ABC1s, readers of broadsheet newspapers and users of the internet. Borders has a strong urban bias, with a strong customer base amongst the 35–44 age bracket and the AB socio-demographic group. WHSmith is popular with two age groups in particular, from 15 to 19 and from 45 to 54 (Mintel 2005).

Targeting the Reader

Through industry or company research, firms can identify which types of segmentation are important to their publishing, and target market segments that prove to be attractive. This then influences the marketing mix chosen for their books – what combination of product, price, place (distribution) and promotion. Publishers that aim to sell to a mass market, for example through supermarkets, will decide to play safe with their cover design. 'It is in this market that publishers cling on to the design shorthand or cliché that acts as a simple signifier to potential buyers – such as the gothic black and gold lettering on thrillers or sci-fi schlock' (Baxter 2005). With volumes destined for a literary market, there is far more leeway for the designer and their creativity, and the type will be more restrained.

An example of targeting was the publication by HarperCollins of *Blood of Angels* by Michael Marshall in 2005. Its promotion, format and price were designed for a particular reader, in what was described by the marketing director as 'a carefully orchestrated military operation'. The target audience was mainly female, ABC1 and 'serious crime aficionados'. Published first in hardback, the book was promoted in the press – there is a link between reading crime and newspaper readership – but not with outdoor advertising – travellers prefer paperbacks (McCormick 2005, 28). The hardback jacket had a menacing black design with the strapline: 'There's a killer in all of us.'

The Harry Potter books have a considerable adult readership and once this was noticed the publisher, Bloomsbury, issued the stories in adult as well as children's editions. This led to a growth in crossover fiction, with titles aimed at both markets. Mark Haddon's *The Curious Incident of the Dog in the Night-Time* was published in the UK with two different designs for the hardback, and again with two designs for the paperback. Mark Haddon commented on the approach: 'The same book is reviewed in different places, advertised in different places and, most importantly, placed on two different shelves, and often in two different rooms, in the same bookshop. So I guess it may be happening a lot more often from now on' (Dean 2005, 26).

Publishers have come up with other ways of targeting more than one segment of the market. *The Little Friend* by Donna Tartt was originally published with a disturbing cover image of a doll's face with a cut-out eye. A second version, published two years later, appeared with the image of a child on a swing – this new cover, less terrifying, aimed the book at a summer reading market (Dean 2005). Jess Foley's saga novel, *No Wings to Fly* (2006), appeared in two editions. The original cover had been aimed at supermarkets, but when Waterstone's became interested in the title, a parallel edition took a more upmarket approach, described by the in-house design team (Ogle, 2005) as more in the style of Sarah Waters (author of *Tipping the Velvet*).

Some authors, such as the thriller writer Chris Ryan, will undoubtedly appeal to a male market, but with readership for fiction stronger amongst women, publishers may prefer to concentrate on books which appeal to a female readership. They have to make this choice because men are reluctant to read what they perceive as books for women. Research for the Orange Prize for Fiction found that, if knowledge of the author or book is excluded, the cover is the most important factor in whether readers would like to start reading a book. 'The front cover/title is taken to be a strong indicator of the sort of fiction a book is and whether or not it might be of interest, and – very importantly – whether the book is intended to be a male or female read' (Orange, 2000). The study showed that nearly three-quarters of men, and over half of women, thought that a book's cover shows whether the book is aimed at men or women.

A book was regarded as a female read based on the author's gender, the colour and general look of the cover, the title and the blurb about the novel. Whilst women are willing to read titles which they regard as male reads, the converse is not the case. Amongst women in the survey, 40 per cent were interested in reading male reads, but amongst men only a quarter were interested in female reads.

> Ian McEwan, *Enduring Love* is a prime example of a book which, in spite of neutral words in its description (e.g. suspense), sends out signals from the look of its cover (including the use of pink) and from its title (using the word Love) that it is a book which would mainly interest women. Over three out of four men think it is a female read, and less than 30% would be interested in reading it (Orange 2000).

Publishing initiatives may be developed to capitalise on the strengths of particular market segments. In 2005 a new publishing imprint was launched with a specific target readership, women aged 45 and over. This is a sizeable market – around 40 per cent of the female population of the UK. The aim of Transita was to publish a wide variety of contemporary fiction with exciting and inspirational heroines. The imprint's founder and director, Nikki Read, wanted to 'give women of this age-group storylines they can relate to and fictional characters with whom they can empathise. Until Transita, the majority of published fiction has centred around younger women's lives and experience' (Pauli 2005).

Positioning

Once an appropriate group of customers has been identified, the next stage is to position the product in the customer's mind.

> Positioning starts with a product. A piece of merchandise, a service, a company, an institution or even a person … But positioning is not what you do to a product. Positioning is what you do to the mind of the prospect. That is, you position the product in the mind of the prospect (Ries and Trout 2001, 2).

In a famous example of positioning, the carmaker Volvo became known throughout the world as the manufacturer of safe and reliable cars. For books, the cover offers the opportunity to position the book in the mind of the manager buying stock for their bookshop, the casual purchaser or the prospective long-term fan of an author. Positioning strategies can concentrate on the usage occasion (summer reading), the benefits offered (a thriller) or how the product relates to the competition (the 'new Catherine Cookson'). In larger shops fiction will be divided up by genre, and the cover may be the best clue as to where the book should be stocked – whether literary fiction, crime or romance.

> The bookshop is almost colour coded to make selection easier. Bubblegum cartoon covers for girly relationship novels. Cold-war thrillers, horror, sci-fi, all dressed in gothic black with melodramatic gold lettering. It's design shorthand. Publishers have just a few seconds to catch your eye, as you promiscuously scan the shop floor. Let your eye rest for a second, and they've almost got you. Make contact, read the blurb on the back and, most importantly today, clock the face of the author (Dyckhoff 2001).

Covers can suggest different types of benefits, for example a light read or more serious, literary fiction. The covers of chick-lit titles position the books as reads for younger women – with feminine colours and a distinctive type of illustration. Purple came to rival pink as publishers sought to make their books look different from what was in danger of becoming a cliché. 'Gone are the quirky little cartoon girlies and in their place are legs sticking out like stumps from sofas and beds … A debut chick-lit title needs to have resonance with the rest of the genre so that potential readers will want to pick it up, but it should not merge into other titles as so often happens' (Kean 2005a, 28).

In the area of saga fiction, authors are positioned in the market through the cover illustration, which reflects the period and location of the novel. Shoutlines locate the author more precisely in the reader's mind, from Harry Bowling, 'the King of Cockney sagas' to Lyn Andrews, 'the Catherine Cookson of Liverpool'. There is a sizeable market for sagas set in the north-west of England and publishers position their authors by location – Liverpool is a lucrative readership – and against other writers – most are promoted as the 'new/next Catherine Cookson' (Williamson 2004).

New Authors and Developing a Brand

Authors new to the market have to be carefully positioned. This can be done in press releases to the media, author interviews, but also through the cover. In 2004 Andrew Rosenheim's novel *Stillriver* was published by Hutchinson, an imprint of Random House. The protagonist, Michael Wolf, returns from Europe to his home town in Michigan, Stillriver, after his father is murdered. His first love, Cassie, has also returned to Stillriver and their feelings for each other are reawakened. The setting for the town is beside a lake and the River Still. In a pre-publication interview in *The Bookseller*, the British trade magazine, the book was described as part mystery, part love story (Clee 2003, 26). The interview suggested that the book is similar in appeal to Sebastian Faulks and Douglas Kennedy, and that the jacket image evoked that selling point. Those successful authors were also published by Hutchinson, and this is a useful positioning exercise for the book trade. As viewed by the in-house team, the market was seen as the 'upmarket end of commercial', 30 plus, and predominantly female (Ogle 2005). When looking at the jacket design – a woman in a dress is seen walking along a landing stage – one is reminded of Anita Shreve, and indeed the review of the novel in *The Independent* newspaper described it as spanning 'the troubled waters between Harlan Coben and Anita Shreve' (Hagestadt 2004). The paperback appeared with a stronger illustration, of a woman in a boat, and the shoutline, 'Death, Jealousy and Forbidden Love'. The soft cover edition is clearly positioned in the market by the use on the front cover of the review quote from *The Independent*.

The success of a cover design can help an author break through into mainstream success. Douglas Kennedy's *The Pursuit of Happiness* was published in hardback by Hutchinson in 2001, and in paperback the following year. The paperback cover has a woman sitting on a beach, reading a letter (see Figure 2.1). The key target market for the design team was a female audience, aged between 30 and 40. The core theme of his novels was seen to be relationships, and Richard Ogle, the art director, described the look of the cover as evoking 'how … you want to feel when you are reading it'. The designer, Glenn O'Neill, had tried out designs using photographs of couples from the 1940s, with locations in New York such as Central Park in the snow (Ogle 2005). These designs had the pitfall of placing the novel in a particular period, and also the overall look was felt to be 'retro' and quite cold. The woman on the beach, by contrast, had a warmer and timeless feel. The success of this look led to other Kennedy novels appearing with what amounted to a series style. Even his thrillers, in print with another publisher, were reissued in this style.

Launching and developing a new author is an expensive process, unless word of mouth recommendation turns the book into a hit, and so publishers must look to optimise their investments in existing authors. Whilst there is little consumer awareness of publisher brands (Sexton 2002), author brands are of increasing importance. If familiarity with the author is the factor most likely to persuade someone to buy, then getting the author branding to work effectively is imperative. Jonathan Hubbard of Interbrand says that the cover is at the forefront of building author brands, since it is so vital to the sales of a title: 'The first 20 to 30 feet of the book store is where most of the sales are … The jacket is stirring up for you an experience that you've possibly already enjoyed or you've heard from someone else that you will enjoy' (Ray 2005). As seen with Douglas Kennedy, the books should have designs that tie in with each other. Customers then choose a book based on the author's name and style, rather than the specific title. Research into John Grisham in 2004 revealed that his brand is based on gripping stories with David and Goliath struggles set in the southern US states. 'Author brands are about delivering a consistent package to the reader, where the ending may be a surprise but the elements that lead them there are familiar and comforting' (Ray 2005). In the case of crime writing, the brand may develop around the character rather than the author, such as Inspector Morse in the books by Colin Dexter.

Problems for a brand can develop, for example when the author decides to write in a different style or genre. Readers may be disappointed to discover that the book is not what they are expecting. A solution is the use of a pseudonym – Ruth Rendell, the writer of detective stories, writes psychological thrillers under the name Barbara Vine with a different style of cover. Some brands continue to expand after the author's

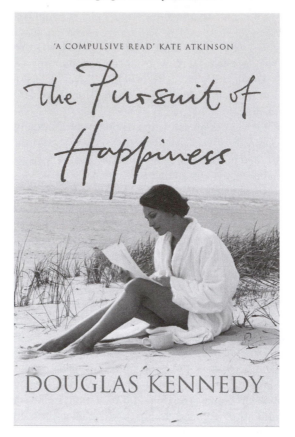

Figure 2.1 The 2002 paperback edition of *The Pursuit of Happiness*

death – a prominent example is Virginia Andrews, who died in 1986. New titles have continued to appear, written by a ghostwriter, with her name on the covers.

Refreshing the backlist for an author is a regular part of successful publishing. Book covers rarely acquire the iconic status of album covers – two exceptions are *Captain Corelli's Mandolin* (Louis de Bernières) and *Everything is Illuminated* (Jonathan Safran Foer) – and there is nothing to stop a publisher redesigning the whole list for an author. For Anita Shreve, her publisher, Time Warner, took another look at her covers:

> We did some market research, not into the covers but into the people who do and don't read her books. It came across very clearly that people associated her with emotions and human feelings – yet there wasn't a single human in sight on her covers. So we went back to the drawing board, put people on the covers, and the idea has gone down very well (Bury 2005a, 7).

Quotes on the new covers come from the upmarket newspapers that are read by her target readers.

Beginning in 2004, Georgette Heyer was repackaged by Arrow from A to B format paperback (an increase in the book's size), and the new covers presented her novels in the style of Jane Austen, reinventing her as a more sophisticated, upmarket read (Ogle 2005). The new positioning included quotes on the covers from Margaret Drabble and the romantic novelist Katie Fforde.

The Queen of Crime

Agatha Christie wrote over 70 detective novels, and her name is 'synonymous with the genre' (Bloom 2002, 132). Her stories continue to sell in large numbers, and her detectives feature in both TV and screen adaptations. The covers have to be re-examined from time to time to assess how they influence perceptions of her writing.

In the 1980s her publisher, Collins, faced with a decline in sales, commissioned research into her readers and their views of the covers. The market research included focus groups composed of Christie readers and readers of general paperbacks. The results of the research showed interest in crime writing, and that Christie was viewed as the 'Queen of Crime'. The covers, however, were thought to be unrepresentative of the qualities of the author. By concentrating on the gory aspects of the crime, the covers were presenting the books more in the horror genre rather than as mysteries: 'horror style covers were repelling her natural market' (Williams 1989, 5). For example, the image for *The Murder of Roger Ackroyd* was a painting by Tom Adams of a knife sticking out of a bloodstained piece of clothing. New covers were then commissioned that repositioned the stories as mysteries. The pictures on the front were 'seen to link with the title … without giving any of the story away. The covers also gave the impression of quality. Most importantly, the name of the author was presented in large lettering' (Williams 1989, 5). Seen as intriguing and subtle, they reflected the 'nice' murders described by the focus groups. Sales of her novels increased by 40 per cent in the first year of the new covers.

Repositioning Agatha Christie has been a continuing process over the decades. Alan Powers describes how when she was still alive, the covers 'sustained the illusion that even the older stories were taking place in the present' (Powers 2001, 104). After the venture into horror, a period approach gradually took over, and following the success of the *Poirot* TV series the covers assumed an 'unequivocally nostalgic approach'. In 1998 the rights to the Christie titles were bought by Chorion for £10m, who set out to manage her characters as a brand. Once again, detective work was carried out into the market for her books.

The company began with quantitative research which showed a high level of awareness of the author amongst the general population (98 per cent). It was discovered that her readership was concentrated in two age groups: children of around 11 or 12 starting on adult fiction and readers returning to her stories in their 50s or 60s. Overall Christie was seen as suitable reading for previous generations, and the period covers reinforced this point. Phil Clymer, the director at Chorion, decided to commission a new template design for the covers, giving continuity across Christie but recognising the sub-brands of Poirot and Miss Marple. These were to reflect what was viewed as the real brand values of Christie – ingenious puzzles that are entertaining and accessible.

Figure 2.2 An example of the 'more upmarket, grown-up' Agatha Christie covers

A joint venture with HarperCollins provided Chorion with more control than if they simply licensed the titles to the publisher (most author contracts are licences granting control of the publishing rights to the publisher).

Focus groups were shown the new design alongside the old versions, and the results were a strong endorsement for the new approach. The old design had been deterring readers and consumers said they would be 'embarrassed to read Agatha Christie on the bus … because of what it said about them' (Clymer 2005). The new covers offered a 'more upmarket, grown-up' feel. Black was used as the base colour for both the Poirot and Marple books, and the modern look was completed by the typeface and the use of photography. The two detectives were given different treatments. For the Poirot covers the aim was to produce 'edgy, slightly sinister' covers and to remove some of the cosiness associated with the author; and for Miss Marple the images suggested 'things hidden', emphasising the mystery and the detective's ability to see behind the obvious. A key part of the brand identity was the use of Agatha Christie's signature on the covers (see Figure 2.2) – also used for the TV adaptations.

Additional research into book buying was commissioned by Chorion. This showed the importance of covers as the packaging that influences purchases. A good cover will encourage the consumer to pick up a book, and the consumer is then five times more likely to buy (Clymer 2005). Potential purchasers also view the endorsements on the back cover, and will check out the type inside the book to assess its readability.

The primary market for Christie is seen as female, with the books providing an escape, 'my time', from work or family commitments. The more sophisticated, contemporary look led to a strong increase in sales – up 50 per cent for the titles in new covers – and the consumer response to the new design was that 'it didn't look like a Christie' (Clymer 2005). By 2004 turnover to Chorion from print publishing across the Christie intellectual property was £4m (Jeffries 2004).

Reading the Cover

How can we read the cover of a book? Although this chapter has discussed covers in the light of marketing theory, the everyday practice of cover design is a creative and sometimes serendipitous process. A number of draft designs may be tried out on the path to a successful design. In the minds of those creating the covers, issues of targeting and positioning are unlikely to be thought of in those terms. Few companies can afford on a regular basis the kind of market research that has been invested in the Christie brand. Publishers will consider comparable authors, key target markets and series style, but not necessarily view their authors as brands or worry about the precise demographics of the target audience.

In general, however, publishers are increasingly aware of their markets and will canvas internal and external opinions to inform the development of new projects. In the publishing industry of the twenty-first century, marketers are developing more sophisticated plans, in which the cover has to work well with other aspects of the book's promotion, and meet the needs of the proposed market and selling channels. Markets can be segmented in a variety of ways, for example by the demographics of the consumer or by bookshop chain.

> Like the automotive industry, book publishers have long been adept at tailoring the outward appearance of their products to suit tastes in different geographical markets. But today there are increasing pressures on publishers to be both more fastidious and more flexible when it comes to deciding on different book covers for different markets and market segments (Baxter 2005).

How developed is the thinking will depend on the importance of the title – for literary fiction with low print runs, there is little need to consider the target market in any depth. Yet even basic distinctions, such as literary or commercial, male or female, do reflect underlying assumptions about consumers and how markets can be segmented.

The cover plays a vital part in positioning a book or author in the market. The retail environment for books has become highly competitive and covers have to be correct for the chosen market, whether a supermarket audience or a Waterstone's customer. Covers have to work in a variety of environments, from on the web to face out in the bookshop, in a poster on the Underground or on television. Good designs help sell the book to the retailer, and encourage them to place the book prominently at the front of the store. The growth of central buying amongst the retail chains means that a few key decision-makers determine how widely a book is stocked – whether they love or hate the cover really matters. These head buyers may be shown draft designs, and the sales and marketing staff who present titles to them play a key part in the approvals process for covers within publishers. According to Phil Baines, 'Marketing is a lot more important than it used to be and the fiction market in particular is very, very cut-throat … The feedback from salespeople, after they have visited retailers for pre-order meetings, is taken very seriously' (Baxter 2005).

Covers position the book so that when it is unpacked in the bookshop, the title is placed in the correct part of the shop. The cover can determine whether the book is displayed face out in the shop, and whether it is picked up by a browser looking for their next purchase. The reader needs to be comfortable with how the author is presented, and happy to be seen with the book when on the bus or in the company of friends. For major author brands such as Agatha Christie, incorrect positioning has a direct impact on sales. Consumers are exposed to a wide range of influences from all kinds of media, and book covers run the risk of dating as fashions change. Today's fresh look can become outdated or clichéd, and publishers are accustomed to changing the covers for an author on a regular basis.

Angus Hyland, from the design company Pentagram, commented on the contenders for the Booker Prize in 2005: 'Judging the covers on their own is difficult, because the cover designs of books are conceived as part of a much wider marketing strategy' (Hyland 2005, 14). Deepening our understanding of how covers relate to their markets enables us to make that fuller judgement.

Chapter 3

Relocating Liverpool in the 1990s: Through the Covers of Regional Saga Fiction

Val Williamson
Edge Hill University

The escalating prominence of regional sagas in fastseller lists significantly increased the commercial importance of women authors in British publishing in the 1990s.[1] This discussion will look at a specific group of saga novels, the Liverpool group,[2] and seek to elucidate how the discourses and semiology of their covers become developed between the tensions posed by the exigencies of the London-based publishing industry and the superior local knowledge of local authors and artists. Radway (1984) indicates 'the effectiveness of commodity packaging', that is the relationship between cover and content, for the mass-market romance, (Radway 1984 in During 2000, 565) and similarly effective packaging has been particularly significant in the development of the saga sub-genre. This chapter offers an analysis of 1990s practices in book titling, cover art semiology, book cover paratexts and some author and reader epitexts. This will include consideration of how Liverpool saga covers constitute paratextual thresholds (Genette 1997) to the narratives within, and how and why specific themes are indicated on this primary marketing medium for these bestselling fictions. Further semiotic and textual analysis of covers will interrogate contradictions posed by publishers' juxtaposition of representational artwork and the thematic indicators in back cover 'blurbs'.

Between 1974 and 2000, a dozen authors provided 102 Liverpool saga fictions set mainly in the twentieth century before 1955, 88 of these published in the 1990s. The Liverpool sagas have developed alongside other large bodies of similar novels

---

1   Throughout the nineties, books categorised as 'sagas' in Alex Hamilton's annual list (*The Guardian*, December, reprinted in *The Bookseller*, January) of the top 100 fastsellers (sales over 100,000) in Britain. Sagas, their authors or their marketing are mentioned in the editorial most years after 1994, when Hamilton featured sagas in the column 'Clogs By The Aga'. Hamilton notices an increase in woman-authored bestsellers from 25 in the early 1990s, escalating to 40 in 1997, with women authoring over 45 per cent of top sellers by the end of the decade (Hamilton 2000, 21). Close analysis demonstrates that between 12 and 25 of these titles are saga fictions.

2   In Hamilton's list for 1999, Audrey Howard's total reported sales at 83rd and 92nd were worth £1,740,340; that year, Liverpool saga authors Lyn Andrews, at 89th, and Ruth Hamilton, at 91st, are reported with sales totalling £1,686,137. That is, over £3.4 million being spent mainly in Liverpool and Merseyside, in addition to four other Liverpool saga titles published that year. Liverpool saga authors Andrews, Howard, Jonker and Baker are all in the Public Lending Right top 20 most borrowed authors for 2003–2004.

similarly 'placing great emphasis on the location for the narrative and the community of the protagonist' (Moody 1997, 310), while giving expression, as Ken Worpole suggests, to what working people 'do know [and] the value ... of their experience and knowledge' (1983, 23). This type of narrative, 'has as its subject the popular culture of women' (Fowler 1991, 1). Fowler's examination of the work of Catherine Cookson discovers that, 'The roots of her story-telling lie in using the conservative romance with a "labourist" or social democratic inflexion, evident both in the lower-class perspective and her alternating strands of realism with redemptive utopia' (Fowler 1991, 3). Cookson's popularity (albeit that it took 50 years to develop) reached a peak in the late 1980s, sustained throughout the 1990s until her death in 1998. Cookson had by then become a brand name in her own right, indicated by the supersession of cover art by her 'logo': 'writers become their own categories ("Have you got any more Catherine Cookson?"). Their names are printed in large letters *above* the titles of their books' (Kerton 1986, 4; see also Bloom 2002, 75).

At this time the numbers of Cookson imitators, writing 'clogs and shawls' or 'rags to rickets' sagas, proliferated rapidly, recruited by a publishing industry aware of her age and frailty and the escalating popularity of the saga genre generally. These nicknames, commonly repeated by agents and literary critics, betray both a sense of class and its urban location, with a suggestion of narratological tropes. By the late 1980s, regional saga covers had developed a distinct semiology conveying that same information.

Genette (1997) is interested in the relationship between books and readers, a relationship that apparently begins with the display of a new book in the shop; but for the publishing industry this relationship begins many months before final printing (Blake 1999, 240–42). Books, or at least the idea of them, first have to be sold to the trade. Sample jackets (flat, not folded, constituting a 'card' for handing out) are used both to test reactions to, and to market newer authors at book trade fairs.

> Time, place, title, cover – we do judge by it. A publisher has one and a half minutes to sell the idea to distributors – the cover will tell them far more than the publisher can say in the time, and so will the title. This is where the 'shout' lines count, and the knowledge of the '*controlling idea*' (such as 'love conquers all') [*sic*] (Going, 1994).[3]

In bookshops and supermarkets in the 1990s the practice of displaying paperbacks with the front cover rather than the spine facing outward becomes ubiquitous.

> by the 1990s bestsellers were sold as any other products in supermarkets, where female purchasers spent 80 per cent of their book purchasing on impulse buying of famous named 'author' brand.[4] ... Supermarket sales are equally affected by marketing, so displays, good covers and clear 'blurb' (user instructions!) help, but the effect must be immediate ... Throughout the mid-1990s, much emphasis is placed, therefore, on good jacket designs which can be clearly displayed on shelves, tables and in store windows. (Bloom 2002, 75–6).

The process of jacket design therefore, far from remaining the realm of the house art department, becomes a focus of editorial concern from early in the publication

---

3   Going is an editor at Headline Books, now Hodder Headline plc.
4   Bloom references *The Bookseller* December 1998 for these figures.

process (Blake 1999, 240). It may therefore be deduced that the process of design for jackets on Liverpool sagas has been equally carefully approached. In the case of Liverpool and London sagas in the 1990s, identifiable landmarks are shown on their covers, but all covers feature clothes, setting and sense of time just out of memory. Covers usually feature a lone woman in period dress foregrounded over terraced back streets typical of the industrial towns of England.

> a (Corgi) saga cover for a mass market paperback ... [which] ... clearly shows the character, the place and the clothes that define the period ... The cover is shouting 'woman's historical novel' and appeals very strongly to the traditional sector of the market (Laczynska 1997, 49–54).

Genette distinguishes four book covers: front cover, inside front cover, back cover and inside back cover (1997, 23–32). 'The name of the author, publisher, title, laudatory comments, excerpts from reviews, biographical notices, indication of genre ... and publisher information pre-dispose readers to opinions of the literary work before they commence reading the work' (Koenig-Woodyard 1999).[5] As HarperCollins take Helen Forrester into the 1980s, they begin to print thumbnails of her previous book covers inside the back covers of their Fontana paperbacks. By the end of that decade, they are printing thumbnails of her fiction covers inside the front cover of her fiction paperbacks, and thumbnails of her four autobiographies inside the back cover. Except for Forrester, on Liverpool sagas generally, the title of the novel is given more emphasis than the name of the author. Tropes for titles include phrases from popular songs of the past, old-fashioned homilies or references to locale, where 'past' may be 1920 to 1955. Hence *Mist Over the Mersey* (Andrews 1994), *Going Home to Liverpool* (Francis 1996) and *Lights Out Liverpool* (Lee 1995). Liverpool 1990s titles increasingly refer to place, except for those of Joan Jonker and Elizabeth Murphy, whose titles more commonly refer to theme, such as *Honour Thy Father* (Murphy 1996) and *When One Door Closes* (Jonker 1991). Where locale is not strongly emoted by the title, either 'Liverpool' or 'Mersey' will be in the cover comments:[6] for instance 'A heartwarming saga set in wartime Liverpool' (Howard, *There Is No Parting*, 1993); 'The new Liverpool saga from the author of *A Wise Child*' (1994) (Murphy, *Honour Thy Father*, 1996).[7]

Titles and cover images form thresholds intended to reflect content, intimating character, historical moment, locale and theme. The narrative morphology of saga fiction encompasses four types of saga developed throughout the twentieth century. A 1990s regional saga, such as these Liverpool examples, is a single-volume work, with a narrative formula combining themes of nostalgia and ownership, usually set in an urban landscape. British regional saga fiction features a working-class woman as its central character, and sets the story in the past just out of memory, often in

---

5   An analysis elsewhere, of author research method, contains consideration of some of this paratextual information, such as author forewords (Williamson 2000b, 163–78).

6   One of Headline's Liverpool saga authors reported in 2001 that her editors believed that the word 'Liverpool' on the cover sells 10,000 more copies.

7   The book cover engages strong reactions from readers; for example *All About Romance, the Cover Controversy part ii* at <http://www.likesbooks.com/covers2.html>.

the grim slums of a chronically depressed northern industrial town. Her quest is to attain or retain economic control, and clothes, furniture or mobility may provide the forum for discussion of this quest. It is in that northern grime that these 'regionals' and their current popularity are most strongly rooted, although by the early 1980s publishers had broadened the potential for sales by encouraging writers from other regions, London especially, the legendarily impoverished East End particularly (for example, Lena Kennedy, Mary Jane Staples and Philip Boast, joined in the 1990s by Harry Bowling, Dee Williams, Helen Carey *et al.*).

Paratextual design, Genette suggests, embraces the spine of the book and dust covers on hardbacks, too (Genette 1997, 23–32; Sutherland 1991, 3, 6), which becomes relevant when considering how popular saga fiction is among library borrowers (Public Lending Right statistics 1990–2004). As Bloom points out, (2002, 74) hardback sales to libraries may number between 50 and 2,000 per title; I suggest that saga authors often sell the higher figure, 1,200–2,000 copies, to libraries, with reprints of backlists to replace worn out stock taking place every eight to ten years. It is notable that both the paperback and the hardcover library editions of Liverpool saga books either offer an extension of the cover illustration wrapping around to the back, and/or often include a thumbnail reproduction of the front cover illustration on the spine. An analysis of themes foregrounded in back cover blurbs reveals several important ones, from an aspiration toward 'the leaving of Liverpool'[8] through the skills developed by enduring World War II to a strong focus on poverty.[9] Asked, 'What is your favourite book with a Liverpool connection?' Liverpool library users[10] put the founding text of Liverpool sagas, Helen Forrester's *Twopence to Cross the Mersey* (1974), first and Silas K. Hocking's ([1876] 1968) *Her Benny*, second. Both are tales of the grinding poverty and depredation of childhood on Liverpool's streets. Robert Tressell's ([1914] 1955) *The Ragged Trousered Philanthropists* is included, but 13 of this 'top 20' are sagas, some authors having several titles listed. *Twopence to Cross the Mersey*, 'Helen Forrester's poignant story of her poverty-stricken childhood in Liverpool during the 1930s' (back cover, 1995) has been published by three different publishers; HarperCollins first published it in paperback in 1981 and reprinted it 24 times up to the special edition in 1995.

As we follow the promotional progress of Liverpool sagas through the 1990s, we find, in back cover shoutlines, a decreasing emphasis on 'the leaving of Liverpool' (Moody 1997, 311) and an increasing emphasis on rags: 'In spite of her poverty' Lyn Andrews's heroine sails on *The White Empress* (1989). Prior to the 1990s the poverty theme is implied rather than made explicit, especially by June Francis (1990) – 'For young Flora Cooke the misery of the Second World War and the hardship it brings is both real and unrelenting …' – and Elizabeth Murphy (1991): 'But despite the grim years of the Depression, … she finds the resources to survive an era of

---

8   Revealed in Forrester's title, *Twopence to Cross the Mersey* (1974) for instance.

9   Williamson 2000a, 268–86.

10   The City of Liverpool Libraries and Information Services poll, November 1997. Results, Pool's Winners, were published, listed in different categories, as colourful bookmarks. The bookmark 'Liverpool books chosen by Liverpool readers', features the top 20 authors and their most popular titles.

economic hardship and social upheaval.' But by the mid-1990s the detail of poverty is emphasised, as in Katie Flynn (1993), 'Life is tough in Liverpool in the years after the First World War and Kitty is always hungry and dressed in rags.' By 1997 Katie Flynn invites the reader to 'Let yourself be swept away by this warm and delightful story of two families struggling through poverty and hardship to reach their Rainbow's End.' The issue raised here is the logical contradiction between 'warm and delightful' and 'struggling through poverty and hardship'.

> The city has a nationally recognisable profile as a place of hardship and conflict, but more importantly the writers who use it as a setting are themselves very self-aware and reflexive. ... The Liverpool family sagas lay common expressive claim to their writers' experience of Liverpool, their credentials and their further research or inspiration from the community are part of the formula' (Moody 1997, 311–12).

Reflecting the continued impact of Helen Forrester's *Twopence to Cross the Mersey* (1974), a tale of a well-to-do young girl reduced to poverty in the 1930s by alleged parental fecklessness, most Liverpool authors devise at least one plot or subplot where a young girl is similarly plummeted from boarding school in the south of England to a working-class home in the back streets of Liverpool.[11] Unlike the real Forrester, the fictional character is taught how to cope by the Liverpool working-class experts among whom she is fortunate enough to have been welcomed. In this instructive mode the fictions also inform the 1990s Liverpool reader, an important aspect of the saga's project, which strives to portray the city's vast working-class community, and they do so very satisfyingly, as far as their readers are concerned.

> The fictional space of Liverpool is increasingly being used to interrogate the past ... Liverpool is used as a point of connection between the fictional past and the readers' present' (Moody 1997: 312–15).

Epitexts accruing during interactions between authors and readers seem to confirm this. Such meetings, observed as part of ethnographic research, certainly encourage formation of epitexts, 'elements "outside" the bound volume' (Genette 1997, 8) and these are as likely to come from the reader as from the author. For example, in November 1998, at a 'Meet your favourite Merseyside author' session at Skelmersdale Library Arts Centre, with Lyn Andrews and Katie Flynn, one reader expressed thanks and delight that the road she lived in as a child was 'in a Katie Flynn'; another proposed a vote of thanks, saying 'everyone gets comfort and love out of your books'. Liverpool sagas are 'a point where text and lived experience overlap, provoking a discussion of the [reader's] material reality' (Radway 1986) and this is one of the primary pleasures of these texts for their readers. That material reality includes acute awareness of the gap between present and past realities, and of the gulf between desire and gratification in that past reality (Fowler 1991, 152). Regional saga texts resonate strongly with the known reality of working-class Lancashire to elderly and middle-aged readers now dis-located from backstreet communities, which are yet remembered for their specific exigencies. This dis-location was brought about not

---

11 For instance, *Going Home to Liverpool* (Francis 1996).

only by World War II, and an ensuing national awareness and guilt at the effects and widespread existence of poverty, (Calder 1969, 41), but also by the post-war welfare state. Sagas constitute a recovery of experience for many working-class women now temporally and often geographically dis-located from their past.

In the 1970s, Liverpool de-industrialised and, in the 1980s, became a tourist city (Urry 1995, 154–7), a set of curiosities and spectacles for the outsider to come in and marvel at (Urry 1990; Urry 1995, 189). The Albert Dock in its current tourist-friendly condition, a typical 'heritage' site, function redefined from workplace to site for leisure, both symbolises and problematises today's cognitive map of Liverpool.[12] As a symbol, the Liver Building had particular meaning for anyone who returned to Liverpool by sea, signifying 'home' and now serves as the principal sign for the city, its statues incorporating the city's crest – the Liver Bird. An incalculable amount of local Liverpool pride remains invested in this sign. The railway, tram, ferry and liner traffic and the Mersey Tunnel traffic that converged on this spot meant that mass translocation of both local and transitory populations occurred daily, if not hourly, imbuing a sense of the Liver Building being the heart of the city. From the mid-1950s a series of traumatic transformations to Liverpool traditional industry, and therefore the Liverpool waterfront, took place. Edwina Currie (in her sole attempt at a Liverpool saga) cites: '… seventy four shipping companies registered in Liverpool this year [1963]. Within twenty years there'll be hardly a dozen' (Currie 1998, 43). The 7-mile-long overhead railway, the 'docker's umbrella', was demolished; the liners were replaced by aeroplanes (to Manchester); the tramway was replaced by buses; dock work practices were transformed by new designs in machinery and shipping; tenement populations were relocated; markets and 'slum' communities along the nearby artery, Scotland Road, were replaced by a multi-lane highway. But the Liver Building remains, a significant Liverpool waterfront icon, and has become the focus of today's tourist map of Liverpool.

The Royal Liver Building is part of a group of iconic buildings on the Liverpool waterfront recently awarded World Heritage Site status. With the Cunard Building and the domed Mersey Docks and Harbour Board Building, this 'trinity' seems classical, historic and demonstrative of international influence and Empire. In fact they are comparatively recent (the 'long' Edwardian period), and symbolise the renewed hope of Liverpool at the end of the nineteenth century, before the cycle of boom and bust economics that characterise the decline of Empire during the first half of the twentieth century. The vista presented by these three buildings has continually symbolised Liverpool aspiration since.

> Liverpool reached its zenith at the turn of the 20th century, becoming one of the richest cities in the world. … This wealth is vividly expressed in the trio of buildings erected … at the Pier Head: the Royal Liver Building, the Cunard Building and the Mersey Docks and Harbour Board Building. … The Pier Head group of buildings typifies the money that was spent by those who felt confident that Liverpool was a genuine rival to London. This is also reflected in street names such as Covent Garden, the Temple, Islington and The Strand which echo the streets of the capital (Morris and Ashton 1997, 15).

---

12   Ken Worpole's 'Out of Hours' study and report for Comedia, financed by the Gulbenkian Foundation, published as *Towns for People: Transforming Urban Life* (1992), offers discussion of government and capitalist intervention in town politics and planning at that time.

These buildings, rather than the Albert Dock complex, increasingly dominate cover design for Liverpool and Merseyside sagas during the 1990s, as Liverpool's post-industrial renaissance as a tourist city gathers pace.

Figure 3.1 The front paperback cover of *The Girl from Penny Lane* (1994). Reprinted by permission of The Random House Ltd

Closer analysis, however, reveals continued gradual changes in cover iconography that concur with thematic shifts in the narratives. At the same time as Liverpool becomes transformed into a knowledge culture city, a very large group of its residents turn to identities from the past for reassurance or information to help them to endure the present, and I suggest that saga cover de:sign evolved as it did because it attracts this reader. For instance, the cover art of Forrester's autobiographies (1974–85) featured locally significant Liverpool buildings such as the Town Hall rather than the waterfront, so that the iconography impacts as universal, of poverty, girlhood and the city. I suggest that the 'map' of Liverpool that now interests the readers of Liverpool sagas is located away from both iconographic waterfront and city centre. Those readers live in or, after relocation, warmly remember having lived in, the many miles of Victorian terraced streets that remain to the north and east of the city, especially in Everton and Anfield. It is these districts and their red-brick streets that constitute the locales for fastselling and steady-selling British regional saga fiction. Lynch asserts that

Environmental images are the result of a two-way process between the observer and his environment. The environment suggests distinctions and relations, and the observer – with great adaptability and in the light of his own purposes – selects, organises, and endows with meaning what he sees (Lynch 1960, 7).

The saga editors, and the cover artists they commission, understand this in a social as well as environmental sense, as true for their readership. The generic nickname for working-class regional sagas, 'clogs and shawls' (Hamilton 1994), allows a useful social visuality, suggesting a particular iconicity for the regional working-class saga. By the late 1980s, regional saga covers had developed a distinct semiology (Chapter 2 above), often conveying that same information and a 'visual quality of the ... city which is held by its citizens' (Lynch 1960, 2).[13]

Cover iconography on Liverpool saga fictions evolves as public perceptions of Liverpool may be envisaged to have evolved during the 1980s 'renaissance'. So we find the maritime heritage illustrated at first; then, on saga covers, came the sanitised 'tourist' iconography. It is well into the 1990s before covers demonstrate the personal cognition that is at the heart of British regional sagas everywhere, and this (the depiction of the housewife) begins with covers depicting World War II (Figure 3.2). By 1986, Audrey Howard had joined Helen Forrester with Liverpool-based saga-like fictions published both with Century/Arrow and with Hodder/Coronet. There is a notable ambivalence by her cover artists between the nostalgia of the working mid-century waterfront, of 'clogs and shawls' and the days of sail, Liverpool and Albert Dock tourist status having been publicised internationally by twice hosting the Tall Ships Race in that decade. In 1989, London publishers Headline and Corgi made their first foray into the Liverpool saga market with Elizabeth Murphy (*The Land Is Bright*) and Lyn Andrews (*The White Empress*) respectively; the cover artists for each foregrounded a young woman in period dress against a distant maritime background; each sold in excess of 90,000 paperbacks.

By 1993 these two authors had published a total of ten similar books in which the Liverpool waterfront 'tourist' iconography – the Liver Building, the pierhead 'trinity', if present – was distant/remote.[14] They were joined by Anne Baker (Headline 1991), Joan Jonker (Print Origination/Headline 1991), June Francis, (Piatkus/Bantam 1992), Sheila Walsh (Century/Arrow 1993), Katie Flynn (Heinemann/Mandarin 1993) and Maureen Lee (Orion 1994), making the market highly competitive and cover symbolism a significant factor impacting on sales figures. The semiology of Liverpool saga covers of the early 1990s appeals to similar local nostalgia for the lost mid-century Liverpool, but internationally understood iconography for Liverpool features increasingly.

---

13   Hence the sailing ships in dock as a backdrop to Howard's (1992) heroine (Liverpool's last sailing ship was constructed in 1948) and the transatlantic liner intimidatingly belching smoke beside Murphy's (1991) family. In spite of these novels' resonance with cultural memory, which is aware of the importance of the liner industry to the city between the wars, very few saga covers bear this image.

14   For instance, the shawl-wrapped woman foregrounded against a distant sea traversed by diminutive sailing ships on Murphy (1990) and Andrews (1991).

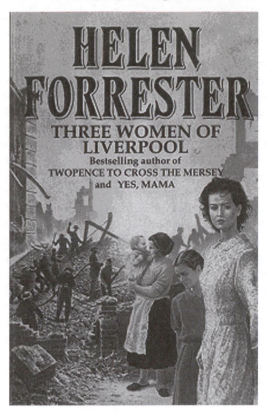

Figure 3.2 The front paperback cover of *Three Women of Liverpool* reprinted by permission of HarperCollins Publishing Ltd © ([1984] 1994) (Helen Forrester)

In 1993 ten authors published 12 new Liverpool sagas, the most ever in one year. From this point, such strong competition for the same readership precipitated a number of changes in approach to saga production. Cover artists begin to be named on individual sagas, revealing the use of local freelance artists. For instance Gwynneth Jones, a local further education teacher, has provided illustrations for a number of sagas by Katie Flynn, June Francis and Joan Jonker. Other artists include Gary Blythe, Nigel Chamberlain, Chris Collingwood, Gordon Crabb, Gary Keane, Nick Price, George Sharpe, Andy Walker and Len Thurston. The fact that the artists are usually named on the books from 1993 onward, and that the authors of highest status, such as Katie Flynn, are shown preliminary sketches for approval[15] implies continued publisher recognition of relevance to the potential customer with strong local or regional affiliations.

---

15 Observed at meetings of the Romantic Novelists' Association North West Chapter meetings, from 1998 to the present, where artists' preliminary sketches and completed cover designs are circulated.

The work of the port is no longer the primary focus and Liverpool as a fantasy setting becomes foregrounded in publishers' insistence on unrealistic pristine white buildings against a fabulous blue sky (a fact that artists and authors alike bemoan), an interesting intersection of recognisable tourist iconography with signification of the utopian ideal typical of saga and other popular fictional fantasies (Fowler 1991, 31–3). The fictions themselves then begin to diverge between those that sell through the icons and historical references of Liverpool locale and those that sell by a more subtle sense of theme. At this point the saga market nationwide was diverted into a plethora of World War II scenarios to cash in on a national nostalgia.

The pace of social change for women has, since the 1970s, been so rapid and so radical that the profoundly organic, and socially determined, role of housewife has virtually vanished. So these fictions map a wider reality, and their semiology and central topography are common to a wider than local readership; the Liverpool saga therefore interpellates both a large body of local readers, and a wider readership in other post-industrial locations with whom its central concerns particularly resonate. Generally, in actuality, either the place or the sense of identity attached to it has been displaced or erased during sudden rapid change. The fiction generates a convincing sense of the identity of a specific place that concurs with how readers may remember it, or may wish to experience it again; and the success of British regional working-class saga fiction has developed through the sense of recognition, or perhaps, what Worpole calls 'respect', for their emotional involvement with that place.

> Local identity remains one of the strongest emotional ties left in secular life, one of the most powerful 'imaginary communities' in which we live. It deserves serious consideration and respect (Worpole 1992b).

In twentieth-century Britain everywhere, inner city demolition led to the post-war relocation of entrenched populations, the dispersal of established communities and the development of new 'problem' housing developments and estates. The destruction caused by bombing is dealt with comprehensively within the remit of British regional sagas generally, and by relocating lost spaces into the *Imaginary*, constitutes an important aspect of the concept of cognitive remapping for this genre. As Jameson points out, Lynch found that,

> Disalienation in the traditional city … involves the practical reconquest of a sense of place and the construction or reconstruction of an articulated ensemble which can be retained in memory and which the individual subject can map and remap along the moments of mobile, alternative trajectories (Jameson 1991, 36).

Post-war mass rehousing with traumatic relocation came very late to bankrupt Liverpool, and the personal implications of that in the early 1980s became the focus of a whole other range of fictions, plays and soap operas (for instance, Russell 1983; Redmond 1984) attempting to assist the emotional negotiation of the new map of Liverpool.

By the mid-1990s even those Liverpool sagas not catering to the World War II anniversary market began to deviate from the earlier elements of specific Liverpool cover iconography. Nationally, the terraced street had been the working-class regional saga's iconography from the late 1980s. Indeed, new publishing house Orion had concentrated on soap opera-like backstreet community sagas set in a variety of English cities, with covers reflecting that locale rather than specific landmarks. But it was the mid-1990s when the publishers finally realised that the icon for the 1990s British regional working-class saga is actually the working-class woman, albeit often encoded as her younger self in training for her ultimate role as 'the housewife' (Williamson 2004).

There seems little doubt that the use of universally recognisable iconography for Liverpool constituted, in Genette's terms, a particular kind of threshold to Liverpool sagas at the point in time when six new authors begin to compete with the four who first published before 1990. Self-conscious referencing of authenticity in paratexts explicating author research activity in local Liverpool archives (Williamson 2000a) is also indicated as drawing the potential reader across that threshold and into the text. The shifting, or nebulous, nature of the cover as threshold is suggested in the rising success of Jonker and Lee, whose covers concentrate on a more universal sense of neighbourhood and home. This indicates that, by the mid-1990s, readers were seeking to repeat a particular experience of the text to which specific Liverpool iconography is irrelevant. The significance of the woman dressed in 'period' (up to 1950s fashion) then becomes coherent when comparing covers for regional sagas, wherever set. While the practice of referencing a specific city continues in front cover straplines, the heroine of a Harry Bowling London docklands saga does not appear very different from the heroine of a Joan Jonker, June Francis or Anne Baker Liverpool saga. The cover iconography, then, has finally caught up with the typical reader, who is a woman over 50 years old, negotiating her way through a cultural remapping of her life and her mother's life that concurs with scores of similar fictions set in other regions and other cities of industrial/colonial Britain.

Chapter 4

Empirical Studies of the Bookshop: Context and Participant Observation in the Study of the Selling and Marketing of Science Fiction and Fantasy

Nickianne Moody
Liverpool John Moores University

One of the distinguishing characteristics of science fiction considered as a commercial genre is the way that publishers have orchestrated a relationship between illustration and text. The value placed on illustration has taken place in order to both widen and sustain its market appeal at different stages during the genre's popular development. As such the iconography and visual nature of the narrative is a prominent aspect of the genre's history and movement across media forms. Interviews with artists and science fiction editors in publications such as *Foundation, Extrapolation Vector* and the *Science Fiction Research Association Newsletter* can provide empirical insights into publishers' perspectives about the use of cover art and illustration. However, this discussion is concerned with understanding the way in which booksellers and consumers make use of this specific marketing of the genre especially within mainstream rather than specialised retailing. Interaction with consumers and the context of their consumption contributes to an understanding of science fiction as a cultural product. Such a premise enables the researcher to be self-reflexive about their interpretations of texts. Moreover the questions that are raised by the discovery of cultural practices associated with reading and book buying shapes an understanding of how popular fiction's social impact can be subject to further study.

Science fiction has a long lineage, from tales about vanished civilisation (Atlantis) in Plato's *Timaeus* (*c.*427–348 BC) and Lucian of Samosata's (*c.*AD 115–200) satirical accounts of warfare and extraordinary interplanetary voyages in *A True Story* and *Icaro-menippus*. The line of descent lays claim to Renaissance utopias and covert scientific discussion in Johannes Kepler's *Somnium* (1634) and Francis Bacon's *The New Atlantis* (1626). Modern science fiction is usually dated from the popular edition of Mary Shelley's (1818) *Frankenstein*: *or The Modern Prometheus* published in 1831 (Fredericks 1982, 7). It became consolidated as a commercial genre in the late 1920s through specialised magazine publication. Part of that process took place through the use of imagery to signify the form as well as content. There are precedents to the way science fiction magazines used illustration, but the style that develops in the 1920s is fully focused on the specificity of the genre. Highly detailed and clearly identified illustrations of the far future, interplanetary locations and technology had already appeared on the covers of miscellaneous story magazines during the teens.[1] Earlier drawings used by pulp magazines in the 1880s also concentrated on narrative episodes which could be construed as science fiction.[2] Moreover, the images which accompanied the work of French authors Jules Verne and Albert Robida invited the popular imagination to speculate more directly on the relationship between technology and the future.[3]

The science fiction magazines that proliferated during the depression era in North America established a distinct market and relationship between writers and readers. Although specialist magazines in fantasy and science fiction existed in Europe prior to the launch of Hugo Gernsback's *Amazing Stories*, this magazine created a product and form which united readers and commercial opportunities for writers.[4] Gernsback repackaged H.G. Wells, Jules Verne and Edgar Allan Poe as 'scientifiction' in April 1926, reprinting these stories and locating a twentieth-century market which could sustain publication of a genre magazine and encourage new speculative fiction about science and technology. The slogan that Gernsback gave *Amazing Stories* was 'Extravagant fiction today … cold fact tomorrow'. The first cover is striking largely due to its use of colour and narrative contingency.[5] The sky is yellow, dominated by a red, yellow and blue ringed Saturn-type planet below which smiling furry humanoids skate in the foreground; behind them sailing ships are marooned on piles of snow and ice. The cover designs featuring red, yellow and sometimes blue skies and a particular iconography which made *Amazing Stories* (as well as Gernsback's subsequent magazines) so distinctive were created by a regular contributing artist, Frank R. Paul.[6] Artist Vincent di Fate's assessment of Paul's contribution to the genre sees his work as:

> The very centrepiece of science fiction's early allure to America during the 1920s and 1930s, with vast, sweeping cityscapes, great spaceships and intricate machines, he established the legitimacy of such subjects as a way of visually identifying the field at a time when science fiction was not yet a fully established form of specialised literature (1997, 237).

1　　See Robinson 1999, 20–21 for examples of these cover illustrations.

2　　The most notable of these are various illustrations and covers for Edward F. Ellis (1868) *The Steam Man of the Prairies* whose sequels and imitators became an entire subgenre of the dime novel.

3　　Robida's best-known illustrated books are *Le Vingtième Siécle* (1883) and *La Vie Electrique* (1887) in which he collected together his earlier slightly satirical speculations about a mechanised future portraying the prospect of everyday life in the 1950s, including warfare, flight, the telephone, the videophone and advancement in female equality.

4　　*Der Orchideengarten* was an Austrian-German magazine published between 1919 and 1921. The Swedish magazine *Hugin* was even earlier, first published in 1916 celebrating scientific achievement and anticipating future discovery including short stories and reviews. Both had illustrations but neither generated a sustainable commercial market.

5　　See Robinson 1999, 28.

6　　Frank R. Paul became the major illustrator for *Amazing Stories*, creating all of the interior design and cover art for the magazine, while Gernsback remained as editor 1926–29. He continued to work with Gernsback for the *Wonder Stories* magazines and other titles.

Paul's cityscapes are iconic and evocative, grounding both the aspirations and anxieties of the modernist imagination of the future. Di Fate argues that Paul's approach to representing the subject of the stories rendered the magazine unmistakably science fiction (1997, 29). This was through his assessment that the work had 'conceptual brilliance' (Di Fate 1997, 29) but I feel that it is also significant that Paul's work engages with the ordinary as well as the exotically alien. Moreover Paul's understanding of the pulp magazine as an artistic medium enabled him to refine and intensify his style. Pulp magazines are named after the cheap woodpulp paper which was very lightweight and suitable to mail to subscribers as well as display on newsstands. The paper was inferior and reproduction generally unsophisticated, which meant an artist had to develop a technique to suit the material. Di Fate refers to this as posterisation, which is 'highly saturated primary colours and large flat areas and employ[ing] a minimum of modelling relying instead on heavy outlining to define form' (1997, 234). However it was Gernsback's decision to employ Paul as a consistent cover artist that allowed him to develop this particular style and technique which become definitive for the emerging genre.

The nineteenth-century serialisations and short stories of Wells, Poe and Verne that Gernsback used as models to establish the twentieth-century genre had also been illustrated, but this artwork was not commonly reproduced when the stories were republished. Instead artists were asked to reinterpret the stories in a manner appropriate to the expectations of the new readership. Alongside nineteenth-century writers of the scientific romance, Gernsback and other editors published established popular writers such as Abraham Merritt, who were keen to take up the opportunity of writing for the new genre, and the work of authors altogether new to publication but who were interested in the scientific and creative impetus of this particular narrative fiction, such as E.E. Doc Smith. To encourage new writing and a fan culture that would sustain interest in the magazine, a Paul cover for one of Gernsback's later publications, *Science Wonder Stories* (November 1929), offered '$300 for the best short, SHORT story written around this picture'.[7] The dramatic cover illustration was dominated by a circular shaped spaceship (a flying saucer) with metallic tentacles extending from it which are wrapped about a skyscraper building that is being carried out into space. Such artwork and the discussion of scientific discovery were intrinsically linked in Gernsback's invitation to readers to become both critics and writers and contribute to an interactive culture forming around the new genre. These cultural practices have always marked science fiction out from other genres, especially their impact on the production and consumption of narrative.

Fan culture is one of the reasons why it is possible to research the role of key cover artists in shaping the generic conventions of science fiction and its marketing. Popular paperback publishing is extremely remiss in acknowledging cover artists. Fans and collectors of science fiction, however, have compiled lists of artists associated with particular eras or writers and confirm their work through discussion with editors or publishers and the artists themselves at conventions and through commercial and fan periodicals. Today it is a little easier to trace cover artists via the display of these collections and annotated descriptions of books on personal

---

7   See Di Fate 1997, 235.

internet sites. The interest of fans in documenting the history of the genre and its achievements has led to publications and the archiving of material by local, national and international science fiction associations. For other genres this process is not so straightforward and often requires oral history interviewing and access to publishing archives to understand professional as well as cultural practice.[8]

The covers of science fiction magazines as they competed with one anther during the 1930s and 1940s became distinct from each other. Yet at the same time their iconography transcended the genre, becoming part of the broader process of how western culture imagined the future.[9] Specifically science fiction illustration depicted and provided an imaginative focus for cultural speculation on future and alternative cities, warfare, relationships between people and machines, social engineering and the practicalities or ethics of interplanetary travel. These ideas were then taken up by other media, particularly film, reaching larger audiences. Therefore when novellas and short stories from the magazines were repackaged for the paperback market of the 1950s publishers drew upon a well-established iconography of science fiction kitsch for their cover art which has been deplored and resisted by its readership who already possessed a conduit and forum through which to speak to editors.[10]

In the original magazines fantasy and science fiction mixed relatively freely. However, by the 1970s distinct commercial products had been established for the market which were regulated by the publishers' categorisation on the book cover alongside their recommended price. As major industrial changes prompted by recession and the impact of new technology became apparent in publishing in the post-1974 era of economic recession, a battle for ascendancy between the category of fantasy and that of science fiction began to take place in British bookshops.

---

8   For this research I used the archive of the Science Fiction Foundation housed at the University of Liverpool, which has a policy of collecting and recording where possible the cover art used for different editions of science fiction books. I am extremely grateful for the support of Andy Sawyer, the collection's librarian, during the research for this chapter.

9   In contrast with other science fiction pulps *Astounding Science Fiction* was distinguished by its more sober covers. First published in January 1930 but very much connected with John Campbell's editorship between 1938 and 1971, *Astounding* was an extremely influential magazine within the field and sometimes outside it. 'Campbell was the linear and logical successor to Gernsback. He was technology-minded and application oriented as the rest of the field in the thirties, with this difference: that he had a broader concept of the scope of "science" (technology and *engineering*); he wanted to explore the effects of the new technological world on *people*' (Merril 1971, 67). This was evident in cover design for the magazine. In particular Campbell used artwork by the astronomical illustrator Chesley Bonestell for a series of covers. Bonestell had produced background paintings for films, and illustrations for popular science books, but was best known for features in magazines such as *Life* speculating on the practicalities of working in space and reaching the surface of planets during the 1950s.

10   The Hugo Awards are given by fans to professionals. The first award ceremony was made at the 1953 World Science Fiction convention. The Hugos, named in honour of Gernsback, include categories for editing, artwork and fanzines. The Nebula Science Fiction Award has been given by the Science Fiction (and Fantasy) Writers of America since 1966 for professional writing. Debate about these awards (and the many others that exist) and their use as an endorsement have provided an arena for feedback and exchange between writers, editors and readers.

This differentiation was made evident by cover design, art work, blurb and the classifications made on behalf of the bookseller and the prospective reader but was experienced as largely ambiguous. At the end of the 1970s booksellers saw the success of J.R.R. Tolkien's *The Silmarillion* (1978) in paperback following equally good hardback sales. Tolkien's place at the top of *The Bookseller*'s rankings was then taken by *Star Wars* and prominent advertising campaigns for Frank Herbert and Michael Moorcock sustained further interest in this minor but well-performing genre of science fiction which included fantasy.[11] *The Bookseller* (1978, 34), addressing the bookselling trade, reported these books and authors as among the most frequently requested. Articles and reports in *The Bookseller* related such books to the category of science fiction, but the sheer volume of sales meant that they would remind booksellers that although belonging to this genre the fiction commanded a more heterogeneous readership.

As the publishing and bookselling crisis intensified in Britain during the mid-1980s, I was carrying out a textual analysis of how science fiction in this period accommodated distinctly gendered groups of writers, which I referred to as cyberpunk and feminist fabulist. Both groups of authors were interested in fictional extrapolations of the near future, the impact of communications, information technology and commodity capitalism on the social and material environment of their fictional worlds. I was curious to see how these books were sold and the nature of their audience. To do so I took up the ethnographic practice of 'lurking', watching the cultural practice of book browsing and buying, first as an observer and then gradually through interaction with booksellers and their customers.

Ethnography is an empirical research process. Its complexity is (a consequence of) the rigorous requirement of different stages of the research such as initial methodological impetus, ongoing research planning and judgement during execution of the research plan, ethical practice and finally communicating the findings to those who have little knowledge of the cultural environment which has been investigated. This perspective, an empirical rather than experimental observation of cultural life, has been adopted by different humanities and social science disciplines from physical anthropology. Longitudinal ethnographic fieldwork which in the early twentieth century took the anthropologist three to four years of total immersion in tribal life started with learning the language. Meaning of the cultural practice was then understood from an insider's perspective. One of the principles of anthropologist Bronislaw Malinowski's ethnographic method was the application of 'strategies to observe and record the imponderabilia of actual life and typical behaviour' (1967, 109). The emphasis here is to document cultural phenomena which are 'uncountable' but can be understood by qualitative research analysis.

For those working in the field of popular fiction extensive empirical research is often too costly for consideration in research plans. The seminal study *Reading the Romance* (Radway 1984) complements contextual analysis of the romance genre and textual analysis of Harlequin (Mills and Boon) fiction with reader

---

11 A novelisation of the film was published prior to its release as part of the marketing campaign. See Sutherland 1981.

questionnaires, observation, guidance by a key informant and interviews.[12] The study revealed significant material about the cultural practice of reading. The scope of this study has rarely been repeated.[13] Nevertheless the standard of social science's use of ethnographic method does not preclude empirical assessment and surveys of the environment in which popular texts are bought and sold. These contextual considerations are a vital aspect of how science fiction finds its market.

At some stage any researcher in science fiction will have to attempt to define the genre and one of the ways in which this is frequently fought out is by making the distinction between science fiction and fantasy. For my own part (at the start of my research) I was perfectly happy with John Clute and Peter Nicholls's definition:

> Science fiction is a label applied to a publishing category and its application is subject to the whims of editors and publishers (Jakubowski and Edwards 1983, 257).

The process of choosing a definition for the genre is a rite of passage in science fiction scholarship. Originally this definition was attractive because it allowed me to accommodate both groups of gendered writers and also another emergent and unavoidable innovation in the practice of the genre, that of fantasy role-playing games. In the field, what the definition enabled me to do was to recognise that a particular struggle over categorisation was being played out through book covers, booksellers' shelving decisions, categorisation on the back of book covers and more significantly the relationship between readers and sales staff of independent bookshops in this period, just prior to the attainment of dominance by bookselling chain stores on the British high street. Nevertheless because this distinction between fantasy and science fiction is so important to the ensuing discussion it may be useful to flag up the way that influential academic commentators have defined these genres. The most useful critical definition comes from Manlove (1987), whose work on fantasy fiction is concerned with its complexity and differentiates between types of modern fantasy through clear literary analysis, giving an account of the characteristics of the popular which is referred to disparagingly as anaemic (1987, 106). In his preface to *The Impulse of Fantasy* he includes a definition that comes from his earlier work:

---

12   Radway's empirical research was carried out specifically to avoid assumptions made from solely conducting a semiotic analysis of the text. She interviewed romance readers who bought their books from a bookshop in a Midwestern town in the USA which was notable for the expert knowledge and welcome advice given by the bookseller. Radway found that these readers shared their cultural knowledge of these books, forming a critical and interpretive reading community.

13   William Sims Bainbridge distributed questionnaires to the delegates at the Iguanacon World Science Fiction Convention held in Phoenix, Arizona in 1978 and received 595 completed forms. Bainbridge was particularly interested in the fandom subculture and the opinions of expert readers. The questionnaire listed 140 authors who were ranked on a preference scale. They were also asked to make a preference ranking for 40 different literature types largely but not wholly related to science fiction and its subgenres. Further questions looked at favourite periods of writing, topics and protagonists. From this data Bainbridge looks at the distinctions between the hard science tradition, the new wave and the fantasy cluster and identifies a major variable for this period of women writers and readers making an impact on the genre.

A fiction evoking wonder and containing substantial and irreducible element of supernatural or impossible worlds, beings or objects with which the mortal character in the story or the readers become on at least partly familiar terms (1987, iv).

Incorporated into this definition is the privileging that fantasy gives to the supernatural and the fantastic as a journey and an immersion in a fictional world which is different to the extrapolative and rational discursive exploration in science fiction texts. Fantasy book covers therefore use distinctive visual signifiers which foreground these qualities and emphasise the supernatural rather than the technological. They have 'a sense of individuality that comes from making things strange and luminous with independent life in a fantastic setting' (Manlove 1987, iv) which is apparent in the internal narrative, language and address to the reader, making it distinguishable from the work of science fiction which is more often interested in rendering the strange as a form of verisimilitude.

My observations of the way definitions of science fiction and fantasy (or variations of those four words) were employed in the field took place in five different bookshops in the West Midlands – one commercial chain, the bookseller and stationer WHSmith, three independent bookshops and a specialist science fiction bookshop – between 1984 and 1987. The shops were visited at least once every six weeks for 18 months and interviews took place with 14 different shop personnel. Shelf categorisation changed quite regularly as reviews of sales and planning meetings by staff redefined what was selling and what needed to be brought to the attention of this group of readers.

About ten years earlier bookshops in Britain may not have been selling books by generic category at all and would have been more likely to sell by publisher or imprint. So science fiction readers would have known to look at Panther, Mayflower, Gollancz, Orbit, Sphere, New English Library and Pan for their one or two monthly publications in this category. If they were buying new books they would know the publisher of favoured authors and be aware of that publisher's list supporting front-, mid- and backlist science fiction writers. These readers would rely on reviews from science fiction magazines, author promotions at conventions and local science fiction groups rather than relying on the bookseller. However in the 1980s generic categorisation became increasingly important and books were labelled by publishers to help bookshop staff place them in their correct stands or shelving. All of the bookshops except the specialist shops found science fiction a difficult category to manage. Even so the booksellers often felt that they did not agree with the category stamped on the spine and were discomforted by arguments with readers about these definitions.

One of the older members of the WHSmith's branch found the genre particularly difficult because of the ban that the chain had enforced on the British fiction magazine *New Worlds* following its serialisation of Norman Spinrad's *Bug Jack Baron* in 1968. He was extremely suspicious of the genre and its power to offend ordinary readers. Others saw it as juvenile or male-oriented fiction and had difficulty with the category of science fiction and fantasy when it was suggested by The Women's Press or Virago. Booksellers were frequently frustrated by requests for books that had only been published in the US or the return of books that had been reprinted under different titles. Nevertheless they were unanimous in why they wanted to persevere with the genre. Firstly, although they did not have a category definition for it, they were still in awe of the way the *Star Wars* novelisation and tie-in series had sold during the late 1970s across a visibly heterogeneous audience. Secondly they knew that this audience was returning to the bookshop and continuing to buy from the science fiction and fantasy genre. They also saw it as the one genre which could sell hardback books, especially fantasy trilogies. They were also impressed that paperbacks sold even though they did not have access to reviews. Booksellers saw the genre as one which was promoted through media reference, new films, radio plays, television and a common awareness of science fiction which would bring new and regular customers into the shop. Nevertheless during interviews and informal discussions nearly three-quarters of the booksellers revealed themselves to be, in varying degrees, contemptuous of the genre.

In retrospect this was an extremely interesting period of transition in the book trade. The independent bookshops that I visited during that period were taken over by the emerging bookshop chains or put out of business by them. The empirical research that I carried out took the form of observing the culture of the bookshop. Participant observation provides ways of understanding common beliefs within a culture: it avoids dependence on assumptions and complements theoretical models about cultural experience and practice. Interaction with sales staff and browsers meant that my understanding of the bookshop culture was derived from informal interviews, a method which needs to be differentiated from simply gathering anecdotal information.

> Informal interviews are most common in ethnographic work. They seem to be casual conversations, but where structured interviews have an explicit agenda, informal interviews have a specific but implicit research agenda. The researcher uses informal approaches to discover the categories of meaning in a culture. Informal interviews are useful throughout an ethnographic study in discovering what people think and how one person's preoccupations compare with another's. Such comparisons help identify shared values in the community – values that inform behaviour. Informal interviews are also useful in establishing and maintaining a healthy rapport (Fetterman 1989, 48).

As well as in the bookshops I was carrying out similar interviews within fan culture and reading communities. However, with the bookshop staff the issue of reciprocity and exchange, which is important in maintaining rapport, was much clearer.

> Trusting and cooperative relationships among the participant observer and the insiders in the field setting, in short, are necessary for obtaining access to the daily existence of insiders and for accurate, dependable, high quality information about their world. Trust and cooperation are matters of degree. The participant observer should seek to maximize cooperation with at least a few key people in the field setting. Trust and cooperation constantly are problems and depend on ongoing interactive work in concrete situations. You will have to decide while in the field and doing fieldwork when there is sufficient cooperation and trust to support truth claims. You, in other words, constantly must interpret and evaluate information in terms of who is providing it, the degree and character of the relationships involved, and the situations and setting in which you interact with insiders (Jorgensen 1989, 70).

The booksellers were willing to talk to me because I was familiar with a variety of fantasy role-playing games that were bringing new readers and young readers into the bookshops as potential customers. Sales staff were aware that they had to increase their understanding of all potential readers and this was an area about which they could find very little information.

The recession of the 1970s and 1980s put increasing pressure on publishers and booksellers. Library budgets were no longer able to sustain the hardback sales of popular fiction. Poor sales and public debate about science fiction associated with *New Worlds* and moves by science fiction writers to become part of contemporary literature encouraged publishers to see science fiction as a problematic, waning and unstable genre. Several stories circulate during the mid-1980s in both British and American fan circles to support the idea that highly specialist knowledge was required to identify successful science fiction such as the unprecedented commercial success of *The Chronicles of Thomas Covenant the Unbeliever* (Stephen R. Donaldson 1977).[14] It was believed that the book had been turned down by 47 different publishing houses until it gained the support of the Del Rey imprint run by an influential husband and wife editorial team at Ballantine.[15] Lester Del Rey was a well-received science fiction writer, critic and editor, his wife Judy-Lynn an important editor particularly of fantasy fiction. Throughout the 1980s science fiction does not feature on the British fastseller top 100 list except when it is referred to as fantasy. Booksellers remembered that the recognition of this crisis had been an intervention by the Book Marketing Council in 1983 which launched a science fiction promotion where it had been very obvious that only half of the books were by contemporary authors.

Publicity budgets, which were shrinking in the wake of the Organization of Petroleum Exporting Countries (OPEC) crisis, became focused on the genre's bestsellers, Asimov, Clarke and Heinlein. New writers in North America were forced into short and declining print runs amongst smaller presses and imprints alongside successful writers from the 1960s and 1970s. Writers would then attempt to renegotiate publication of their work once they had proved that there was an audience for it. So at the beginning of the 1980s the trade perceived three main initiatives in the publication of this genre which booksellers and professional writers had to address. The fantasy trilogy was attractive to the publisher because it guaranteed hardback sales and demand from libraries. The commercial track record of Frank Herbert's 'Dune' series, Michael Moorcock's 'Elric' series, Anne McCaffrey's 'Dragons of Pern' and Marion Zimmer Bradley's 'Darkover' novels encouraged the return of the 'three-decker novel'. However, concern was expressed that the fantasy trilogy used

---

14 Booksellers often used this series as an example of ambiguous marketing, the book was labelled as a fantasy series, used the coding of landscape associated with fantasy but was also seen as an exemplary example of contemporary science fiction when reviewed in trade magazines. The dual categorisation which was acknowledged by the booksellers is probably evidence of the achievement of marketing for the Del Rey science fiction and fantasy list.

15 The material being referred to here and at other stages of this discussion is anecdotal but drawn from a large number of interviews with writers, editors, publishers, fans and readers at science fiction conventions in Britain and America between 1984 and 1987.

cover art that was distinctive from science fiction, fragmenting a potential market. Shared world and themed anthologies were popular at this time influenced both by the success of collections based on *Star Trek* and *Dr Who* as well as fiction related to the game worlds of fantasy role-playing games. Writers who were new to the genre felt pressured into accepting contracts which required three-volume serials or sequels if sales merited it. Various commentators found this form of serialisation was damaging to the development of the genre. It was connected to a third trend prompted by the convergence of different media industries and the desire to identify brands which could be heavily promoted rather than the riskier route of developing the career of a range of newcomers. Charles Platt saw this as the decline of the midlist:

> 'Midlist' means the middle range of a publisher's list of books. The ones at the top of the list are the best-sellers heavily promoted, selling 100,000 copies or more. At the bottom are westerns, cheap romances, and other types of formula-fiction mass-produced with minimal expectations. Somewhere in the middle are reasonably thoughtful novels for reasonably thoughtful readers – the literary equivalent of BBC2 television (Platt 1989, 49).

Predictability for the publishing industry was now more than ever a key concern. Editors were looking for books which would return their costs and make a profit as projected. The margin for experimentation and offsetting books that failed to make their costs or made their profit at a slower pace on the backlist had been completely eroded. Science fiction had protected itself from what it perceived as a hostile publishing and critical environment through a fan association and then a professional association which awarded prizes and published anthologies of new work in order to promote and sustain the genre and enhance acceptance of midlist writers. However, publishers began to use the shortlists for these prizes and anthologies of new fiction to locate writers who were seen as acceptable to the established genre audience or who would be able to initiate and continue science fiction which could be sold as a series of books. Older science fiction concepts were seen as potential franchises which would satisfy new audience demand.[16] Increasingly science fiction was returning to a definition aligned with adventure rather than overt political comment, experimental writing or introspection, the audience for which seemed unpredictable. The mass publication of fantasy adventure seemed semi-programmable in that it could meet and satisfy a larger audience demand. These two concerns led to the most cogent change in publishing during the period: the move to fantasy and the reliance on the quasi-medieval diegesis which predominates during the 1980s.

Umberto Eco (1986) makes an argument for the rise of medieval locations in popular media (not just science fiction) as a form of new millennialism which responded to a particular cultural climate. Such location could negotiate social anxieties about changes in working life (de-industrialisation and information technology), political and national certainties (ending of the cold war, power of Middle Eastern oil producers, Asian technological innovation and in Britain membership

---

16   For example Platt (1989, 50) cites several examples including Robert Silverberg's deal with Bantam Books to expand three Asimov novellas into novels. Other published and well-acclaimed science fiction authors were being commissioned to write sequels to successful novels published by writers from the genre's golden age.

of the European Economic Community [EEC]), gendered power relations and the prospect of institutional change and modernisation. He saw the persistent use of the medieval as a setting for narrative as a way that a culture could explore the roots of capitalism during a time of transition and crisis.[17]

The success of fantasy, as distinct from science fiction, can be accounted for in several ways that are adjacent to Eco's thesis. The first is that this type of fantasy, the quest, is suitable for the trilogy format. Material for the fantasy trilogy can be drawn from other generic categories. Fantasy fiction sat alongside romance, mystery, horror and mainstream fiction far more happily in booksellers' and publishers' minds than science fiction seemed to do. Existing trilogies could also be repackaged and republished in slightly different generic packaging. Demand for fantasy reading material arose from subcultural activity that accompanied fantasy role-playing games. This was very clear from interviews with readers who wanted to put fantasy novels and/or series to use in other cultural practices than just individual reading. Such novels formed the basis for game playing and shared storytelling beyond actual commercial products sold specifically for role-playing games.

This generation of readers in Britain also made connections with children's television of the previous decade which had been fascinated with the relationship between technology and magic, creating a predisposition to read the fantasy adventure in the new young adult market. Publishers' interest in the serial provided a means for the science fiction writers to earn a living. Publishers also found writers who would produce television and film tie-ins and novelisations which sometimes offered fans opportunities to become professional writers. Relationships between print and televisual fiction have become central to the reformation of the genre across new media forms. At that time the fantasy serial and books based on television programmes and films appeared to disrupt earlier traditions and critical perceptions of science fiction's integrity (Platt 1989). The distinction between science fiction, fantasy fiction and the emerging hybrid science fantasy became clear to readers and booksellers by virtue of its cover design rather than through publishers' designated categories which struggled to maintain the coherence of the genre during a time of very troubled economics for transforming publishing houses.

The style and design of science fantasy book covers in the 1980s reversed the trend of 1970s science fiction illustration, which had developed into abstract, symbolic and metonymic imagery. This was seen as appropriate for the type of dystopian and speculative narratives that were being published at that time especially those associated with new-wave science fiction. In Britain the movement originated with Michael Moorcock's editorship of the magazine *New Worlds* in 1964. Scholes and Rabkin's characterisation of this movement finds coherence between many diverse writers predicated on two concerns: a new literary self-consciousness

---

17 Various academics, publishers and critics have debated why fantasy as a genre was so successful in this period. Sutherland's (1981) reading of *Star Wars* sees it as the perfect product to offer escapism to a population culturally exhausted by the Vietnam War. I have argued elsewhere (Moody 1991) that it was attractive to female writers and readers because it could used to represent strong female characters. Alternatively Eco seems to suggest that it becomes a narrative location which can dispense with political correctness.

that encouraged experimentation within the writing and corresponding criticism; and secondly a social awareness that marked the work as anti-establishment and iconoclastic (Scholes and Rabkin 1977, 88).[18]

The style of artwork used to promote publication marked this new science fiction from the iconography that had been borrowed from the magazines of the 1940s for paperback republication during the 1950s. Di Fate (1977, 56–78) looks at the transition from magazine to paperback editing by considering the finds of two successful publishing houses from this period, Ace and Ballantine. Each had taken on science fiction editors – Donald Wollheim and Lester Del Rey respectively – who had been writers and moved into publishing although they had very different approaches to cover design.[19]

Familiarity with the pulp magazines of the 1940s and 1950s, Di Fate asserts, led Wollheim to preserve the predominant flamboyant style of cover art designed to appeal to an audience for science fiction which he believed comprised largely 'unworldly' teenagers (1997, 59). The covers for *Amazing Stories* and its downmarket imitators developed science fiction clichés that became culturally iconic through film posters and parody especially: femme fatales in metal brassieres, bug-eyed monsters, phallic rocket ships, adventurous rescues and lurid design which was seen as suitable for an adolescent male readership. Alternatively Ballantine assigned Richard M. Powers to design the cover for Arthur C. Clarke's (1958) *Childhood's End*. Powers was influenced by surrealist artists Yves Tanguy and Joan Miró and was original in his use of this imagery for science fiction and commercial art (Di Fate 1977, 60).

> The distinguishing quality of Powers' work was its sophisticated and abstract, non-representational style which set a precedent for a great diversity of approaches by other artists (Di Fate 1997, 59).

This cover created 'a sensation but also helped greatly to increase the sales of the book' (Di Fate 1997, 59). Following the successful illustration for Clarke's speculative fiction Powers's approach to cover design was used for New Wave science fiction. However Di Fate argues that the use of this imagery fell out of favour because as it was developed it produced covers which were 'jarring and distasteful to consumers' (1997, 78) prompting a re-evaluation of marketing strategies. This was to be a return to artwork which possessed a strong narrative quality and made use of a different and distinctive spectrum of the acrylic paint palette which had been developed in the

---

18   In terms of his own writing Moorcock was more commonly associated with the 'Sword and Sorcery' subgenre of commercial fantasy. In the United States Judith Merrill was the main proponent of the movement through her editing and criticism rather than her own writing.

19   Wollheim was very much involved in fandom as well as writing. He is best known for the creation of Ace doubles, two novels in one with different cover art which eased the cost of promoting new writers. He formed his own company, DAW Books, in 1971. As previously discussed Lester Del Rey came from a background of science fiction writing in the late 1930s and early 1940s, magazine editing and reviewing. He joined his wife as a science fiction editor at Ballantine in 1974. Judy-Lynn Del Rey was instrumental in forming the Del Rey imprint through her ability to market science fiction and fantasy to audiences large enough for the books to enter bestseller lists.

1950s and 1960s. I will refer to the colours being used for fantasy fiction in the late 1970s and the 1980s as a 'muted acrylic palette', which is darker but more delicate when compared with the primary colours used by pulp and abstract science fiction covers while retaining an intensity of colour.[20]

Booksellers I talked to in the mid-1980s did indeed recognise distinctions in the use of colour in cover art as marking out a category of science fantasy. The covers largely concentrated on the fantasy world or landscape which formed the setting for the narrative, its diegesis, and very often included detailed depictions of the protagonist or characters in the story. The booksellers all described the change that was taking place as a shift of colour and in quality of artwork, but they were hesitant about whether this signified fantasy or science fiction and were happier to refer to the fiction as science fantasy. One book that was singled out as being particularly emblematic of the hybrid science fantasy genre was the British paperback edition of Gene Wolfe's *The Shadow of the Torturer* (Arrow, 1981).[21] The front cover announces that the book was the winner of the World Fantasy Award, the British Science Fiction Award and the Nebula Award. The design very definitely contains the formula for the new diegetic covers. It depicts an armed hooded figure with a swirling cloak walking away from a stone-built hillside town. The wraparound cover is designed so that we can see that the figure will move through an ancient forest towards ships anchored at shore. The clouds in the sky on the front cover are a muted orange and the land below is phthalo turquoise. The back cover is darker than the front, concentrating more on the land than the sky. The book's categorisation is clearly given on the back cover as science fiction.

The cover for Michael Moorcock's *The City in the Autumn Stars* (Grafton, 1986) uses a similar division of colour.[22] The sky is bright using violet quinacridones of rose and magenta. The protagonists are associated with a steam-driven airship which has an oval balloon of banded yellow, red and green contributing to the brightness at the top of the design. The ship is flying over a muted violet patchwork river valley to a darkened turreted city within a forest. *The City in the Autumn Stars* is not clearly labelled as a part of a series but it is categorised as fantasy. The intense violet sky fades to the darkness of mountain and city with the spine trisected by three graduations in colour from rose to magenta to ivory black. The cover for the Gene Wolfe book is as sharply bisected between the raw umber and orange of the sky and darker phthalo turquoise of the mountain range of the fictional world. However the effect of Geoff Taylor's wraparound cover for the Moorcock book is dissipated by a yellow box which emphasises the narrative summary for the cover blurb and endorsements from

---

20   This is a use of colour which is very evident on the covers of *The Magazine of Fantasy and Science Fiction* during the same period.

21   Cover artist Bruce Pennington, unacknowledged on the actual cover.

22   Cover artist Geoff Taylor. Scholes and Rabkin's comment on the author's 'reactionary fictional form' is that 'if there is a theme that runs through Moorcock's fiction, that theme would have to be parody ... Moorcock's end of the world is simply England's *fin de siècle*, extrapolated: a world of dandies and darlings, living for pleasure. It is amusing, fantastic and wildly escapist. Social consciousness intrudes not here' (1977, 89–90).

The Guardian and *The New Statesman*.[23] Although the booksellers were disparaging of the genre, they appreciated the covers aesthetically and as effective marketing tools and would display books face forward on the shelves if they thought they were particularly attractive. They would display promotional posters indefinitely as part of the interior décor of the science fiction and fantasy section and they would include books in coveted window displays because they could make connections between them using the iconography.

Trading on the establishment of this iconography and its distinctions from previous science fiction illustration were two series which booksellers found difficult to characterise effectively: 'The Thieves' World Saga' edited by Robert Asprin and Lynn Abbey and Terry Pratchett's writing as a whole. Pratchett was associated with irreverent and comic writing which is an established sub genre in science fiction – for example *Strata* (1982) a parody of Larry Niven's *Ringworld*, a classic science fiction series. However, what was emerging as his most popular creation was the 'Discworld' series set in a fantasy world. The cover design for the second edition and subsequent paperback publication was produced by one of the most notable British science fiction and fantasy cover artists, Josh Kirby.[24] Kirby had a long and prolific career creating covers for a range of different publishers and types of genre fiction in the 1950s and 1960s. His preference appears to be for science fiction and fantasy artwork but consistent commissions in this field did not materialise until the late 1970s.

Malcolm Edwards's evaluation of science fiction's place in the economics of publishing in 1984 noted structural changes taking place in the industry as a whole and the genre in particular. Although he states that 'science fiction publishing has never been more profitable' like Platt he feels this is because of the promotion budgets given to the top end of the market (1984, 292).

> A gulf has developed between the superstars and the rest which many publishers find hard
> to bridge; and that 'rest' represents marginally profitable publishing, in which the more
> serious and demanding works are increasingly pushed aside in favour of simple-minded
> fantasy (Edwards 1984, 292).

Evidence of the promotion budget can be found in Kirby's output beginning to focus exclusively on science fiction and fantasy paperbacks. In the 1950s Kirby comments that paperback science fiction design was 'watered down' because publishers wished covers to be ambiguous, possibly science fiction but definitely containing an adventure story in order to attract both markets (Langford 1999, 74). Artists therefore

---

23   The endorsements on the back of the Wolfe book use bold white type on a suitably darkened sky, so the back of the book does not have the contrast between bright colour at the top of the design and dark below. Therefore it emphasises the fictional world and comment from *The Times* and critically acclaimed science fiction/fantasy writer Ursula K. Le Guin.

24   Colin Smythe's original publication of *The Colour of Magic* used artwork by Alan Smith. The colours Smith uses are reminiscent of Power's work and although the cover is representational of the narrative content it is also quite abstract. The American first edition (St Martin's Press) used the same cover. More importantly the US paperback edition did not use Kirby's artwork.

were constrained by these demands. Kirby worked across the science fiction and fantasy spectrum producing covers for *Authentic Science Fiction Magazine* in 1967, the Panther editions of Asimov and Corgi's editions of Arthur C. Clarke. However his association with comic and fantasy series also connected him to Ray Bradbury, Ursula K. Le Guin, Andre Norton, Robert Silverberg, Robert Sheckley, Tom Holt, Robert Rankin and two writers of significant and long-running serial science fantasy fiction, E.C. Tubb (*Dumarest*) and Philip José Farmer (*Riverworld*). In 1984 his covers were used for the immensely successful paperback versions of Pratchett's Discworld novels as well as producing covers for Corgi's two fantasy role-playing book series *Wizards, Warriors and You* and *Tunnels and Trolls*.

Although Kirby's work is distinct from the fantasy cover formula and does not use the muted acrylic palette, it is the connection Kirby's illustration makes to fantasy fiction which was significant to the booksellers. Kirby's illustration places emphasis on characters as well as the quasi-medieval fictional diegesis of the Discworld.

The British edition of the Thieves' World series did not use the highly regarded Walter Velez artwork which drew upon the more firmly established imagery in North America for a fantasy role-playing game (FRPG) diegesis. Instead they used the work of Bruce Pennington who did use the muted acrylic palette, the perspective of a centred protagonist from which the reader looks down into/over the city or a narrative encounter.[25]

The Thieves' World books were shared world anthologies comprising short stories by many established science fiction and fantasy writers using characters (mainly outlaws) who coexisted in the city of Sanctuary. In 1981 the games company Chaosium Inc. released an outline of the fictional world and its characters which could be adapted for use with nine major fantasy role-playing systems from that period. *The Shadows of Sanctuary*, which again uses phthalo turquoise, depicts a confrontation with a FRPG thief/assassin and a man with a crossbow taking place within a medieval stone 'laboratory'. More interestingly the wraparound cover for the first book in the series, *Thieves' World*, uses the rose and magenta colour scheme to show a warrior facing a flying monster.[26] This scene is continued on the back cover where we see the expressions of characters who are behind the warrior watching the scene. Their expressions and medieval dress are reminiscent of the Discworld characterisations, especially the way in which they respond to the situations in which they find themselves.

Rather than just accepting and displaying the covers, booksellers made use of them to advise potential readers and group genre products together. The iconography, use of particular colours, viewing the landscape from above, representations of

---

25 Pennington was awarded the British Science Fiction Award for artwork in 1982 and 1984. He produced science fiction covers for Ballantine, Corgi and Sphere. He produced covers for the game book series 'Signs of the Demonspawn' and the game *Warhammer*. He is mainly known for his artwork for the British Arrow paperback editions of Gene Wolfe's *The Book of the New Sun* series. Currently these can be viewed at <http://easyweb.easynet. co.uk/~ajellis/WolfeArt.htm>.

26 The cover art illustrates the story *The Gate of Flying Knives* by Poul Andersen. The front cover invites readers to 'Enter a new and magical realm created by the world's top science fiction and fantasy writers'.

protagonist and integral characters, wraparound covers and medievalism which dominate the bookshelves in the middle years of the 1980s were part of an expansion of what was being offered by this genre. It stands in contrast to the popularity of more conventionally defined science fiction films: the *Star Wars* series in 1977, *Star Trek* series 1979, *Alien* (1979), *Mad Max* series 1979, *Blade Runner* (1982), *The Terminator* (1984), *Dune* (1984), *Back to the Future* (1985) and *Robocop* (1986). The next trend responding to these films created in turn the need for new signification and the resurgence of science fiction over fantasy. Currently we have the dominance of fantasy films and fantasy books, particularly for a juvenile market; the struggle in taxonomy is no longer between fantasy, science and horror but in finding ways that this fiction can be put before a mainstream audience.

In an article on the potential of radical fantasy, Fredric Jameson (2002) speculates on the difference between fantasy and science fiction. He dispenses with the 'tricky process' of accessing the readership and proposes in its stead a structural analysis of generic difference. His discussion claims that the distinction 'is not an academic or scholastic issue, for the readership, with a few interesting exceptions, are significantly different and do not tolerate each others' tastes' (2002, 278). Science fiction and fantasy is mass produced and has to have a readership which is a little more omnivorous than Jameson suggests in order to sustain its sales and inclusion on publishers' lists. Studies of science fiction fandom on which such assertions are often based only touch the surface of the genre's readership. Therefore, consideration of cultural practice and the circuit of relationships which determine the choice and reading of fiction points to moments when fantasy and science fiction become interchangeable and swap their dominance on bookshop shelves. During this process cover designs and the marketing of books as a cultural product have had a critical impact and contribute to how texts are used culturally. To understand how that readership is formed and how cultural values are transmitted and negotiated then researchers need to involve themselves in the messy and time-consuming habit of finding ways to encounter the reader and challenge academic assumptions about how spaces of consumption are actually used.

The once colourful covers for Terry Pratchett's Discworld novels now have new designs so that they can pass out of science fiction and fantasy categories and on to general fiction shelves. They have now assumed sober photographic covers which eschew their generic origins and seek out a mainstream adult audience in the same way that Bloomsbury's alternative covers for 'adult versions' of the Harry Potter series. However, in the case of Pratchett what is taking place here is a shift in genre. The cover blurbs make no reference to science fiction or fantasy; instead they emphasise humour and use endorsements from national newspapers. At the beginning of the twenty-first century fantasy film is dominant at the box office and serial fiction has allowed writers in many different genres to build up an audience willing to follow the exploits of unlikely protagonists. Detective, fantasy, horror, science fiction and romance readerships can be targeted in different marketing campaigns through regular changes in cover design.[27] How readers locate the texts that they want to read in the age of Amazon.com, the arrival of major bookstores in out of town shopping malls in Britain and publishers' interest in promoting generic fiction to a general rather than specialised readership needs to be understood and included in the analysis of popular texts. It does not need to take the form of a longitudinal social survey, but an understanding of how the popular text as research subject is placed in bookshops, marketed and packaged will always produce insight into the context in which the text is being consumed.

---

27 Laurel K. Hamilton's 'Vampire Hunter' series is a good example of this trend: her books are shelved as horror, fantasy, romance, science fiction and general fiction sometimes simultaneously.

PART 2
What Makes a Book Popular?

Chapter 5

Literary Prizes, Production Values and Cover Images

Elizabeth Webby
University of Sydney

Although lacking the international recognition of The Booker Prize, the Miles Franklin Award is Australia's most prestigious literary prize. It was established in 1954 through a bequest from the Australian novelist Miles Franklin. She had spent time in America and so was aware of the lack of any Australian equivalent to the Pulitzer Prizes. For six years I had the pleasure of being a judge of the Award and this chapter's reading of the covers of some recent Australian novels in relation to their production and reception was inspired by the many examples I saw each year. Initially I was concerned about the impact a less than enticing cover might have on the sales of a book I considered deserved more notice. Subsequently I became interested in the reasons why covers of Australian novels were almost always altered when these works achieved release in Britain and the USA. This occurs even when covers and other paratextual elements make a significant contribution to the meaning of a postmodern text, as with the Flanagan and Hooper novels discussed below.

For the 2002 Miles Franklin Award, my fellow judges and I ended up with a shortlist of five novels. Three happened to come from the same publishing house – Pan Macmillan Australia – and we could not help remarking that much more time and money had been spent on the production of two of the titles than on the third. These two, by leading Australian writers Tim Winton and Richard Flanagan, were hardbacks with full-colour dust jackets and superior paper stock. Flanagan's *Gould's Book of Fish* (2001) also featured colour illustrations of the fish painted by Tasmanian convict artist W.B. Gould, the initial inspiration for the novel, at the beginning of each chapter, as well as changes in type colour to reflect the notion that Gould was writing his manuscript in whatever he could find to use as ink. The third book, Joan London's *Gilgamesh* (2001), was a first novel, though by an author who had already published two prize-winning collections of short stories. It, however, was published in paperback, with a monochrome and far from eye-catching photographic cover that revealed little about the work's content.

One of the other judges – the former leading Australian publisher Hilary McPhee – later wrote a newspaper article reflecting on what she described as the 'under publishing' of many recent Australian novels. This in turn drew a response from the publisher of another of the shortlisted novels, horrified that our reading of the novels submitted for the Miles Franklin Award might have been influenced in any way by a book's production values. To those who work in book history rather than publishing this reaction will seem naïve to say the least. Yet many successful novels now appear in quite different formats as they are sold into different markets and different countries. These varied formats suggest that publishers are quite aware of the way that the covers, illustrations and other elements of the production of books shape their reception. This chapter will examine a number of Australian literary novels to explore how their various formats might influence their national and international readers' interpretations of them.

In addition to Winton, Flanagan and London's work, this chapter will look in particular at Peter Carey's multi-award-winning *True History of the Kelly Gang* (2000), which has appeared in five different formats in Australia alone. Like Flanagan, Carey bases his novel on an Australian historical figure, the bushranger Ned Kelly, who is supposedly writing his life story. And like Flanagan he has some fun with the materiality of the text, in this case via detailed bibliographical descriptions of the supposed Kelly manuscript. I will also be considering a more recent novel, Chloe Hooper's *A Child's Book of True Crime* (2002), which as its title indicates also draws on the current popularity, in Australian fiction at least, of mixtures involving history and fiction, with more than a spice of sex and violence. Like Flanagan's novel, Hooper's is set in Tasmania, allowing for some additional frissons thanks to that island's Gothic associations, though also attracting the wrath of those like Flanagan who actually live in Tasmania rather than just exploit it in their novels. Like Flanagan's novel, *A Child's Book* also includes illustrations, in this case mock-childlike drawings of iconic Australian birds and animals, which are an essential part of the text. And, at least in some editions, it featured a cover, also using Australian fauna, which made parodic reference to the covers of some early twentieth-century English children's adventure stories set in distant parts of the Empire, such as Australia. This cover seemed such an essential part of the work's meaning that I was very surprised when I discovered that the American editions of the novel had very different ones.

My initial interest in the disparity in the amount of money being put into the covers, dust jackets and design of novels by name authors as opposed to new or unknown ones was as part of an investigation of what we know to be happening with promotion and marketing generally. Name authors now get such big advances that publishers have to keep throwing money at their books to ensure that they do not end up with even bigger losses. It then becomes even harder for a new author, or a not-so-new one who has not yet managed to become a name, to attract the attention of buyers, readers and perhaps even judges. As I have delved further into the differences between these book covers, however, some intriguing issues have opened up with respect to the ways in which these differences might affect the readings of texts. This seems to be especially crucial in the case of texts which deliberately play with notions of history and fiction, truth and lies, and where paratextual elements are used as part of this play. Even where this is not the case, as with Tim Winton's *Dirt Music* (2001), the differences between the Australian, British and American covers raise questions about the ways in which texts from elsewhere are presented to British and American readers. While one might have expected a playing up of the exotic element – as certainly happens with Australian film and television programmes – the reverse seems usually to be the case. Indeed, it would seem that publishers have even attempted to conceal the fact that Winton's and Carey's novels are set in Australia, perhaps because quality fiction is not usually associated with Australia in the way that crocodiles and the outback are.

Covers of both the hardback and paperback Australian editions of Winton's *Dirt Music* feature the same beautiful image of a single large boab tree, set against a cloudy sky. The dominant colour is brown, from the dried grass making up the bottom half of the image, as well as the clouds and the tree trunk. This attractive image is resonant for any Australian reader of the northern Australian outback where the novel is set, as well as being in a colour well attuned to the novel's title. A small black-and-white drawing of the boab tree is also used as part of the internal page design. And, in reading the novel, one finds that at a certain stage, when the hero is alone in a very isolated part of Western Australia, boab trees become surrogate humans for him – more particularly, surrogate women. So I was very surprised to find that the covers of the British hardback and paperback editions of *Dirt Music* had nothing whatever to do with boab trees, dirt or, it would seem, with Australia. Both are predominantly blue in colour, with the hardback featuring an empty rowing boat with sea behind and the paperback showing part of the back of a male figure standing by a road. While both covers have a connection to some of the novel's events – the hero does on occasion hitchhike and also row in a boat – these are minor compared with the centrality of the boab tree to the narrative. Both covers, but especially the paperback's, also say nothing about the interconnections between man and environment, which is such a strong theme in all of Winton's work, and is indicated here even in his title of *Dirt Music*. And, furthermore, neither cover indicates that the novel has any connection with Australia. While the material on the inside dust jacket flap of the British hardcover edition is mostly identical to that on the Australian hardcover there is a crucial change in the last sentence, which refers to Winton as 'one of the finest novelists of his generation' instead of 'the pre-eminent Australian novelist of his generation'. The American hardcover blurb, in contrast, uses the Australian version of this last sentence, though in other respects is very different, presenting the novel's story from the perspective of the leading male character instead of the leading female one. Both the US hardcover and paperback editions feature aerial shots of what could be part of the Australian coast and, with brown, red and yellow predominating, are at least a little more authentically Australian with respect to their colour. Even though the focus is still more on water than dirt, one does get a sense of the immensity of the landscape, another theme in the novel. Without the small line drawings of the boab tree to break up the text, the page design of each of these non-Australian editions is also much less attractive to the eye.

In the case of Richard Flanagan's *Gould's Book of Fish*, there is much less difference between the images used on the covers of the various Australian, British and American hardback and paperback editions. All the designs feature one or more of the paintings of Australian sea creatures actually made by the Tasmanian convict artist William Buvelow Gould in the 1830s which are so intrinsic to the novel: its subtitle is *A Novel in Twelve Fish*. Indeed, apart from their differently designed jackets, different coloured bindings and different title and imprint pages, the US Grove Press and UK Atlantic Books hardback editions of *Gould's Book of Fish* are identical to the Australian Picador hardback. All were in fact printed in Australia, presumably to help spread the cost of what was a very expensive piece of book production, featuring specially designed marbled endpapers as well as full-colour illustrations of the twelve fish, plus a text printed in six different colours, supposedly reflecting Gould writing his journal in whatever he could use as ink. In 'A letter from Richard Flanagan', part of the initial promotion of his novel to bookstores, Flanagan explains how he came upon Gould's fish paintings and developed a story based on them. He also justifies the expensive production in terms of a reaction to Microsoft's Bill Gates's pronouncements about the death of the book, writing, 'Far from technology making books redundant, it opens up new possibilities, both creative and commercial.' This is followed by a lengthy description of what the use of different coloured inks adds to his novel's meaning:

> Billy Gould thinks in colours and consequently the book is printed in six different coloured inks. These colours reflect the difficulty of his making his book, an activity for which the direst punishment is reserved. The red ink chapter, for example, Gould pens in his own blood; the purple with ground-up sea urchin spikes; the blue chapter with the pulverised lapis lazuli necklace of the man he has just killed – but the colour also propels the story on, as colour does in a good movie. Thus the purple chapter is written in purple prose and tells the story of a failed tyrant; while the green chapter, written in green laudanum, tells of hallucinations and jealousy and pregnancy; and the red chapter is a tale of murder and horror.

In fact, the differences in print colour of the chapters are not as great as this might suggest and could even be overlooked by readers, though the narrator does draw attention to them in passages recounting how he gets his different inks. And just how vital the different colours of the chapters are to the novel's meaning is put into question by the fact that the cheaper paperback editions of *Gould's Book of Fish* are not printed in different coloured inks. Readers of the paperback just have to imagine the differences in colour – arguably more in keeping with the novel's magic realist approach. And, of course, in either version readers are actually looking at print rather than Billy Gould's manuscript. More of a loss to the reading experience, however, is that in the Australian paperback the coloured plates of the twelve fish, because of the need to use better paper stock, are all collected together at the back of the book rather than each appearing at the beginning of the appropriate chapter. Readers of the British paperback do get each fish at the beginning of its chapter but not in colour, since this edition is a black-and-white photocopy of the text of the hardback. As Flanagan's novel demonstrates, despite the advantages of new technologies, financial considerations still limit what can be done by an author who attempts to use the materiality of the book as part of its textual meaning, especially when trying to go beyond the simpler manipulations of layout or typeface found at least as far back as Sterne's *Tristram Shandy*. All sorts of things can be done in artists' books for a select group of readers but taking these into the mass market is another matter.

  Since the drawings of Australian birds and animals which head each chapter of Chloe Hooper's *A Child's Book of True Crime* are in black and white, there are no such major differences between the internal texts of the hardcover and paperback editions of her novel. Here the big difference is between the covers for the American editions as against those of the Australian and British ones. As already noted, the covers of the latter were a clever parody of typical covers for English children's books from the early decades of the twentieth century, books that were widely circulated in Australia as well. The Australian hardback did not have a dust jacket but instead a dark blue cover elaborately embossed in red and gold, with a central vignette foregrounding the now extinct Tasmanian tiger and a kookaburra, with a mob of kangaroos hopping across a red and yellow plain in the background. A larger version of this illustration, extended upwards to include a koala looking out of a gum tree, appeared on the covers of the Australian paperback and the British hardback. The American hardback edition in contrast featured a very attractive red and black cover whose main motif was a highly stylised drawing of a black swan. A black swan also appeared on the back cover of the Australian hardback, though it was drawn in the same naïve realist style as the animals on the front cover and in the chapter illustrations. The covers of the American editions of *A Child's Book of True Crime* seem, in contrast, to have been designed to remove any reference to earlier children's literature and also to downplay the novel's Australian references. The cover of the American paperback is in much cooler tones, predominantly blue, while its main motif, a woman's naked arm and shoulder, positions it as very much a book for adults. The only reference to Australia is a very tiny image of a kangaroo at the bottom margin. The fact that the American covers were so different from the Australian and British ones suggests that American readers were assumed not to be familiar with the earlier children's book covers being parodied in those editions. Perhaps there is also a suggestion that American readers were perceived as less sophisticated than British and Australian ones, and so likely to assume that a book with a garish cover and the word 'child' in the title was indeed just a book for children.

Peter Carey is now, of those catering to the more literary end of the fiction market, probably the Australian novelist with the most significant international reputation and sales. He has twice won Britain's Booker Prize, the second time with the novel I am focusing on here, *True History of the Kelly Gang*, closely based on the life of Australia's most famous bushranger, Ned Kelly. Like much of Carey's fiction, including his most popular works, this is set in the nineteenth century. It presents what is supposedly Kelly's own first person account of his life, written for a daughter he will never see. The daughter is an invention of Carey's, however, as is Kelly's distinctive narrative voice. Though a long letter containing Kelly's own justification of his life and crimes does survive, its highly idiosyncratic syntax and language would have proved too taxing for readers of a novel, so Carey provides his own version of Kelly's voice, as of his life.

While he has lived in New York since 1989, Carey has until recently remained faithful to his original publisher, the University of Queensland Press (UQP), which brought out his first collection of short stories, *The Fat Man in History*, back in 1975. Given that he has been one of the authors mainly responsible for helping to keep them in the black, the UQP naturally has to make every effort to market and promote Carey's works. *True History* was initially issued by them in a beautiful limited edition hardcover which, with its plain cream covers and light brown imitation-leather spine, was designed to look like a nineteenth-century book in half-leather binding. This resemblance was reinforced by a stiff, semi-translucent paper dust jacket. A large-format paperback released at the same time featured a cover design based on an 1880 engraving of the Victorian country town of Benalla, near where the Kellys lived, rather than depicting the type of bush landscape more usually associated with nineteenth-century Australia, and especially, for obvious reasons, with bushrangers. The engraving has, however, been coloured in a deliberately stylised way, as seen especially in the clouds in the bright blue sky, which contrasts strongly with the predominantly orange town, so that the cover presents itself as a combination of aesthetic object and historical artefact, in much the same way as the novel does.

Two smaller format paperback versions followed. The cover of the earlier one, in contrast to the seemingly deliberate ahistorical stylisation and rejection of conventional assumptions about Kelly seen in the cover of the large paperback, included a small photograph of Kelly combined with a reproduction of part of his actual handwriting, so providing a reading frame which stressed the historic figure rather than the fictionality of the text. The other Australian paperback, with a much more stylised cover featuring a large letter K and so this time stressing textuality rather than history, was issued after the novel had won the Booker Prize, and has been by far the biggest seller in Australia – over 100,000 copies. Another hardback edition was also issued in 2001 to celebrate Carey's second Booker Prize. Apart from a less elaborate binding and an illustrated frontispiece – the verso lists the seven other literary prizes won by the novel – this is identical to the earlier hardback. All in all, the University of Queensland Press sold more than a quarter of a million copies of their various Australian editions of *True History of the Kelly Gang*. Sales of the K paperback were considerably helped by it being chosen for a special promotion by the city council of Brisbane to encourage reading, called 'One Book, One Brisbane'.

In Britain, where Carey is published by Faber and Faber, the decision was obviously made to emphasise the historical aspect of the text, with a cover using a photograph of Kelly's mother outside her hut with her family. Readers of this edition of the novel would therefore be less likely to question the truth claims made in the title, one assumes, and more inclined to believe that this actually is the true history of the Kelly gang. Indeed, for many readers both inside and outside Australia, Carey's Ned Kelly will now be *the* Ned Kelly. An historical reading also seems to be encouraged by the British hardback edition's title page, which features a documentary photograph of men standing outside bark huts. As against this, the English edition of *True History of the Kelly Gang* was the only one not to include a map of Kelly country. The layout of the text, designed in the US and so identical with that for the American edition published by Knopf, on the other hand perhaps works against a reading of the novel as a collection of documents, something encouraged by the page design of the Australian editions.

While the illustrated title page and general design of the US hardback edition is very similar to that of the British hardback, the American publishers obviously saw the need to provide their readers with more information about Ned Kelly. So the endpapers featured a map that was larger and more detailed than the one in the earlier Australian editions, showing Kelly country in relation to the rest of Victoria. The superiority of this map was acknowledged when UQP adopted it for their most recent paperback edition. The US edition also includes an illustration, based on a nineteenth-century engraving, of Kelly in typical helmeted pose on the verso facing the start of the main text, and another of a steam train between the end of Kelly's first person narrative and the final sections of the text. An enlarged section of the same illustration, but featuring only part of the engine, appears in the same place in the UK hardback.

In contrast to Faber and Faber, however, the US publishers of *True History of the Kelly Gang* chose covers which stressed neither the historical aspects of the text nor its connections with Australia. The jacket of the hardcover edition features an illustration of a landscape that, at best, could be seen as making some vague iconic reference to Australia. The real surprise is the cover of the US paperback edition, with its two rearing white horses. While the Kelly gang did include horse stealing among its nefarious activities, it would be hard to think of a less appropriate cover than this one. Again, this cover suggests that American readers are assumed to be less sophisticated than British and Australian ones, with the novel being promoted as a western on the strength of its title.

After the publication of *True History of the Kelly Gang*, Peter Carey announced that he was leaving University of Queensland Press for Random House, in part because Carol Davidson, who had looked after the marketing of his novels in Australia for many years, was now working for the Australian branch of Random. In a final attempt to ring the last possible sales out of *True History of the Kelly Gang*, UQP marketed the big K paperback edition along with a similarly styled edition of *Oscar and Lucinda* (1988), Carey's other Booker Prize winner, packaged together in a little black paper bag with red ties. UQP rightly prides itself on being one of the few independent publishers of Australian fiction but it is noticeable that this nationalism does not extend to promotions featuring its authors' Australian literary prizes rather than his British ones. Carey has won the Miles Franklin Award three times, for his first novel *Bliss* (1981), and then for *Oscar and Lucinda* and for *Jack Maggs* (1997), though he did not win it for *True History of the Kelly Gang*. For some readers, all this ferreting around in the past has become a little wearying, even when the setting is not Tasmania. At a time of increasing globalisation, there have been questions as to why so many Australian novelists have turned to the colonial period for their stories. Are they, and their readers, retreating to the greater certainties of the past where it is easier to portray the white Australian male hero as victim of malign forces outside his own control? Is the supposedly postcolonial present too full of stories which challenge this comforting image? One might be tempted to assume that an emphasis on the more exotic aspects of Australia's past is designed to appeal to international audiences but, as this chapter has demonstrated, British and American publishing houses are usually concerned to play down the origins of their Australian texts. So, as we have seen, Australian authors are still very much presented as the colonial other when it comes to packaging their novels for overseas audiences. They may not be subject to quite as many editorial changes to the actual words on the page as in the days when nearly all Australian novels were published in London without authors being able to correct proofs. In 1901, for example, Miles Franklin herself was horrified to find the title of what was to become her best-known novel, *My Brilliant Career*, lacking the intended question mark after 'Brilliant', only one of numerous changes to her text (Webby 2004, vii–viii). She was probably equally horrified by the illustration on the front cover, showing the heroine cracking a long stockwhip over the backs of a few very docile-looking sheep! Today, Australian authors do have a local publishing industry, even if one dominated by multinational companies, which gives at least some of them some say in how their works are presented to the public. The worry is, that if current trends in publishing continue, writers of Australian fiction may once again have to rely on publishers outside the country. And then Australian readers would again have to put up with covers that not only contain inaccuracies but also diminish rather than enhance their reading experiences. While there can be arguments about the respective merits and reading effects of each of the Australian covers for *True History of the Kelly Gang*, any one of them must be preferred to American white horses.

Postscript

After presenting the original version of this paper at the Society for the History of Authorship, Reading and Publishing conference in Los Angeles in July 2003, I flew to New York to spend a few days with my son and his wife. He had kindly kept me a copy of a full-page review of Joan London's *Gilgamesh* which had recently appeared in the *New York Times*. It was a most appreciative review of a book that had been unjustly overlooked in Australia, in part because of lack of promotion and an unappealing cover. I later found the American edition of London's novel in a bookshop: a beautifully designed small hardback with a cover which was not only eye-catching but, with its image of a young woman looking out of a train window, evocative of her main concerns in a way that was not true of the cover for the Australian edition. So in this case, with a novel not so obviously Australian as most of those discussed here, the American edition was definitely the best!

Chapter 6

Book Marketing and the Booker Prize

Claire Squires
Oxford Brookes University

One night every year, in the month of October, printers and binders stand at the ready. They are awaiting a verdict from the literary establishment, which is gathered together for the evening in London. As the printer Clays writes of this nail-biting moment:

> Tension is as high in Bungay [the Suffolk town where Clays is based] as it is in the Guildhall on the night The Booker Prize winner is announced. Traditionally, the publisher of the winning book immediately rings the printer to arrange an instant reprint. In 1997, for example, the Clays Account Controller watched The Booker Prize presentation on television and at 9.59 pm saw that *The God of Small Things* had won. By 10 pm a 20,000 copy reprint had been confirmed and Clays went into overnight production. Within 24 hours the books were printed and on their way into bookshops all over the country. Sales were so strong that, three days later, HarperCollins placed an order for a second reprint of yet another 20,000 copies, this time with 'Booker Prize Winner' emblazoned on the cover (Clays 1998, 58).

Winning the Booker Prize is big business for publishing companies, as the rush to extra production referred to in this account, and the ensuing extra sales, makes evident. For not only do printers receive an instant mandate to produce more copies, but they will also be asked to put through amended reprints. These reprints will – like the example of *The God of Small Things* mentioned here – include an additional strapline on the cover: 'Booker Prize Winner'.

This chapter explores the impact of the award of literary prizes, and particularly the Booker Prize, on the production and reception of books. The strapline on the cover becomes part of the marketing mix of the award winner. It also leads to these books' commodification and – as is frequently the case with Booker Prize winners – canonisation. Using the examples of Yann Martel's *Life of Pi* (2002) and John Banville's *The Sea* (2005), the chapter investigates the signification of the 'Booker Prize Winner' strapline. It examines the role of literary prizes both in popularising 'literary' fiction and in defining which books become 'popular', as well as investigating the impact of marketing in situating books in the literary marketplace and in creating cultural value via the medium of the book cover. It addresses the central question of what, in a publishing environment where a Booker winner equates with both literary and commercial success, is the influence of book awards on the notion of 'popular' fiction, and finally considers the reflection back to the Booker Prize from the cover straplines it sanctions.

The Impact of the Booker Prize

Yann Martel's *Life of Pi* won the Booker Prize – or rather the Man Booker Prize, as it had been renamed to reflect its new sponsor – in 2002.[1] Looking back on his October night, Martel writes about the impact of the Prize on his career:

> *Life of Pi* is coming out in close to forty countries and territories, representing over thirty languages and counting. I now have the attention of the book-reading world. My creative act, conceived like a whisper, is ringing across the world (Martel 2003, 32).

As the biographical note for Martel adds, *Life of Pi* 'became an instant bestseller' on winning the Prize, and its author set off on 'a worldwide author tour' (Martel 2003, 33). Evidence shows that winning the Booker Prize has an undoubted commercial impact, meriting the extra reprints put through by Clays and its fellow printers. In the first week after the announcement of its Booker win, *Life of Pi* sold 7,150 copies in the UK, making it the bestselling hardback fiction title in that week. The following week, it sold 9,336 copies. Previously, it had sold only 6,287 copies in total since its May publication, about half of which had been after its shortlisting (*The Bookseller* 2002a; 2002b; 2002c). Not all Booker titles undergo quite such spectacular sales, but nonetheless every year a marked increase can be noted. D.B.C Pierre's *Vernon God Little* (2003), which won the Prize in 2003, went from a sale of 373 copies in the week before the announcement to 7,977 in the week after, although its ongoing sales were lower than those of *Life of Pi* (Book Sales Yearbook 2004, 93). In 2000, sales of Margaret Atwood's *The Blind Assassin* (2000) also jumped, from fewer than 200 a week to more than 3,000 (Book Sales Yearbook 2001, 91). The strapline 'Booker Prize Winner' – and its associated promotional activity – has a marked impact on book sales and production.

In his book-length study of the Booker Prize, *Consuming Fictions: The Booker Prize and Fiction in Britain Today* (1996), Richard Todd not only emphasises the role of the Booker in making commercial successes of its winners, but also assesses its impact in commodifying and canonising them. Todd's thesis is that the post-Booker period (that is from 1969, when the Prize was first awarded) has seen a growing commercialisation of literature, commenting that literary novelists have 'worked in an increasingly intensified atmosphere, one in which both the promotion and the reception of serious literary fiction have become steadily more consumer-oriented' (Todd 1996, 128). He does not see the Booker Prize as the sole factor in this changing environment: other elements, including the promotional activities of trade publishers and the retail chains, have also contributed. However, statistical evidence clearly demonstrates the impact of the Booker Prize on sales figures of Booker winners and also shortlisted titles. Moreover, as others have argued, the Prize has had a role in the formation of a canon of contemporary English-language fiction, which has been as pertinent a force in overseas markets, and particularly in the US, as it has in the UK. It has also made a concerted contribution to the promotion of postcolonial fiction, by

---

1   This chapter refers to the award as the Booker Prize, except in the case of specific post-2002 instances.

bringing to prominence writers including Salman Rushdie in 1981, Ben Okri in 1991 and Michael Ondaatje in 1992 (Niven 1998).

The Booker Prize has also been taken as an indicator of the continuing health of the literary marketplace. In *British Book Publishing as a Business Since the 1960s* (2004), Eric de Bellaigue takes the Booker Prize judges as 'arbiters of excellence in the matter of fiction' in order to provide a seemingly objective way of assessing the impact of conglomeration on the ten or so foremost literary imprints. These imprints, de Bellaigue concludes, have consistently produced works of quality throughout the Booker's existence and their own change of corporate ownership (2004, 18, 185). Jonathan Cape is a particular case in point: its company history has been a series of corporate takeovers, latterly by the global conglomerate Bertelsmann, and yet throughout it has continued to have a high tally of winners. De Bellaigue's argument is therefore that corporate takeover does not necessarily affect the quality of literary output. Whether the Booker Prize can really be taken as an objective gold standard is debatable, and the often negative commentary that greets the judges' decisions are assessed later in this chapter. What is worth taking from de Bellaigue's argument, however, is the way in which the Booker Prize is perceived by many to be an indicator of quality, and hence the Prize's aim of awarding the 'very best in contemporary fiction' is seen to be a sign of the health of the literary marketplace (The Man Booker Prize for Fiction 2005a).

The award of the Booker Prize, then, holds the key to both commercial and critical success, and is hence an effective weapon in the book marketer's armoury. Alison Baverstock, in her practical guide to book marketing, advises that, 'If one of your titles is a front runner for a forthcoming prize you will be required to put together a plan of action to support and sustain media interest, and further capitalise on it if the book … wins' (Baverstock 2000, 224). If the book does win, Baverstock continues, the publisher could produce stickers for book covers announcing the win, and also prepare point of sale material for retailers' use in bookshops. The strapline 'Booker Prize Winner' thus becomes part of a wider marketing mix set to build on the book's achievements in the eyes of the judges. Hence, particularly with the bigger literary awards and certainly with the Booker, floor and window space is given over to displays of the shortlist and to the eventual winner.

The organisers of the Booker Prize stress the importance of marketing the Prize and its chosen titles. The conditions for the award stipulate that publishers must comply with co-promotional activity if one of their books should be shortlisted. In 2005, this included a contribution of £3,000 to 'general publicity' for any book reaching the shortlist, and an undertaking to 'spend not less than £1,000 on direct, paid for media advertising of the winning book, including a winning poster or showcard, within three months of the announcement of the award' (The Man Booker Prize for Fiction 2005b). In 2005, the Man Booker Prize website also offered public libraries free promotional packs consisting of 100 bookmarks, five A3 posters, 100 stickers and a wallchart in order to create displays to attract borrowers to the shortlisted and prize-winning books (The Man Booker Prize for Fiction 2005c). This promotional material is in addition to anything the publisher would create themselves, bookshops' own branded marketing and the media coverage that the Booker Prize always generates.

On a grand scale, then, and on the scale of practical marketing activity, the Booker Prize has had an important impact on the production and reception of literary fiction in the latter part of the twentieth century and the early part of the twenty-first century, an impact that has been analysed in a variety of critical and academic arenas. Book-length academic analyses include Todd (1996), Huggan (2001), Strongman (2002) and English (2005). There also exists a host of shorter academic, trade and general media commentary. This chapter, however, aims to look specifically at the role of the strapline 'Booker Prize Winner' on the cover, and it is to this element of 'judging on the cover' that the chapter now turns.

'Booker Prize Winner': the Uses of a Strapline

Copies of *Life of Pi* printed subsequent to winning the Prize feature the strapline 'Winner of The Man Booker Prize 2002' in both hardback and paperback editions. Moreover, all the other titles on the shortlist in 2002 incorporate a strapline into their covers to indicate their shortlisting (paperback editions of Mistry 2002, Shields 2002, Trevor 2002, Waters 2002 and Winton 2002). These straplines demonstrate the marketing value of being on the shortlist of big literary prizes, let alone winning them (Shields' and Waters' novels mention their additional shortlisting for the Orange Prize). The Edinburgh publisher Canongate, who had lured Yann Martel away from his original UK publisher Faber & Faber to publish *Life of Pi*, has used the Booker win to market later publications by Martel. *The Facts Behind the Helsinki Roccamatios* ([1993] 2004), a short story collection which was originally published by Faber & Faber but reissued in 2004 by Canongate subsequent to *Life of Pi*'s Booker success, appends to Martel's name on the cover the strapline 'Winner of The Man Booker Prize' as well as 'The Author of *Life of Pi*'. The two Canongate covers use the same artist, and have a similarity of subject matter and perspective, thus contributing to the author's visual branding. Faber & Faber's edition of Martel's first novel, *Self* (1996), also has the strapline 'Author of *Life of Pi*, Man Booker Prize Winner 2002' in post-2002 print runs. The Booker association is hence used to market the winning author and their book, shortlisted authors and their books, and future and reissues of other works in winning authors' oeuvres. The Booker strapline, and the design decisions made after the Booker win, become key elements in the branding of the author.

Paperback reprints of *Life of Pi* now feature two straplines. One, at the bottom of the book, indicates that the book is 'Winner of The Man Booker Prize 2002', while at the top of the cover are the words 'The Number One Bestseller'. These joint straplines are – as the chapter has already argued – closely interrelated, as *Life of Pi*'s Booker win undoubtedly contributed to making it into an international bestseller. The literary 'excellence' perceived by de Bellaigue thus transfers into economic excellence.

By so clearly conjoining elements of critical and commercial success, the cover of *Life of Pi* encapsulates James F. English's development of Pierre Bourdieu's concept of the field of cultural production. In *The Field of Cultural Production* (1993), Bourdieu posited the concepts of 'economic capital' and 'cultural capital', in which the economic stands for success in the marketplace: sales, box-office takings, mass popularity. Cultural capital, on the other hand, is conferred by those 'who recognize no other criterion of legitimacy than recognition by those whom they recognize', even if the award of such capital is still 'affected by the laws … of economic and political profit' (Bourdieu 1993, 38–9). In Bourdieu's theory, this creates a principle of inversion. This principle runs into problems when encountering commercially successful artworks. As Bourdieu continues, 'some box-office successes may be recognized, at least in some sectors of the field, as genuine art' (Bourdieu 1993, 39). Bourdieu does not resolve this statement, which is particularly problematic for the late twentieth and early twenty-first century field of literature in Britain. Indeed, the construction of value enacted by literary prizes is a prominent example of how, in this period, cultural and economic capital combine.

James F. English, in his essay 'Winning the Culture Game: Prizes, Awards, and the Rules of Art' (2002), contemplates how Bourdieu's work might be applied to a study of artistic prizes in the latter half of the twentieth century through a consideration of the Booker and Turner Prizes (the latter for art rather than books). English introduces the concept of 'journalistic capital (visibility, celebrity, scandal)' as the mediating – and transforming – force between economic and cultural capital in the late twentieth century. He contends that the 'rules … no longer apply', and that the 'two discreet zones' of cultural and economic capital 'must be set aside' as a means of understanding the production of value (English 2002, 123, 125–6). As the cover straplines of *Life of Pi* so briskly enunciate, cultural and economic capital come together with the award of the Booker Prize. That Martel went on to become embroiled in an argument about whether he had based his novel too closely – close to the point of plagiarism, some suggested – on the Brazilian writer Moacyr Scliar's *Max and the Cats* (1981) only goes to confirm English's addition of 'journalistic capital', and its attendant 'scandal', to economic and cultural principles (Blackstock 2002).

Cover straplines mentioning literary awards, then, signify the conferral of popular and literary success on books, and the particular combination of economic and cultural capital that prizes such as the Booker are capable of bestowing on their winning and shortlisted titles. This combination also generates substantial journalistic capital. For a book such as *Life of Pi*, whose place in the market had not been assured, despite the validation of positive reviews (for example Atwood 2002, Jordan 2002 and Massie 2002), the Booker Prize performs a situational role. It ushers in a book's commercial and cultural success, and states that it is a possibly paradoxical entity: a popular literary title. It also physically places it in the marketplace: in Booker Prize displays, for example, and in 3 for 2 promotions. By the book's placement within such prominent promotions, its marketplace visibility is increased yet further, assuring further sales and a Booker book's centrality to debates about literary value. The Booker strapline is one that lifts the title above the mass of other books in an extremely crowded marketplace, one that in the 2000s in the UK produces over 100,000 titles every year (Book Facts 2001, 17). The judgement delivered by the Prize panel and heralded on the cover is a prime piece of marketing, and plays a role in defining cultural value that should not be underestimated.

'Pop Goes the Booker'

And yet, despite the literary gold standard that the Booker represents to many, it is apparent that the Prize is not without its critics. Every year, there are those who think the wrong title has won, and its place as prime arbiter of literary excellence questioned. Some think that the wrong title inevitably wins every year, as a correspondent to the newspaper *The Sun* wrote the day after *Life of Pi*'s win:

> The great thing about the Booker Prize is it gives us a list of books we would NOT want to read, as the Turner Prize gives us a list of art we wouldn't want to see.
>
> It's a pity the arty establishment is so out of touch with reality (Brown 2002).

It is entirely possible that this letter, and its placement within the largely conservative, jocular tabloid *The Sun*, is a knee-jerk reaction. The correspondent quite probably had not had the time to read *Life of Pi* so swiftly after the announcement of the win. Nevertheless, there is a legitimate point being made here, beyond the supposition that the accolade of the Booker Prize may turn some people against reading a particular title as well as towards it. No large-scale consumer surveys currently exist to clarify the attitudes of book buyers to prize-winning books, although evidence from the increased sales of titles certainly suggests that they, and their associated marketing activity, have a much stronger positive than negative impact on sales.

The debate that this letter enters is one to do with the Booker's negotiation with the concept of the 'popular', and its evident yet non-formalised role in popularising the literary. This is the argument of Todd's work on the Booker in *Consuming Fictions*, investigating the way that 'serious literary fiction', as he terms it, has been commercialised, and hence popularised, in recent decades, with the Booker Prize as central to that process. Todd's thesis tracks the same period as that of English's article, in which the dissolution of the opposition between cultural and economic capital is discerned. English's argument concentrates on the media and publicity impact of prizes, whereas Todd's looks more broadly at the marketing environment in which literary fiction is published. Both these studies, though, refer to an environment in which literary fiction has intersected with concepts of the 'popular', be it either as having popular appeal, receiving popular acclaim or being widely known, or, in other words, subject to popular knowledge.

In *The English Novel in History: 1950–1995*, Steven Connor provides a preliminary definition of literary fiction in the post-war period, which is useful in trying to articulate the negotiation between the literary and the popular:

> Literary fiction is usually defined by negation – it is not formula fiction or genre fiction, not mass-market or best-selling fiction – and by subtraction, it is what it is left once most of the conditions that obtain in contemporary publishing are removed. Typically, though, the question of whether the literary novel will survive, or can be protected, tends to obscure questions about the relations between the literary (with it customary or conventional meanings, values and powers) and the commercial (Connor 1996, 19).

Connor's explanation of literary fiction as 'negation' provides a series of synonyms of what the literary is not: formula, genre, mass-market, bestselling or commercial. 'Popular' could be added to this list. One of the roles that the Booker Prize has taken on during its history, then, is to disrupt this opposition between the literary and the commercial. The Prize, through its contribution to the marketing mix of literary fiction, and its media-worthy aspects, has made literary fiction more 'popular', but has also negotiated with the category of the popular and, as the final part of this chapter discusses, is itself subject to changing perceptions of its populism.

The timing of the letter to *The Sun* was ironic, given that the Prize judges in 2002 had set out explicitly to popularise the Prize. This coincided with the change of sponsor, and the Prize's consequent renaming. The judges, headed by their chair Lisa Jardine, declared that their agenda was to award books that they deemed to be readable and popular, as the press reports following the announcement of the shortlist in September 2002 make evident. *The Times*'s report was entitled 'Booker judges attack "pretension and pomposity"' (Alberge 2002), and the *Daily Telegraph* repeated the comedian and 2002 judge David Baddiel's comments that some of the books entered by publishers '"were big and serious, with gravitas, not very funny books. Some of them had a vulgar and obvious seriousness"' (Reynolds 2002). In the same article, Salley Vickers, another judge, was quoted as saying that some of the entries were '"pompous"'. An *Observer* commentary from literary editor Robert McCrum later in the week mentioned Jardine's 'claim that this year's short-list marked "the beginning of a new era"', a claim that went on to 'ignite ... a debate about "literary fiction"' (McCrum 2002). Martel's *Life of Pi* was the title that the judges then decided would best represent this 'new era', and – at least in terms of sales figures – the panel was vindicated. The following year, the literary critic James Wood picked up on this debate in his *London Review of Books* review of the 2003 winner, Pierre's *Vernon God Little*:

> There used to be something thought of as 'a Booker novel' – a big, ambitious balloon sent up to signify seriousness and loftiness of purpose. Such books were not always very attractive or even very interesting, though we may learn to miss them just because their elevation already seems old-fashioned. Last year, the prize's new sponsors let it be known that it was time for a shiny new populism, and so far the judges have concurred. Neither prize-winner, under the new regime, has been a crowd-displeaser, nor a crowd-puzzler.

> John Carey ... chaired this year's jury, and announced that he was in favour of 'widening what might be looked on as the Booker's scope'. He and his judges had, he thought, a preference for 'books with a strong storyline, a strong plot, a compulsion to go on turning the pages' (Wood 2003a).

Wood's comments proved to be controversial, not least because of the implication that the new sponsors (a financial investment group) had intervened in the judging process. John Carey and Martyn Goff, the Prize's administrator, speedily responded in the Letters pages of the *London Review of Books*. Carey wrote that Wood's accusation of meddling was 'serious, defamatory and false', and that the sponsors did not influence the judges' deliberations in any way. The decisions made 'reflected our estimate of literary quality and nothing else'. Goff added that Wood's implication was 'completely false and damaging', and that the Man Group's sponsorship was one of 'unconditional generosity' (Carey 2003; Goff 2003). Carey and Goff were quick, in other words, to assert their belief in primacy of autonomous cultural capital over the laws of the literary marketplace and the world of global finance.

Wood replied in the same issue, clarifying his comment that the judges '"concurred" with the new sponsors by saying that he 'was being idly figurative'. He went on to write that he was 'happy to retract any imputation that the sponsors influence in any way the outcome of the prize'. However, he reasserted his belief that:

> The juries of the last two years seem to have fallen in – unconsciously, of course – with a perceived new zeitgeist. When Man plc took over sponsorship last year, there was a good deal of speculation that what Lisa Jardine … called 'a new era' had begun … At the time, journalists wrote of 'a very British coup on behalf of Booker's new sponsors' … and that 'the administrators want to control the prize's image, and any debate about changing its constitution'.

> Most of this was probably just journalistic hot air. Still, both this year's and last year's judges laid new emphasis on the importance of choosing accessible, plot-driven novels, and the two books chosen would seem to comport with that emphasis. Next year a rebarbative Maori epic as winner? We shall see (Wood 2003b).

The 'journalistic hot air' of which Wood makes mention is precisely the kind of journalistic capital that the Booker Prize has thrived on, making its decisions media-worthy and hence with a forceful impact in the marketplace, combining cultural and economic capital. With regards to the issue of populism, it is evident that whatever the influence of the new sponsors, conscious or unconscious, the judges, and particularly Jardine's 2002 panel, set out to choose a winner that could not be accused of being pompous, portentous or pretentious – as they claimed some of the entries from publishers were. As it can only be assumed that these submissions were made by publishers reacting to earlier winners celebrated by the Prize, there is also an implicit criticism of previous winners and judging panels. Jardine and her panel wanted to shift the Prize into a populist framework, and with *Life of Pi* found a suitable winner. Indeed, even before the addition of the cover strapline, the novel's packaging reflected this new era of the Man Booker: an unintimidating design featuring a simple, colourful, even childlike painting of a boat, the sea, a tiger, a boy and some fish.[2]

Wood's clash with the Booker Prize authorities signals the ongoing debate about literary seriousness and populism, and the role of the Prize in creating and defining those terms. Inherent in this debate is the question of whether the Booker, either in its pre- or post-Man incarnation, can really be seen as an objective arbiter of literary value (as de Bellaigue would have it), setting aside its undoubted impact on sales and reputation. To assess this question fully would necessitate a more comprehensive

---

2 The chapter is not concerned specifically with the cover *design* of Booker winners. For two brief assessments of the 2005 Prize from this perspective see Hyland (2005) and Thorpe (2005).

history of the Booker Prize than space allows for here. Nevertheless, the negotiation between the literary and the popular continues with regard to the Prize, and this chapter will conclude with one further example: that of the 2005 Man Booker Prize winner.

'Not the Normal Kind of Booker Book'

In 2005, media analysis would seem to suggest that the Prize had turned back to seriousness by choosing John Banville's *The Sea*. From a shortlist of novels by Julian Barnes, Sebastian Barry, Kazuo Ishiguro, Ali Smith and Zadie Smith, the judges picked Banville's, the fourteenth in a career of complex, serious and unpopular works – if popularity is calculated in terms of sales (Brockes 2005; Fay 2005). This choice prompted a vehement reaction from Boyd Tonkin, *The Independent*'s literary editor, who wrote that the choice was 'a travesty of a result from a travesty of a judging process', and 'the worst, certainly the most perverse, and perhaps the most indefensible choice in the 36-year history of the contest' (Tonkin 2005). The report in *The Guardian* was more moderate, but still proclaimed Banville's win 'one of the biggest literary coups', taken from 'under the noses of the bookies and the literary insiders'. The novel is described as 'a victory of style over a melancholy content which makes his book one of the least commercial on the … shortlist' (Ezard 2005). Seriousness rather than popularity would seem to have risen to the fore once more.

John Sutherland, the chair of the 2005 panel, wrote about the media's reaction to his team's decision, which he clearly knew would be unexpected, and even, possibly, provocative:

> What, one wondered, would the epithet be? 'Controversial'? 'Safe'? 'Eccentric'? 'Grotesque'? In the event the papers next morning settled on 'surprising'. Surprising not just because it was a turn up for the book, but because this particular novel had been preferred over shortlist rivals that, on the face of it, had more reader appeal, more energy, more human interest, more punters' cash riding on them – more everything, except, possibly, art (Sutherland 2005).

Sutherland defends his panel's decision to choose the 'best' novel in terms of 'art' against any other claim that may be made for the Prize, including that of popularity, or 'reader appeal'. This is an explicit refutation of the combination of cultural, economic and journalistic capital that the Prize has come to develop, although ironically, and inescapably, this refutation would be of interest to the media. In an interview after being given the award, Banville himself addressed the question of the 'literary' nature of his text, the popularity of winners and Booker's interaction between these two terms:

> *The Sea*, says Banville, 'is not the normal kind of Booker book', and he hopes its success will send a long-overdue message to publishers that 'literary fiction can make money. That's very important in this image-obsessed age.'

Surely, I suggest, all Man Booker prize winners are literary fiction?

Banville grimaces. 'Yeeees, the Booker winner will be a literary book. But I feel over the past 15 years, there has been a steady move towards more populist work. I do feel – and of course I'm completely biased – that this year was a return to the better days of the 80s and early 90s. It was a very good short list and a decent jury; it didn't have any stand-up comedians or media celebs on it, and I think that's what the Man Booker prize should be. There are plenty of other rewards for middle-brow fiction. There should be one decent prize for ...' he pauses, '... real books' (Brockes 2005).

Banville's comments contribute to the ongoing debate between concepts of the literary and the popular generated by the Booker, but also to a struggle for definition of the Booker itself, in which various different interest groups (including the judges, the sponsors, the book trade industry, journalists, critics, writers and readers) vie for control over the direction taken by the Prize. This reflects back to James Wood's response to Carey and Goff's letters, in which he also observed a 'new emphasis on the importance of choosing accessible, plot-driven novels', and 'a shiny new populism'.

To reinforce his point, Wood glancingly refers to an earlier, much less 'populist' Booker winner in the shape of 'a rebarbative Maori epic': Keri Hulme's *The Bone People* (1985). This novel is frequently cited as one of the more controversial choices made by the Booker judges. In *Consuming Fictions*, Todd quotes the *Evening Standard*'s description of the book as 'the most commercially disastrous winner ever', although he then interrogates this claim because the newspaper failed to take into account New Zealand and Australian sales (Todd 1996, 76). Nevertheless, *The Bone People* tends to stand in Booker mythology for a type of difficult, non-commercial literature that is an aberration from the more typically successful blend of the cultural and the commercial chosen by the judges and celebrated by the book trade.

In his negative commentary on the 2005 award, Tonkin states that, 'For the reputation of the Man Booker Prize, it may count as nothing less than a disaster' (Tonkin 2005). This line may seem extreme, but the principle was echoed in less excitable language by the author Tibor Fischer in *The Guardian*:

No one can dispute Banville has earned the right to the award; he has sweated nobly in the engine room of fiction. His first book was published in 1970 and he has written a string of highly-regarded and highly-decorated novels since. He is an intelligent, gifted writer and an astute critic, and perhaps his win is for lifetime achievement. Yet his selection surprises me because *The Sea* is a book, I fear, that won't do the Man Booker's reputation too much good. Of course the Man Booker prize shouldn't be allotted to a work on the basis of its probable readership, it should be awarded on quality, but nevertheless the Booker winner is one of the few titles that readers will pick up this year (Fischer 2005).

Fischer rightly identifies the strategic difficulties of the judging panel of a prize as influential as the Booker. Ostensibly the panel makes its award to the 'very best in contemporary fiction', within eligibility requirements, published that year. Yet such a criterion is nebulous, and inevitably leads commentators, and judges, to query and then construct their own concepts of quality and readership, as Fischer does in his article. In addition, because of its position as the UK's prime literary award, the Booker does play a role in heavily influencing book sales, and quite what the impact of this is on the judges during their deliberations is unclear, and perhaps may never be fully discovered. (Information on this may be promised in the memoirs currently being written by Martyn Goff and, it may be supposed, via the archives of the Booker Prize at Oxford Brookes University, but the extent to which either of these will fully reveal the intricacies of the judging process remains to be seen.) But the judges must, even on an unconscious level, at least consider the extent to which readers will appreciate their choices, as well as thinking about how their choices reflect back on Booker tradition.

For the Prize is caught in a paradox: in order to be able to fulfil a mission of rewarding and promoting the 'very best in contemporary fiction', it must sustain its place in the public eye and – even when choices are sometimes unexpected or even controversial – it must, over the years, retain its aura of the pre-eminent arbiter of literary value. Journalistic capital must be created alongside economic and cultural capital. Booker thus has an investment in popularity, in order to maintain itself as the highest profile literary prize in the British marketplace. The choices of winning books reflect not only on the books themselves, then, but also back on the Prize, affecting its reputation and creating journalistic capital which is vital for the Prize to achieve its prominence and impact.

All this may seem some way from the question of covers and the use of the 'Booker Prize Winner' strapline in the marketing of Booker winners. And yet this debate over the role and direction of the Booker Prize, and its intervention in definitions of the popular and the literary, is one that reflects and is reflected by book covers and their influential role in positioning literary products in the marketplace. The strapline 'Booker Prize Winner', as well as meaning that the book will be heavily marketed and prominently placed in bookshop displays, sends out signals to a potential readership. How those signals are received is open to the normal interference of marketing communications: for some, the strapline may be an attraction to buy and read the book, but for others such as *The Sun*'s correspondent, it may be a warning to avoid. The journalistic controversies that accrue to the Prize, and its negotiations with concepts of the popular, contribute to the interference of these signals so that, for example, the strapline 'Booker Prize Winner' on *The Sea* or *The Bone People* is received differently to 'Booker Prize Winner' on *Life of Pi*. There is, moreover, a way in which Booker-winning book covers reflect back, through their straplines, to the Booker Prize itself and thus come to have a role in defining the Prize. As a visual illustration of this, in the volume put together to commemorate 30 years of the Booker Prize, *Booker 30* (1998), the endpapers are decorated with thumbnail front covers of past winners. This offers the most instant, and also long-lasting definition of the Prize. This is that the Prize is most emphatically constituted by the decisions it makes, via the books that have won it. For what else, in the end, is the Booker but a composite of its winners, and the book trade activity and media and critical analyses which have surrounded them?

In conclusion, the signs of judging on book covers play a variety of roles in the literary marketplace. With a prize as influential as the Booker, they strongly affect sales and contribute to the marketing and promotion of literary titles. Through the Prize's construction of literary titles as 'popular' books, these signs of judging also position their award-winning and shortlisted titles, situating them as popular literary books. Finally, in the annual negotiations with questions of value carried out by the judges of the Prize, the eventual straplines on Booker books reflect back on the Prize itself, each year altering its own image, marketing impact and literary credentials. 'Booker Prize Winner', therefore, is a signifier of marketplace success, a definition of literary value and a self-reflexive act in which the books Booker chooses actively construct what is meant by Booker.

Chapter 7

Jerome K. Jerome and the Paratextual Staging of Anti-elitism

Susan Pickford
University of Paris XIII

One of the demands of the book is that we consider just what it is we mean when we attribute to a particular book the quality of being 'literature'. For 'literature' is not the constant we sometimes think it to be. Literature does not have a fixed status; it is part of the larger total world of the book, which includes many forms of expression of which literature is one. Particular books may be regarded as 'literature' at some times but not at others; they may be used by readers as literature or as something else. (Bradbury and Wilson, in Robert Escarpit, *Sociology of Literature* [1958] 1971, 7).

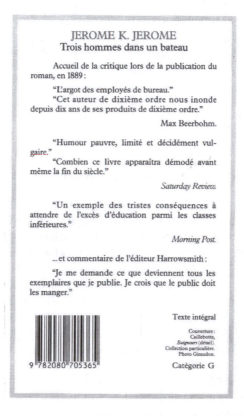

Figure 7.1 The Flammarion edition of *Trois Hommes dans un Bateau* clearly stages its own position in this debate by using negative critical judgements as an appeal to the reader

Escarpit's examination of the publishing industry in this seminal French text for research in popular fiction argued that research should focus on relationships which bring writers, books and readers together. This is a process which he saw as psychological and political as well as aesthetic and economic (Bradbury and Wilson 1971, 7). This discussion considers why it has taken over 100 years since the first publication of Jerome K. Jerome's *Three Men in a Boat* in 1889 for the text to be categorised as a classic. It focuses on the relationship that Escarpit identified by examining the extremely unusual editorial strategy taken by a paperback translation published by Flammarion in 1990, which chose to use a series of negative critical comments as its cover endorsement (Figure 7.1).

The reason why this categorisation did not take place in the late nineteenth century was largely due to contemporary conflicts in the field of publishing, criticism, and the perception of the book's original market. As Q.D. Leavis observed in *Fiction and the Reading Public* ([1932] 1990, 34), some time in the late nineteenth or early twentieth century, there came to be a 'curiously inverse relation ... between esteem and popularity'; highbrow, middlebrow and lowbrow readers were catered for by distinct book markets and the term 'bestseller' became a derogatory epithet among cultivated readers. Jerome K. Jerome fell into the bestseller category – *Three Men in a Boat* sold well over a million copies in the United States, although unfortunately for Jerome mostly in pirated editions – and thus failed to register on the critical horizon. However, in very recent years, Jerome has enjoyed a minor critical renaissance and *Three Men in a Boat* is now available in both Penguin Classics and Oxford World's Classics, thus gaining respectable classic status according to Rachel Malik's definition of classics in terms of publishing categories: 'a set of texts which have been published in specific ways: with a distinctive kind of editorial apparatus, for example (Malik 1999, 28).

Jerome K. Jerome's Contemporary Critical Reception

Jerome K. Jerome was born in Walsall in 1859. At this time, his father – a non-conformist minister – made a disastrous series of coal-mining investments that led the family to bankruptcy. The family's fall from middle-class stability and concomitant removal from the Midlands to the East End of London, where his father worked as an ironmonger, had a great effect on Jerome's outlook. He started the first in a variety of jobs, aged 14, two years after his father's early death in 1871, including a two-year stint as a travelling actor in his late teens. This proved a superb vantage point from which to observe popular cultural practice, enabling him to tap into the emergent market for popular fiction, and he drew on this in his first book, *On the Stage and Off* – the brief career of a would-be actor, published in 1885. The book was mildly successful, but the critical scorn that was to dog Jerome for the next 20 years was already apparent: he noted in his autobiography that the critics 'denounced it as rubbish' (Jerome 1926, 74). In 1886 he published *Idle Thoughts of an Idle Fellow*. *Three Men in a Boat* followed in 1889, published first in serial form in the magazine *Home Chimes* and then in book form by J.W. Arrowsmith of Bristol.

Despite the popular success of many of Jerome's subsequent works, including *The Passing of the Third Floor Back* in 1907, the critics were harsh. In *My Life and Times*, Jerome reflected upon his critical reception in the early part of his career:

> I think I may claim to have been, for the first twenty years of my career, the best abused author in England. *Punch* invariably referred to me as 'Arry K. 'Arry and would then solemnly proceed to lecture me on the sin of mistaking vulgarity for humour and impertinence for wit. ... Max Beerbohm was always very angry with me. *The Standard* spoke of me as a menace to English letters; and the *Morning Post* as an example of the sad results to be expected from the over-education of the lower orders (Jerome 1926, 74).

A typically hostile comment is made by Oscar Wilde in a letter to Leonard Smithers in 1897 about the proposed foundation of a British Academy of Letters:

> I have seen the Academy with its lists of Immortals. It is very funny what sort of people are proposed. ... Personally I cannot make up my mind as to whether the Duke of Argyll or Jerome K. Jerome has the better claim – I think the former. The unread is always better than the unreadable (Batts 2000, 91).

Indeed, none of the lists of authors put forward for the proposed academy included Jerome's name. In 1894, Robert Hichens used a liking for Jerome as a byword for philistinism in his satire on the aesthetic movement *The Green Carnation*. The class-based nature of much of this critical antagonism is evident from *Punch*'s imitation of the Cockney accent and the *Morning Post*'s comment: Jerome's readership, correctly perceived as being drawn mainly from the newly literate 'lower orders', is clearly seen as a threat to prevailing literary standards.

One particular aspect of Jerome's work that attracted criticism was his style of humour, which was influenced by the American New Humour represented by authors such as Mark Twain. This style drew heavily on the use of slang and idiomatic expressions typical of 'the lower orders'. *Punch*'s repeated references to Jerome as 'Arry J. 'Arry is one obvious example of this condescending attitude to an author who, although not a native Cockney, nevertheless clearly revelled in the lively turns of expression of the clerks and shopkeepers he had grown up with. *The Saturday Review* likewise focused on this aspect of the work in its review of *Three Men in a Boat* on 5 October 1889, criticising the 'colloquial clerk's English of the year 1889' and concluding that 'the book's only serious fault is that the life it describes and the humour that it records are poor and limited and decidedly vulgar' (Connolly 1982, 74–5). As late as 1959, George Sampson was still referring to Jerome's humour disparagingly as part of the music-hall tradition beloved of Cockney clerks (Jerome 1990, 13). While this description is far from inaccurate – indeed, J. and his friends conclude their trip up the Thames with a trip to the Alhambra theatre to see a bill including 'world-renowned contortionists from the Himalaya Mountains' (Jerome 1994, 184) – the tone indicates that according to dominant critical discourse, the popular cultural tradition to which Jerome and his readership were considered as belonging was still considered infra dig. It also overlooks Jerome's broader achievement as a man of letters: as editor of *The Idler* from 1892 to 1898, he was a well-connected member of the (middlebrow) literary scene, publishing contributions from authors and friends such as Mark Twain, Rudyard Kipling, George Bernard Shaw and Arthur Conan Doyle. Jerome's friend Israel Zangwill, an American author who also wrote in the New Humour tradition, believed that much of the animosity was simply down to Jerome's success:

> There is a most bewildering habit in modern English letters. It consists in sneering down the humorist – that rarest of literary phenomena. His appearance, indeed, is hailed with an outburst of gaiety; even the critics have the joy of discovery. But no sooner is he established and doing an apparently profitable business than a reaction sets in, and he becomes a by-word for literary crime (Connolly 1982, 114–15).

John Carey examines the broader context of the hostility of certain intellectuals towards forms of popular culture in *The Intellectuals and the Masses: Pride and Prejudice among the Literary Intelligentsia, 1880–1939* (1992). Carey argues that after the 1871 Education Act considerably enlarged the pool of readers, the intelligentsia risked losing the monopoly as the arbiters of taste that their exclusive and expensive university education gave them. As a result, certain sections of the intelligentsia who explicitly figured themselves in class terms as constituting an aristocracy of letters set out to belittle the new formats of reading matter which were evolving beyond their cultural control, including newspapers and magazines – such as *Home Chimes*, where *Three Men in a Boat* was first published. Carey's thesis is that literary modernism was developed as a ploy to exclude the popular readership by producing deliberately hermetic texts. Unfortunately for Jerome's critical reputation, his writings were prime examples of the sort of popular literature that the new readers favoured: his journalistic, anecdotal, slangy style and the short essay format he adopted in many of his works meant that his books were ideal reading for commuters making their way from what the critics no doubt considered their dreary little homes in the suburbs to their dreary little jobs in the city. It is all too easy to imagine Mr Pooter[1] reading *Three Men in a Boat*.

The subject of *Three Men in a Boat* was likewise one likely to raise the hackles of the critics, inspired as it was by the increasing popularity of boating on the Thames, previously the reserve of the wealthy. Carey cites authors including Yeats and Pound who drew on Nietzschean metaphors of the rabble to describe crowds such as the hordes of holidaymakers who ventured out on the Thames in ever-increasing numbers during the 1880s as cheap train tickets made it easy to escape from London. According to André Topia (Jerome ed. Topia, 1990, 19), in 1888, some 8,000 boats were registered on the Thames; by 1889, there were 12,000. In 1888, 800 boats passed though Boulter lock on one day to watch the races at Ascot and the same year, 8,000 people took the train to Henley to watch the Royal Regatta. The river, like the literary sphere, was being democratised, whether the critics and landowners liked it or not. In both cases, a long-held privilege was under attack. In this context, it is interesting, then, that Jerome specifically mentions landowners who chain off backwaters as a scourge of the river:

---

1   The diarist of George and Weedon Grossmith's *Diary of a Nobody* (1892), originally published in *Punch*, who records his humdrum suburban life with self-satisfied simplicity.

The selfishness of the riparian proprietor grows with every year. If these men had their way they would close the River Thames altogether. They actually do this along the minor tributary streams and in the backwaters. They drive posts into the beds of the stream, and draw chains across from bank to bank, and nail huge notice-boards on every tree. The sight of those notice-boards rouses every evil instinct in my nature. I feel I want to tear each one down, and hammer it over the head of the man who put it up, until I have killed him, and then I would bury him, and put the board up over the grave as a tombstone (Jerome 1994, 68–9).

The issue of resistance to the democratisation of access to culture arose repeatedly in the twentieth century in reaction to innovations in publishing which led to the increasing availability of cheap reading matter. Two such moments of resistance with strong parallels with the critical attacks on popular forms of literature of the late nineteenth century took place in reaction to the launch of cheap paperback collections in the 1930s in Britain and the early 1960s in France – Allen Lane's Penguins, launched in 1935, and Hachette's Livres de Poche, launched in 1953. The Flammarion edition of *Trois Hommes dans un Bateau* clearly stages its own position in this debate by using negative critical judgements as an appeal to the reader.

The Use of Negative Cover Blurbs as an Editorial Strategy

It is obviously very unusual for marketing managers to broadcast negative opinions about their product, let alone feature them in such a prominent site as the back cover of a book. Usually, public awareness of such negative opinions leads to a fall in sales. The 1990 edition of *Trois Hommes dans un Bateau* is thus indicative of a very specific and potentially high-risk promotional campaign. Given that a poll published in the French trade magazine *Livres Hebdo* in March 2003 (125) indicated that 42 per cent of book buyers say they are influenced by covers and cover blurbs, we can presume that there is a carefully planned publishing strategy at play here – one that subverts the usual rhetorical stance of the blurb, characterised by hyperbole rather than litotes.[2] So what sort of publishing strategy would lead an editor to sabotage his chances of selling to 42 per cent of book buyers?

One answer would be to look at the sorts of books (and other cultural products) that use this strategy. Although the use of negative cover blurbs is extremely rare, the strategy has been used on occasion. The few examples fall into two categories. The first consists of works that set out to court controversy. In this case, the negative comments are worn like battle scars to suggest that the work is so cutting-edge that even the critics did not understand it. One example of this practice is Iain Banks's *The Wasp Factory*, which reprints extremely negative critical comments on the first few pages before the title page, such as 'It is a sick, sick world when the confidence and investment of an astute firm of publishers is justified by a work of unparalleled depravity' (*Irish Times*) and 'As a piece of writing, *The Wasp Factory* soars to the level of mediocrity. Maybe the

---

2   The Canadian website <http://www.goodreports.net> has set up an award called The Puffies dedicated to the art of the hyperbolic cover blurb, celebrating such gems as 'Eric Bogosian writes like an M-16 ripping through the brainpan of Western civilisation'.

crassly explicit language, the obscenity of the plot, were thought to strike an agreeably avant-garde note. Perhaps it is all a joke, meant to fool literary London into respect for rubbish' (*The Times*). In this case, the audacious publishing strategy is designed to give both the author and the company a maverick image. Another related example would be the biography of Caravaggio, *M*, by Peter Robb which boasts the quote 'Deserves to be pulped' by Brian Sewell, who in this case clearly represents the establishment with Robb and publishers Bloomsbury as the maverick upstarts challenging the art world, which by implication is hidebound by tradition.[3]

The second, related category consists of works in which the negative comments are used to define a target group of potential purchasers that will identify itself in opposition to the group represented by the critics. This strategy can be used in works that wish to define themselves as countering prevailing standards and mainstream tastes. In the case of humorous works, such comments are used to suggest that the critics in question simply didn't get the joke. One such example would be the Tom Lehrer album *An Evening Wasted with Tom Lehrer*, which proudly wears the comments 'more desperate than amusing' and 'Mr. Lehrer's muse is not fettered by such inhibiting factors as taste'. This category also includes the cover of *Trois Hommes dans un Bateau*. The rhetorical intention is to give the potential purchaser the feeling that he belongs to the privileged group of those with a sense of humour subtle enough to understand a joke that all these critics have missed. It also says to the reader that if you appreciate this joke, then you will not be disappointed if you buy this book.

The cover blurb is a relatively recent innovation in French publishing. According to Gérard Genette (2002, 38), it came into widespread use in the 1960s when enormous paperback print runs made the earlier form of the *prière d'insérer* or review slip costly and impractical. At the same time, the cover blurb highlights the book's status as a commodity: as Alan Powers (2001, 6) suggests, 'A book jacket or cover is a selling device, close to advertising in its form and purpose.' The cover blurb thus represents a key element of the process of the desacralisation of the book, which caused a storm of controversy amongst French intellectuals in the early to mid-1960s in a debate which became known as the '*querelle du poche*'.[4] The opening salvo was fired by the art theorist Hubert Damisch in the November 1964 issue of the review *Mercure de France*.[5] Damisch (1964, 45) argued that the paperback was nothing

---

3   I am grateful to Hilary Ely of East Surrey Libraries for bringing this example to my attention.

4   The noun (*livre de*) *poche* is masculine when it refers to a paperback.

5   The debate reproduces many of the arguments put forward in Britain in the 1930s after the launch of Penguin paperbacks. George Orwell wrote in the *New English Weekly* (5 March 1936) that 'In my capacity as reader I applaud the Penguin Books: in my capacity as writer I pronounce them anathema.' The publisher Stanley Unwin wrote in *The Times Literary Supplement* (*TLS*, 19 November 1938) that 'If it could be proved – and it is less certain than is usually supposed – that sixpenny reprints created or fostered a new reading public, the case for them would be overwhelming, but if the evidence shows that their effect is primarily a transference of demand by regular book buyers from 2s 6d and 3s 6d cloth bound reprints, there is not the same cause for rejoicing.' Margaret Cole responded a week later, also in the *TLS*: 'That the modern publishers ... have found and fostered a new *book-buying* public I do

less than a bastardisation of the Book, turning it into a product: '*L'édition de poche accomplit la transformation du livre ... en produit.*' He poured particular scorn on brightly coloured covers, which he believed prostituted the content – even in the case of classic texts reprinted in paperback – by making it immediately available to the reader, who no longer had to work to achieve a sense of gratification from reading. The debate continued in Jean-Paul Sartre's review *Les Temps Modernes*, which invited a number of intellectuals to give their point of view on the issue in early 1965. A few supported Damisch, including the writer Paule Thévenin, who focused her contribution on an analysis of a paperback edition of Montaigne's *Essais*, criticising the 'vulgarity' of the presentation, which reminded her of the credits at the end of a film, and the 'rudimentary' critical apparatus (Thévenin 1965, 1749). However, most of the contributions firmly opposed Damisch, recognising that the low exchange value of the *poche* did not necessarily imply an equally low use value, as Thévenin seemed to suggest. Jean-François Revel, Bernard Pingaud and Jean-Paul Sartre himself all argued against Damisch's elitist view, preferring to celebrate the process of cultural democratisation represented by the *poche*. Jean-François Revel in particular celebrated the fact that access to culture was no longer provided solely in schools and universities: he saw the *poche* as an antidote to the sclerosis that afflicts any form of culture that relies on a long process of initiation whereby a master passes on knowledge to his pupils by a sort of drip-feed. The *poche* gave readers direct access to books, allowing them to bypass formal cultural institutions.

Sharp-eyed readers will have noticed something of a discrepancy in the date of the French *querelle du poche*. In Britain, the debate began almost as soon as Allen Lane launched his collection. In France, there was a gap of over ten years between the launch of Hachette's Livre de Poche collection in 1953 and Hubert Damisch's reaction in 1964. Damisch's article was, however, published relatively soon after the launch of two new paperback collections, *Idées* and *10/18*. These two collections broadened the base of the *poche* by including new titles and non-fiction titles including works of contemporary philosophy and sociology (Penguin started publishing such titles as early as 1937 under the Pelican imprint). Thus in France, *poches* were seen as unthreatening light entertainment for much longer than was the case for paperbacks in Britain. The *poche* was not seen as a challenge to the cultural hegemony until the launch of these two new collections. It is indeed revealing that it was shortly after the *poche* expanded into the field occupied by academic publishing, thereby staking a claim to cultural respectability, that certain cultural commentators began to condemn it. Paule Thévenin's comments are revealing in this context. It is clear that she considers *poches* as little better than trashy magazines or films, their defining feature being the ephemeral nature of the impact of each individual work (indeed, the early *poches* seemed to highlight this feature themselves, declaring

---

not think anybody can possibly doubt ... When a technical book on the ballet ... can sell close on a hundred thousand copies in five months ... it is impossible to believe that even a tithe of this spate has been purchased by the comparative few who used to be reckoned as "the book-buying public" ... it is high time that book-owning should cease to be the preserve of a small class and ... it can only be brought to the others by giving them the best you possibly can.' See Schmoller 1974, 311.

inside the back cover that '*le livre de poche paraît toutes les semaines*', that is are published on a weekly basis). Once the desacralisation of the book began to affect genres that hitherto had been the preserve of serious academic publishing, it was clear that the role of cultural commentators as guardians of the temple was under threat. It became apparent that readers were willing to forego the guidance of the traditional cultural institutions in the form of critical apparatus, scholarly introductions, notes and so on, for cheaper, more accessible editions and preferring to read the classics – even Montaigne's *Essais* – on their own terms. It is perhaps not entirely coincidental that this debate took place in the years leading up to the student uprisings of May 1968. Young people and students were looking for means of cultural emancipation, and that is exactly what the *poche* offered them.

The parallels with the situation in Britain at the end of the nineteenth century are striking. In both cases, there is a sudden expansion of the readership, a process of the desacralisation of reading matter, which became widely available in cheap formats, a situation where reading could become an everyday, banal occurrence, and a threat to the hegemony of the intelligentsia who risked losing their status as cultural arbiters and thus counter-attacked by denigrating the quality of the cultural products available to the new readership.

In this context, the paratext, the cover blurb in particular, is extremely important, as it enables the publisher to position their product on the market. The blurb can be used to stage the process of democratisation of access to culture. The very use of a blurb shouts that the book is a product for sale to anyone who can pay rather than some sacred object reserved for the happy few (which is why more upmarket collections, such as La Pléiade, still eschew them). In the case of the cover of *Trois Hommes dans un Bateau*, this process of democratisation is suggested by the ironic citation of the negative opinions of arbiters of taste long dead and buried, set against the quotation from Arrowsmith – himself a provincial publisher, far removed from literary London – who underlines the enduring popular success of the book. In so doing, he highlights the absolute indifference of public opinion to the rarefied considerations of literary critics and thus calls the relevance of their judgements into question.

Bertrand Legendre has demonstrated how, as a result of modern publishing strategies, the legitimacy of a book in the marketplace is measured as much in terms of its popular success as its validity vis-à-vis the traditional cultural institutions.[6] Thus publishers will use strategies such as the announcement of spectacular sales figures as a means of creating legitimacy – a development noticed by Q.D. Leavis ([1932] 1990, 25) in the early 1930s: '… publishers will advertise simply – "OLD PYBUS by Warwick Deeping. 75,000 copies in six weeks" with the assumption that a novel is more likely to be "good" if it appeals to a horde of readers than to a minority'. By 1990, the year that the GF-Flammarion edition of *Trois Hommes dans un Bateau* was published, such alternative strategies of legitimisation in the cultural marketplace had become so firmly established that the book's editor felt able to make ironic, mocking reference to the traditional structures of legitimisation that not only underestimated the significance of popular tastes in forging lasting success, but were by then also hopelessly outgunned by the economic firepower of the new cultural order.

---

6   See <http://www.u-grenoble.fr/les_enjeux/2000/Legendre/Legendre.pdf>.

Conclusion: How Jerome Came to be Canonised

It is ironic that Jerome finally managed to garner a significant degree of critical acclaim in 1902 for his semi-autobiographical novel *Paul Kelver*. *The Times Literary Supplement* compared *Paul Kelver* to *David Copperfield* and *The Story of an African Farm* and concluded: 'No contemporary writer has been more persistently underrated than Mr. Jerome K. Jerome. The authorship of *Three Men in a Boat* has been a millstone round his neck' (Connolly 1982, 121). Today, *Paul Kelver* has been completely forgotten, and Jerome owes his small corner in the canon to the millstone. It is interesting to note how the reprinting of *Three Men in a Boat* in various classics collections in Britain mirrors the struggle for influence between popular tastes and more traditional forms of cultural legitimacy. *Three Men in a Boat* was first printed under a paperback classics label by Wordsworth Classics in 1993. In fact, it was one of the company's earliest titles. Wordsworth Classics, priced at one pound and with their critical apparatus reduced to the bare minimum, were clearly aimed at a broad market.[7] Penguin Classics responded to the threat posed by Wordsworth Classics by launching Penguin Popular Classics in 1994, again with *Three Men in a Boat* as one of its first titles, despite the fact that it had at that time never been included in the Penguin Classics catalogue. Once Jerome had a toehold in the Classics fold, he was granted a (minor) place in the canon: as Rachel Malik (1999, 28) says, a classic is 'simply any text published in a collection of Classics'. *Three Men in a Boat* entered the Oxford World's Classics catalogue in 1998 and the Penguin Classics catalogue in 1999.

The question of cultural legitimisation has come full circle. As paperbacks have come to dominate the market – in France, two out of three works of fiction are sold in *poche* collections, while in Britain 80 per cent of books sold are paperbacks[8] – it is now the books that formerly embodied cultural legitimacy (academic publishing and Classics collections with a scholarly critical apparatus) that are having to follow the publishing strategies of the paperback collections in order not to lose market share. This may be part of the explanation for the expansion of the canon in recent years to include texts whose primary interest lies not necessarily in their intrinsic literary quality, but rather in what they can teach us about middlebrow taste – authors such as Sir Arthur Conan Doyle, H.G. Wells and P.G. Wodehouse, all now available in Penguin Classics or Penguin Modern Classics. Quite simply, it is the paperback edition of a book which now determines whether the book is a success or failure and if, as in the case of Jerome K. Jerome, the paperback edition proves a success in economic terms, collections that confer cultural legitimacy can either choose to accept the work as part of the canon or decide to leave it out and lose sales of a popular and successful text.

---

7   According to the Wordsworth Editions website, the company changed its strategy in 1996 when it became clear that the lack of critical apparatus was hampering sales to students and academics, who remain a vital sector of the book-buying market. See <http://www.wordsworth-editions.co.uk>.

8   These figures are taken from an article by Olivier Le Naire in *L'Express* (2 January 2003) and an article by Florence Noiville in *Le Monde* (6 January 1995).

The negative cover blurb on the GF-Flammarion edition of *Trois Hommes dans un Bateau* symbolises this reversal of the balance of power between the economic legitimacy of standard paperback publishing and the cultural legitimacy of Classics collections, which are, it seems, increasingly willing to trade some of their cultural legitimacy for a slice of the success of popular texts. In the context of ever greater competition from the broader entertainment industry, in which books are increasingly seen by the giant conglomerates as little more than vehicles for cross-media synergies, the traditional publishing world can survive only by defending the cultural specificity of the book as the principal vehicle of our literary heritage; yet to do so runs the risk of reinstating a elitist approach to the book and thus alienating the principal readership of the mass-market paperback. The solution put forward by the publishers' marketing departments has been to redefine the classic text in terms not of some ideal yardstick of literary quality, but rather in terms of its significance in the social history of cultural taste.

PART 3
'The Record of the Film of the Book': Cultural Industries and Intertextuality

Chapter 8

Pop Goes the Paperback

Gerry Carlin and Mark Jones
University of Wolverhampton

The Environs of Perception

In the 1960s the book as an artefact, and literature as a project, seemed to be in crisis. In 1964 media guru Marshall McLuhan would write:

> The book was the first teaching machine and also the first mass-produced commodity. In amplifying and extending the written word, typography revealed and greatly extended the structure of writing. Today, with the cinema and the electric speed-up of information movement, the formal structure of the printed word, as of mechanism in general, stands forth like a branch washed up on the beach (McLuhan 1967, 185–6).

But intimations of the death of the book actually augured a rebirth, of the literary paperback in particular, as the decade saw books entering new markets and contributing to the formation of new cultural environments. The fortunes of the book and the domain of 'the literary' were caught up in the period's accelerating movements of symbolic exchange and cultural mutation in ways that, while transfiguring books, made them and their iconicity central to the new pop and subcultural environments. In a 1997 radio retrospective on the paperback in the sixties, Richard Neville, once editor of the underground magazine *Oz*, stressed the 'talismanic significance' of books during the period and Andy Martin suggested that 'The key fashion accessories, the badges of enlightenment of the sixties were books. Hesse or Huxley, sticking out of the back pocket of your jeans, were pure spiritual chic' (Paperback Writers 1997). The book came to function as an 'accessory' in the pop environments of the sixties, but an accessory that also signalled access to culture, democratising territories which were previously guarded preserves with controlled functions, becoming iconic reference points on an emerging bohemian cultural map.

A particular volume by Aldous Huxley can be taken as a special case in point. Huxley's writings on his experiences with the hallucinogenic drug mescaline, *The Doors of Perception* and *Heaven and Hell*, were collected in a Penguin volume in 1969 and have remained in print as a popular intellectual exploration and justification of the kind of experiments in consciousness which the sixties promoted. In these essays Huxley is at pains to sanctify and ritualise the psychedelic experience, which as the sixties got underway would hit the streets and leak into the culture at large. Under the influence of the drug Huxley contemplates the transfiguration of the everyday objects of his Hollywood home into radiant statements of 'miraculous facts', which prompt long meditations on the world, the self, their interactivity and, crucially, art. Long polymath digressions prompted by works by Van Gogh, Botticelli, El Greco, Cézanne and Vermeer, in turn produce philosophical and aesthetic themes which reference the poetry of Wordsworth and Blake, classical music, Chinese painting, psychology, Eastern religion and other elements of Huxley's eclectic enthusiasms. What is seldom noted, however, is the location of some of these meditations:

> I was taken for a little tour of the city, which included a visit, towards sundown, to what is modestly claimed to be The World's Biggest Drug Store. At the back of the W.B.D.S., among the toys, the greeting cards, and the comics, stood a row, surprisingly enough, of art books. I picked up the first volume that came to hand. It was on Van Gogh, and the picture at which the book opened was The Chair – that astounding portrait of a Ding an Sich, which the mad painter saw, with a kind of adoring terror, and tried to render on his canvas (Huxley 1969, 25–6).

Despite his disparagement of the tackiness of the 'W.B.D.S.', the chain store that Huxley's illuminations take place in would soon be typical of the retail environments in which art books and other mass-produced printed commodities would be displayed and sold. As a survey of the art scene in the late sixties pointed out, 'The popular design and outlook of many art books and magazines, and their increasing number and variety, reflect their appeal to a wider audience than ever before', and a 'revolution in international publishing' had ensured that such books were cheap and lavishly illustrated (Sturt-Penrose 1969, 142–3). Reproductions of images and texts, available in large suburban stores, were helping to spread the kind of independent intellectualism which characterised the sixties, and in which Huxley would loom so posthumously large.

But Huxley's volume became talismanic in pop environments in other ways too. Huxley had taken the titles of both essays from the work of the radical visionary Romantic poet William Blake. The Romantics, as well as other bohemian and avant-garde authors and artists from all fields of cultural history, became elements of the montage that pop and psychedelic intellectualism was assembling. In 1965 the rock group The Doors would name themselves after Blake's line of poetry via Huxley, and Penguin would later publish *Children of Albion*, an anthology of 'underground' poetry with a title taken from Blake, a resplendent engraving by Blake on its cover, and a long Blakean manifesto from its editor – straight after Corgi Books had published two anthologies of modern poetry with fluid, polychromatic art nouveau-inspired covers by psychedelic artists and fashion designers Hapshash and the Coloured Coat (Horovitz 1969; Roche 1967; Geering 1968). Cheap paperback editions of *The Doors of Perception* would be circulated and read by people who had no previous knowledge of Huxley, let alone Blake, but by such routes Romantic poetry and drug experimentation would become popular topics of subcultural conversation. The Penguin cover of *The Doors of Perception* in the mid-sixties showed a detail from Max Ernst's *The Cocktail Drinker*, and thus signposted Surrealism and its project for a revolution of the mind as another movement that psychedelia and the image-driven culture at large would adopt and heavily cite. Book covers and the images they carried began to indicate where literature and its traditions might fit, and what connections they might make, in the new environments of popular culture.

The significance of such observations shouldn't necessarily be located in changes in literary and intellectual currents, so much as in the incorporation of literary concerns into new environments. It is at this point that the notion of the literary and the domain of the intellectual begin, like psychedelic drug experimentation itself, to escape traditional or authorised hierarchies of use. The fate of Huxley's ideas and the fate of *The Doors of Perception* as a paperback commodity become the same thing, as both enter the loops and references of popular cultural intellectualism. The paperback publication of Huxley's essays (1959) occurred at a time when Penguin, apparently, did 'not deal in those products which aim to excite and contaminate the mind with sensation and which could be more aptly listed in a register of poisons than in a library catalogue' (Williams 1956, 22). But, as Huxley's essays on mescaline ironically prefigure, the mission of Penguin books was, like his own consciousness, undergoing mutation.

Pop Goes Paperback Intellectualism

> And in these very early sixties, before the age of T-shirts and baseball boots, the heavy art-school cults were Ray Charles and Chuck Berry and Bo Diddley, Muddy Waters, Charlie Mingus and Monk, Allen Ginsberg and Jack Kerouac, Robert Johnson. If you were pretentious about it, you might stretch to a paperback translation of Rimbaud or Dostoyevsky, strictly for display (Cohn 1970, 151).

The entry of the book into a new network of social and cultural relationships is evident in the 'paperback revolution' which burgeoned in the late 1950s and early 1960s. Since the war, paperbacks had revolutionised book sales by using news agencies, supermarkets and bookstalls as their commercial outlets, which both broadened their market and offered the book to buyers who would seldom frequent a bookshop or consider a book in terms of a casual purchase. As the range of paperbacks increased in the 1960s – there were 6,000 titles available in 1960 and by 1970 this had risen more than sixfold to 37,000 – so the diversity of outlets and readerships proliferated (Laing 1992, 84). Within this market certain qualitative distinctions held: between pulp fiction and the quality Penguin range for example. But the key issue here is that the paperback explosion actually extended the existence and function of the book in an allegedly post-print culture. A widening education sector and a burgeoning pop culture might suggest that the main audience and market for paperbacks was comprised of young people, but the proliferating force of the paperback revolution itself decreed that distinctions and categories in audience and consumption got lost in the mix; as Malcolm Bradbury wrote in 1971:

> Many of the clear stratifications of the market have either disappeared or become submerged in the enormous scale of publishing activity; today, less than ever, does it seem clear what the social bases of readers are, what kind of cultural assumptions and standards unite them, and what part literature plays in their lives.

As far as the question of 'literature' goes, Bradbury suggests that in such an environment 'the book has shifted much further towards the character of a 'medium' – a broad communications provision which is less specifically committed to literature as such' (Bradbury 1971, 224, 227). Another take on this position might be to suggest that literature was becoming a contributing feature of a new multimedia environment rather than a category distinct from it, and the ways in which the 'quality' paperback was drawn into these new systems of communication and exchange can be illustrated by the post-war history of Penguin Books.

In 1956, 21 years after Penguin Books had started issuing paperback reprints of quality work into the bookshops, a celebratory and self-congratulatory volume called *The Penguin Story* was published. Penguin paperbacks were a success, but a large part of their success was dependent upon their difference within a mass market.

> The most familiar feature of the Penguin look is, of course, the avoidance of pictorial covers. In America the lurid cover is considered essential for securing mass sales of paperbacked books; and in Britain also, most of the cheap reprints are presented in picture covers. It has often been urged that Penguin might do better business if it conformed to this general practice; but whatever truth there may be in that supposition, the decision has been made, as a matter of taste, to reject the American kind of cover (Williams 1956, 26).

The post-war 'pulp' explosion in Britain had proven that there was a mass market for paperbacks with lurid covers that promised sex, violence and generic American themes. By the mid-fifties many of the publishers of such material had vanished, due to successful prosecutions for obscenity (despite the fact that the contents seldom lived up to the cover illustrations), printers' strikes and the lifting of a post-war ban which prevented American publishers from exporting fiction titles to the UK (Holland 1993). But low-grade paperbacks didn't go away, despite the efforts of the Home Secretary; they endured and became symbols of degeneration for a British intelligentsia who, like Richard Hoggart, cited them as the 'ragged and gaudy' evidence that the 'mass art' of 'a candy floss world' was supplanting indigenous popular cultural forms (Hoggart 1958, 206–7). Maintaining a distance from America would become a widespread post-war Anglo strategy which asserted the selectivity of English culture, the quality of its products and its resistance to a market governed by appearance and image – the Penguin cover made even 'relatively new books look like old books' (Sutherland 1991, 7). That *The Penguin Story* itself sported a photographic colour cover showing young people browsing shelves of Penguins is a rectifying irony, as the most notable feature of the cover is the blandness of the books themselves: highly stylised, colour-coded designs, clearly intended for spine rather than cover display and aimed at the intelligent reader whose powers of discrimination are focused on content alone. Crucially, the mass-produced uniformity and asceticism of the Penguin look had come to signify quality, as distinct from the 'lurid' polychromatic diversity of the paperback as commodity. But even as *The Penguin Story* appeared on the shelves a revolution in the appearance of the Penguin book was under way, for as the book went to press full-colour picture covers were introduced into the fiction series as an experiment (Green 1981, 9).

Penguin's full embrace of the pictorial cover in the 1960s can be seen as a response to the changing function of books as much as an opportunistic commercial move, and Tony Godwin becoming Penguin's fiction editor in 1961 is crucial here, as it suggests the cultural currents that Penguin was riding. 'Until 1961 Godwin had been a bookseller not a publisher. He established two London bookshops in the 1950s, the more widely known of which was Better Books in the Charing Cross road, and he soon achieved a reputation as an unconventional bookseller'

(Green 1981, 14). The matrix of connections established by Better Books is indicated by such events as 'Better Books Writer's Nights', and avant-garde exhibitions and groupings (Jeff Nuttall's sTigma exhibition opened there early in 1965, and the alternative theatre group The People Show were based there; see Green 1998, 35–9). Allen Ginsberg read there in 1965, appropriately enough since it was Better Books that had disseminated underground and Beat literature and magazines to the nascent metropolitan bohemia, and in June the activities at Better Books would lead to the International Festival of Poetry at the Albert Hall which many would see as the inaugural moment of the British underground. The Ginsberg reading was recorded and then put out on LP by the shop's manager Barry Miles, a catalytic counter-cultural figure who would help to introduce the Beatles to the avant-garde and the avant-garde into the culture at large through his role as underground intermediary. In 1966 Miles would co-found *IT*, Britain's first underground newspaper. *IT* quickly moved from a largely literary focus (issue two carried a translation of Ezra Pound's wartime radio speeches) to a fascination with pop culture signalled by a serious interview with Paul McCartney in issue six, which boosted sales figures and helped install the pop music artist as the major intellectual prophet of the counter-culture. The underground provided a platform for new cultural intermediaries: editors, critics and commentators who mediated the profusion of new ideas, and instigated 'a widening of the range of legitimate cultural goods and a breaking down of some of the old symbolic hierarchies' (Featherstone 1991, 35). As well as becoming the vehicles for a new bohemian intellectualism the underground press made full use of new printing techniques to incorporate the psychedelic design explosion into their pages. *Oz* magazine especially became known for its prolific use of cover and layout designs by artists like Hapshash and the Coloured Coat and Martin Sharp, whose works also graced posters, LP and book covers (see for example Owen and Dickson 1999, 113–43).

Tony Godwin recognised the potential role of the paperback book in these emergent cultural fields, and the activities at Better Books would suggest the kind of subcultural crossovers that Penguin products were destined to make under his editorial direction. While Penguin Books had been perceived as being in the vanguard of a new 'radical liberalisation' since at least the unsuccessful prosecution for obscenity of the paperback edition of *Lady Chatterley's Lover* in 1960, Godwin 'believed that Penguin, in common with other paperback publishers, was relying too heavily on the work of the previous sixty years and that more radical editorial policies should be pursued in order to nurture new and emerging talent' (Baines 2005, 97). As the decade unfolded Penguin began to thematise a new cultural awareness through the publication of a new kind of cultural analysis. A range of radical intellectuals and New Left thinkers found publication between Penguin covers in the sixties, alongside a host of the rejuvenated Penguin Specials and the 'What's Wrong with Britain' and Radical Education series (Laing 1992, 84–7), so much so that as early as 1962 a commentator in *Estates Gazette* announced 'find a pop socialist work, and the odds are considerable that Penguin have put out an edition of it at some time or another' (cited in Hare 1995, 281). What these reflections on the new cultures suggest is that during the breakdown of consensus that characterised the sixties there was both a confusion and diffusion of the notions of culture and legitimacy which Penguin articulated.

Penguin also revealed the new ground in the arts by publishing the American Beats (Corso, Ferlinghetti and Ginsberg 1963) and later found a bestseller with *The Mersey Sound* (Henri, McGough and Patten 1967) in its Modern Poets series (Hewison 1986, 257). Despite these pop successes the modernisation of the Penguin look was a hesitant process which revealed anxieties about precisely these forms of cultural crossover. In the 1950s graphic designs were incorporated onto the Penguin cover, but remained constrained within the tripartite grid cover design. Early in the 1960s, under the art direction of Germano Facetti, Penguin 'introduced the formula of using a reproduction of a work of art on the cover of the Penguin Classics, Modern Classics, English Library and Science Fiction series' (Green 1981, 23) often featuring detail from known works of art or showcasing new design styles in its fiction series. Following a suggestion by Brian Aldiss, the Penguin science fiction series from 1961 to 1965 sported covers that reproduced surrealist art by such practitioners as Paul Klee, Pablo Picasso, Yves Tanguy and Max Ernst, introducing avant-garde traditions to a reference-hungry audience (Aldiss 1986, 208, 462). This conjunction of cultural influence and critical awareness was recognised by J.G. Ballard, who claimed in 1966 that '[t]he techniques of surrealism have a particular relevance at this moment, when the fictional elements in the world around us are multiplying' whilst simultaneously perceiving the role of surrealism in the construction of this mediatised world of 'publicity and the cinema, not to mention science fiction' (Ballard 1996, 88, 84). The Penguin paperback edition of Ballard's *The Drowned World* was graced with Yves Tanguy's *Le Palais aux Rochers*, which reflected the book's psychoanalytic exploration of human extinction in the face of the mendacious mineral realm. This use of surrealist artworks on Penguin's science fiction list functions to signify them, daringly, as alternative proto-classics, combining a modernist sensibility with an awareness of contemporary iconicity. The usefulness of science fiction in this crossover marketing, simultaneously signifying both high seriousness and contemporary cool, is apparent in Panther Books' 1968 paperback edition of William Burroughs's experimental cut-up novel *Nova Express*, issued in the Panther Science Fiction list, and featuring a cover illustration of a hypodermic needle as an interplanetary rocket.

This collapsing of demarcations between fine art and commercial design, and between cultural production and critical perspective, seems to be particularly present in Tony Godwin's employment of Alan Aldridge as the new Penguin art editor in 1964. Aldridge would later become known as a key sixties pop artist, famous for his graphic designs on cars and women's bodies – he is seen in action on the latter in Peter Whitehead's film *Tonite Let's All Make Love in London* (1967) and, according to George Melly, he conceived the idea of painting designs on a girl to advertise Penguin books (Melly 1972, 137). He would illustrate the cover for The Who's album *A Quick One* (1966), and he was also providing covers for LPs recorded at Better Books' poetry readings which, Barry Miles claims, 'were some of the earliest quasi-psychedelic design work' (Palacios 1998, 34). He worked on posters (including D.A. Pennebaker's Dylan film *Don't Look Back* and Andy Warhol's *Chelsea Girls*), was an innovative and talented illustrator (as the Beatles *Illustrated*

Lyrics attest) and his contribution as designer and illustrator to *The Penguin Book of Comics* brought a ground-breaking graphical critical vocabulary to bear on a significant area of popular culture (Perry and Aldridge 1967). Crucially, Aldridge incorporated into Penguin design the stylistic directions of a new graphic art which would so typify the period, and typify it because a new awareness of art and design was so central to the new culture. Drawing on diverse popular forms (his 1966 design for *The Penguin John Lennon* presents the Beatle dressed as Superman), Pop Art and art nouveau, and highly conscious of the resonant historical stylistic references which his designs incorporated, Aldridge's fluid airbrush style would make him for George Melly 'the period's most inventive graphic recorder' (Melly 1972, 155). Aldridge himself considered his artistic innovations in terms of points of convergence with experimentation in pop music – citing the surrealism of the Beatles' lyrics as a compliment to his own work (Aldridge 1998, 8). His awareness and use of contemporary trends in design allowed Penguin paperbacks to soak into the pop market:

> The multi-coloured psychedelic illustrations he produced were just what Godwin wanted to dilute the connotations of cultural respectability which he felt was losing Penguin a large section of its youthful readership to its rivals (Pan Books in particular). Aldridge was certainly successful in this respect, as Penguin covers looked more like record sleeves than book covers during those years (Green 1981, 24).

In fact, as Phil Baines observes, books became their own poster advertisements, in the process becoming part of the design environment constituted by 'hippy' posters and record sleeves (Baines 2005, 132–9; Barnicoat 1972, 57–69). It was perhaps Penguin's science fiction list, for which Aldridge took on personal responsibility for illustration as well as design, which most benefited from this approach. Replacing the simple appropriation of modernist, surrealistic artworks with a postmodern synthesis of styles, overlaid with contemporary methods, Aldridge located the science fiction paperback as an exemplar of sixties design sensibility. His cover for Ballard's *The Wind from Nowhere* combines Dalí's soft objects with the distinctive seascapes of Japanese woodblock prints, executed with the flat precision of sixties commercial illustration (Figure 8.1).

Paperback cover art can be seen as a guide to the ways in which literature and various artistic traditions might be circulated within the currents of pop culture during the sixties – a redirection downwards and outwards of the independent intellectualism which was part of the Penguin ethos. Citing past and contemporary norms, cover art began to mirror the pluralisation which announced that all fields of culture could now be accessed, and collaged into a configuration of the present. The innovative editing and design team of Godwin and Aldridge would finally incur the wrath of Penguin's founder Allen Lane, for cover designs would become increasingly daring in their use of sexual images and some designs would upset authors, as Aldridge noted: 'Problems: covers with naked tits sent the sales up but upset the authors' (cited in Powers 2001, 91). The ways in which Penguin covers had dived into the circulation of pop-cultural references was seen as a capitulation to vulgar mass marketing by Lane, prompting him to point out that 'a book is not a tin of beans' (cited in Lloyd-Jones 1985, 74). Despite the departure of Godwin and Aldridge in 1967, however, Penguin continued to take innovation and illustration seriously. As Jeremy Aynsley has shown, 'Many of the designs which appeared after 1968 can be considered continuations or extensions of styles established in Aldridge's period' (Aynsley 1985, 128).

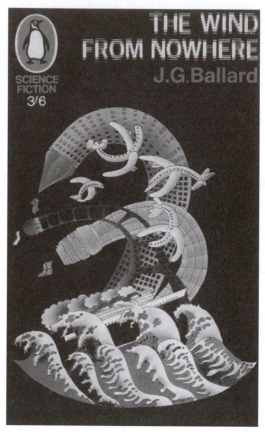

Figure. 8.1 The front cover of *The Wind from Nowhere* (Penguin Books 1967). Copyright © J.G. Ballard, 1962

The impact of the paperback cover is reinforced by the anxiety that such display evoked in conservative commentators. The pictorial cover of the paperback could be regarded as a dire symptom of the dissolution of distinction and the reification of the 'work' of writing into the 'image' of the pop environment, as it was in *The Neophiliacs*, which cites the paperback cover as an index of modern superficiality:

> By the late fifties, the sense that Britain was moving into the future on a tidal wave of change was to a great extent stimulated and kept in being by 'images' of one kind or another – as was shown in the importance of 'modern' design, for everything from the new glass-and-concrete office blocks beginning to rise on the lines first glimpsed at the Festival of Britain, to the covers of paperback books; and in the way that, in order to

surround their products with an aura of up-to-dateness, television commercials were more and more given to using such suggestive contemporary imagery as sports cars speeding down streamlined motorways, as often as not to the accompaniment of a pounding modern jazz soundtrack (Booker 1969, 45).

The paperback appears significant in this discussion of architecture, technology, infrastructure, movement and the mass media, mainly because it so effortlessly participates in the semiotics of the modern. If the rise of the image and 'the look' is the signature of a new commercial culture, then, as Booker's examples suggest, its signs operate by new associations which bricolage 'an aura of up-to-dateness' from the media and technology around them. Here the ideas of endurability and continuity so essential to the traditionally perceived qualities of literature are absolutely negated, for in this new environment only the sensational, the popular and the ephemeral – that which sold on the power of its cover alone – could fully participate. But, to take this another turn, only a culturally sensitive attention to packaging could allow the book to be reborn in this new environment; only by freeing itself from its setting within established traditions could the book and the literary work become a freely exchanged sign of the time.

'Elementary Penguin Singing Hare Krishna'

If the covers of Penguin paperbacks 'looked more like record sleeves than book covers' in the early to mid-1960s, then it might be record sleeves that give us the best indication of the social and intellectual transformations which were modifying the cultural status and iconic function of the book. Dominy Hamilton notes that the sixties album style derived not from the 'teenager' cover of fifties LPs but from their subcultural antithesis; the modern jazz cover which spoke of pose and message:

> The development of modern or 'free' jazz had been helped by the invention of the LP, which made possible the recording of long improvisations and the covers of these LPs proved at least as influential as the music. The intellectuals and 'bohemians' who bought jazz LPs wanted information but they also received style (Hamilton 1977, 11).

As Hamilton goes on to show, the first two Beatles' LPs are a sharp illustration of pop's movement into the styles of intellectualism and bohemia. *Please Please Me* (1963) shows an in-house packaging product photo of the smiling young fabs. Their next album, *With the Beatles* (1963), is presented through a moody existentialist shot of four deadpan faces in high contrast black and white. The shot was taken by the fashion photographer Robert Freeman, who would also produce the *Hard Day's Night* Warholesque sequence of cover images in 1964. As Hamilton notes,

> The starkness of these sleeves connects them with the early jazz covers ... but, to an even greater extent they play upon the record-buyer's definition of and identification with a subtle matrix of visual signals, which were to become increasingly intricate and esoteric towards the end of the decade (Hamilton 1977, 12).

Indeed, by 1967 the cover of the Beatles' *Sergeant Pepper's Lonely Hearts Club Band* would be a suggestive collage of 'people we like', designed and built out of 'found' images, in true Pop Art style, by Peter Blake (who had produced a number of covers for Penguin in the early sixties – most notably for editions of Colin MacInnes's London novels – and whose own *The Beatles 1962* appears on the Penguin edition of George Melly's *Revolt Into Style*). Aldous Huxley is there, as are other writers, artists and thinkers whose works and poses fed into intellectual fields of the sixties – Edgar Allan Poe, Oscar Wilde, Lewis Carroll, Aubrey Beardsley, Aleister Crowley, Albert Einstein, H.G. Wells, Karl Marx, Karlheinz Stockhausen, Laurel and Hardy, William Burroughs, Diana Dors, Bob Dylan, a swathe of Indian gurus, with the presence of a TV effectively suggesting the availability of anyone that has been left out (see Taylor 1987, 31). On the back of the gatefold sleeve, of course, the lyrics were printed, giving the musical text something of the status of poetry for the first time in pop history (Miles 1997, 341). This allowed the recorded artefact to leak onto the cover in a way which signals the package as an integrated aspect of the art object, but it also suggests that the album contained not just ephemeral pop songs which could be consumed at one hearing, but words which deserved to be read and reflected upon, like the literary text. This lyrical display is the final stage in a transmutation of pop into literature which had been prefigured in such texts as the long prose poems which comprised Dylan's sleeve notes in the mid-sixties and Andrew Loog Oldham's 'nadsat' notes for the Rolling Stones (Loog Oldham 1995); John Lennon had already received the Foyles Literary Award in 1964.

While *Sergeant Pepper's* is clearly a 'concept' album it is also an iconic map of uses, crossovers and conjunctions which were no longer proscribed in the new intellectual environment of pop. This innovatory expansion of the pop product into artistically cognate fields was recognised by Alan Aldridge, who commented to Paul McCartney 'It struck me that *Sergeant Pepper* ... has looked at the idiom either like a symphony or a paperback: trying to present a complete show that lasts an hour' (Aldridge 1969, 141). Less than two years after the release of *Sergeant Pepper*'s, in February 1969, this tendency of popular music to appropriate the status of other, more established, artistic fields was signalled by the publication of *The Poetry of Rock*, in which Richard Goldstein ordered 'shove over, Norman Mailer, Edward Albee, Allen Ginsberg, and Robert Lowell – make room for the Electric Prunes' (Goldstein 1969, 1–2). Rock music was becoming 'art', as indicated early in the decade by William Mann's review of the Beatles in *The Times* in 1963 'which put rock 'n' roll for the first time onto the arts pages' (Frith 1983, 168; see also Frith and Horne 1987). By the end of the sixties pop music had become the key form of cultural expression, encompassing the themes, techniques and ideological influence more typically assigned to literature and the arts, while achieving an environmental penetration impossible before the electronic mass media. As McLuhan would recognise, '[t]oday the teenage music is an environment not something to be played inside an environment (McLuhan 1969, 72). This cultural saturation allowed the LP to radiate artistic cachet as much as popular availability, a location which could be casually signified by its extratextual apparatus. For the follow-up to *Sergeant Pepper*'s the Beatles chose Richard Hamilton to design the sleeve, and his minimalist white design would, he hoped, 'place it in the context of the most esoteric art publications' (Hamilton 1982, 104–5). 'It is clear that Hamilton's aim was to mimic the high printing standards of a small press publication' (Walker 1987, 97–8). The convergence of the various artistic forms was, it seemed, complete.

The way was now clear for the newly respectable genre of popular music to lend its commercial and ideological weight to the more established but more exclusive artistic fields. Less than two years after *Sergeant Pepper*'s release, Barry Miles would launch a record label called Zapple, which was intended to introduce experimental music and poetry into the Beatles' Apple Records venture. Essentially a continuation of Miles's innovations at Better Books four years earlier, the project was stupendously ambitious, but would meet its demise amid the acrimonies of the Beatles' musical and commercial fragmentation, and the cultural and political retrenchments of the seventies. However, Zapple made explicit the idealised convergence of the established arts and pop intellectualism, and the pop artist's role as cultural intermediary and facilitator. But the revolutionary hope and commercial rationale of this endeavour drew its inspiration, significantly, from the democratising spirit of the paperback:

> Well-known writer-poets already committed to Zapple releases include: Lawrence Ferlinghetti – America's best selling 'serious' poet; poet-playwright Michael McClure; veteran literary figures Kenneth Patchen and Charles Olson and poet-essayist Allen Ginsberg …. It is the hope of Apple Corps Ltd. that the new label will help pioneer a new area for the recording industry equivalent to what the paperback revolution did to book publishing. The company is now studying new market ideas for the label, which it hopes to eventually retail in outlets where paperback books and magazines are sold (Miles 1997, 475; see also Inglis 2000, 12).

Like the sixties dream itself, the 'paperback revolution' can perhaps most usefully be understood as embedded in and contributing to the era's utopian politics, part of the attempt to reconstruct society towards a more liberal, egalitarian, informed and ideologically aware culture. The 1970s would see a move away from the mass marketing of literature, formatting and jacketing it in ways which would re-establish its aura of prestige. Popular intellectualism went out of fashion, and academic and artistic hierarchies reappeared in paperback publishing (Worpole 1984, 6–9). However, what remains from the period is the importance of recontemporising literary works, indicating their place in evolving cultural mediascapes, through their cover art. Since the 1960s book covers have been sure guides for the autodidactic spirit. As a 15-year-old said in 1965:

> I sometimes get an urge to do some good reading. I've been wading through Kafka's *The Castle* for about two weeks. I wouldn't do it normally but it looked nice. I look around the bookshops and if it's got a nice cover I buy it (Hamblett and Deverson 1964, 188).

Chapter 9

'Now a Major Motion Picture': The Delicate Business of Selling Literature through Contemporary Cinema

Rebecca N. Mitchell
University of Texas, Pan-American

Figure 9.1 2005 *Pride and Prejudice.* The paperback front cover of the 2005 film tie-in paperback cover. Reprinted by permission of Penguin Books. Introduction and Notes © Vivien Jones, 1996, 2003

Figure 9.2 Penguin Classics *Pride and Prejudice.* The front paperback cover, of the 2003 Penguin Classics edition of *Pride and Prejudice*. Reprinted by permission of Penguin Books. Introduction and Notes © Vivien Jones, 1996, 2003, Textual adviser's Notes and Chronology © Claire Lamont 1995, 2003. Appendix: original Penguin Classics introduction © Tony Tanner, 1973

Writing in *Sight and Sound* about the 1986 film adaptation of E.M. Forster's *A Room With a View*, critic Richard Mayne notes, 'We never forget that this is a book' (1986, 134). 'This' was in fact a film – a rather literary film to be sure, with its chapter-like sequencing and its plot and dialogue faithful to Forster's text – but a film nonetheless. Mayne's movement from the visual to the literary is typical of the critical response to film adaptations: to return to the source material to judge whether a filmed version of a novel succeeds or fails is an accepted practice and a common one.

Cinematic adaptation of novels is, however, a two-way street: just as the novel can affect the reception and response of a film, films, especially those with big-budget studio funds for extensive cross-promotion, can affect the reception of the novels on which they are based. Perhaps more significant, although less quantifiable than the critics' reactions to films are the responses of readers to cinema's influence on their books, especially to the primary tool of cross-promotion: the movie tie-in book cover.

Consider an undergraduate English student's reaction to reading Jane Austen's *Pride and Prejudice*, a novel that, at the time of writing this chapter, has yet again been adapted for the cinema:

> The book itself turns me off to the whole idea of reading it. The only version of the Penguin edition I could find had a big glossy picture of Keira Knightley on it with a big ugly circle saying 'Now a new motion picture from FOCUS FEATURES' and I have always been annoyed by people who read for the sake of watching or after watching a terrible translation into film. For that reason, I tore the front cover off of the book so that I could stand to carry it around all day.[1]

This student's disdain of being identified with 'people who read for the sake of watching' occurs before she ever read the novel, and thus before forming her own mental images of characters' appearance. Her disdain drove her purchasing decision, yet this kind of reaction is often overlooked in both the discussion of film tie-ins by the publishing industry, which regards the opportunity for cross-promotion as purely positive, and critical assessments of book covers, which focus on their artistic merit. Phenomenological approaches to the relationship between reader and book can help to clarify the subjective connection to both the text within the covers and to the materiality of the book itself (covers included). Phenomenological readings, and the school of reader-response that they inspired, are experiencing a recent revival (cf. Harkin 2005 for an example in theory, and Warhol 2003 for an example in practice). This critical resurgence of phenomenological readings acknowledges what the reading public has always known: the immediate, emotional and even physical interaction between a reader and their book is the fertile basis for pleasure, for analysis, and – most significant for the publishing industry – for sales.

The present cult of celebrity suggests that sales of a novel would increase if a popular actor or actress were featured on its cover art. Film adaptations of novels do seem to create perfect opportunities for such intertextual promotion: combining the

---

1   Thanks to Molly McGann for her permission to reprint her remarks, composed during an in-class writing assignment during fall 2005. See Figure 9.1.

familiar face of a screen star with the familiar characters of a well-loved story invites new cinema-savvy customers to the literary canon. But in fact, the success of film tie-ins with novels is less straightforward. Publishers must balance two competing desires: courting customers new to classic fiction for whom the familiar stills from a successful movie version would be a tempting lure, and preserving the loyalty of customers who may feel alienated by film imagery on the cover of 'classic' texts.

From Screen to Page: Early Intertextualities

Because fiction provided a ready source of fodder for early film scripts, the relationship between the two modes of artistic production was established from cinema's inception. Plots of popular fiction had been tested by time and their value as intrigue was assured; by using stories with which an audience would already be familiar, filmmakers, especially in the years of silent cinema, could leave ellipses within their story while remaining assured that the audience could follow the narrative line. Seemingly easy, the transferring of novels onto film was based on a series of assumptions regarding the nature of film – for instance, that visual narrative was constructed and appreciated in a manner parallel to reading. Such assumptions were challenged early on, to be sure, and many of the most daring early cinematic endeavours, those that exploited the inherently visual qualities of the medium, were tellingly *not* dependent on novels for their source material (Sergei Eisenstein's *Bronenosets Potyomkin* and Robert Weine's *Das Kabinett des Doktor Caligari* are two examples). There were of course exceptions, the most obvious being George Méliès's pioneering science fiction film *Le Voyage dans la Lune* (1902), which used Jules Verne's novel for its narrative inspiration.

Novels have continued to serve as sustenance for the film industry. In his unpublished 1949 dissertation, Lester Ashiem calculated that, 'between 1935 and 1945, 17 percent of films released by major studios [about one thousand films] were adapted from novels'. Morris Beja calculated that between 20 and 30 percent of American studio productions were novel-based (cited in Giddings, 2000, 21). In 1975, Geoffrey Wagner put the estimate at 'over fifty percent' (27), and the number continues to grow.

One may imagine that since filmmakers have been harvesting material from literary sources for over a century, the bulk of the canon must have, by now, been exhausted. In fact, there seems to be no waning in the industry's enthusiasm for filming the same story even multiple times. Changing conventions, audience desire, social appreciation or response to the original text, and advancing technologies all contribute to the willingness of studios' commitment to retelling stories long since told on page or screen. Directors' dedication to making and remaking adaptations attests to the power of the subjective reading.

Perhaps this collusion of subjectivities has made the practice of filmic adaptation of particular interest for academic consideration (see Giddings, Selby and Wensley 1990; Leitch 2003). The focus of most inquiry on adaptation has been the film that has resulted from the text. Far less attention has been lavished on the effect the release of a film adaptation has on the reception of the book which inspired the film version. This imbalance is due to a number of factors, some related to the nature of the comparison between the two art forms. Robert Stam discusses these biases:

> First, it derives from the a priori valorization of historical *anteriority* and *seniority*: the assumption, that is, that *older* arts are necessarily *better* arts … A second source of hostility to adaptation derived from the *dichotomous thinking* that presumed a bitter rivalry between film and literature … Adaptation becomes a zero-sum game where a film is perceived as the upstart enemy storming the ramparts of literature … A third source of hostility to adaptation is *iconophobia*. This deeply-rooted cultural prejudice against the visual arts is traceable not only to the Judaic-Muslim-Protestant prohibitions of 'graven images,' but also to Platonic and Neoplatonic deprecation of the world of phenomenal appearance (2005, 4–5, author's emphases).

So 'deeply rooted' are these cultural prejudices, it seems, that even Stam predicates his analysis on the relative inferiority of filmed versions of novels – the 'undeniable fact' that many adaptations are 'mediocre or misguided.' Responsibility for the lack of quality in these versions is placed firmly in the hand of the studio and moviemakers, and the publishing house's willingness to adopt the film imagery is attributed to simple market economics (for example Cosgrove 2002, 16).

Films have in fact come to serve precisely as illustrations for novels, most notably on the cover, where an actor's familiar face can function as the illustration of a character within. It is a curiosity that films should send their audience into bookstores to purchase the texts that *lack* the visual specificity of the film they have just seen, but it is a well-documented phenomenon, and one on which marketers have capitalised since film first met the novel.

A Tale of Two Art Forms

One illustrative case study in which a publisher imbued texts with the visuality of a film is the series of hardcover books produced by Lynn Books in the 1930s. Whitman Books' successful 'Big Little Book' series provided a model for Lynn Books and a number of other publishers: inexpensive, illustrated editions of stories starring popular comic heroes (Dick Tracy, Little Orphan Annie) or the occasional abridged literary classic (*Little Women*) marketed primarily to young readers. Lynn Books appropriated the 'Big Little Book' format, but focused their efforts on novels with recent film versions, using film stills as art both on the covers and inside the novels in their line. From mid-1935 through 1936, Lynn produced 17 titles, ten of which were drawn from movies, including Charles Dickens's *A Tale of Two Cities* (1935). Its cover art features an image from the high point of tension in the plot – the moment Sydney Carton is on the scaffold of the guillotine, ready to die in place of Charles Darnay. Far more recognisable to the potential reader than the name Sydney Carton was certainly that of Ronald Coleman, who played Carton in the 1935 MGM film. It is Coleman's name that appears in the largest font on the cover, larger even than Dickens's, and the novel is identified, at the bottom of the cover, as being a 'Metro Goldwyn Mayer Production', raising the question whether Dickens's novel or MGM's movie is contained between the covers.

The Lynn series depended on the integration of the film with the art in ways beyond cover art, and the infusion of visuality into the text created a product desirable to *viewers* as much as to *readers*. Eighty film stills from the movie serve as 'illustrations' for *A Tale of Two Cities*. Eighty-six stills accompany the Lynn edition of *The Call of the Wild*. Authenticity and fidelity were never the primary objectives of the series; the Lynn version of Victor Hugo's massive *Les Misérables* weighs in at only 192 pages, including some 68 stills from the Twentieth Century Fox film production starring Charles Laughton. Much like today's 'Illustrated Classics' (published with only slight variations by a variety of houses, including Modern Library and Abdo Publishing Company), which feature heavily abridged versions of classic novels accompanied by extensive illustrations, the series tells the story of the plot as much through the illustrations – here, the film stills – as it does through the truncated text. Given their illustrated, colourful board covers, their inclusion of extensive movie imagery to illustrate the events of the novel's story, their low price point and their brevity, it is clear that Lynn intended this line for readers who were more likely to attend a movie than to reach for the novel in the first place. They sought a consumer who would read a book version of the film because it was just that: a written version of a film they enjoyed, rather than the original text upon which the film was based. In later years, novelisations of screenplays sought a similar group of readers. This consumer base, especially those new to reading fiction, is invaluable for booksellers; their attraction to the visual medium of film makes the movie tie-in particularly well suited for the cultivation of this market, as Nolan has argued (2004).

Film's mass appeal and the iconography that defined cinema posters provided a steady source of inspiration for the mid-century flood of pulp fiction novels, with their often salacious covers. In certain cases, the inspiration was fruitful both commercially and artistically, as established poster artists applied their talents to book cover or jacket design; in turn of the century France, as Weideman writes, 'the famous poster artists – Toulouse-Lautrec, Steinlen, Forain – saw the book jacket as a poster in miniature and created designs for it' (1969, 6). Half a century later, cover designers capitalised on the marketing savvy of the best poster-makers. While early paperbacks followed the hardcover tradition of simplistic styling (see, for instance, Penguin early lines (1935–38), which featured starkly graphic designs, as discussed by Schreuders (1981, 9), pot-boiler fiction appropriated the sales techniques innovated by the poster-makers; sex sells, and women in tight clothes and cinematic embraces, or provocative perspectives are typical of the period. Recalling the look of the cinema, the covers also often feature movie-style tag lines: 'She was lush as the countryside, as fertile – and as hard to tame', teases the cover of Harry Whittington's 1956 *Desire in the Dust*; the text was indeed filmed in 1960. Whittington knew well how to utilise filmic techniques in fiction, having written novelisations and scripts for film and television in addition to pulp fiction (Lupoff 2001, 172); a consumer looking for the cinematic experience in a book would be attracted to the sales pitch offered by *Desire in the Dust*, and so many books like it.

From the late 1930s onward, once paperback bindings became standard for pulp fiction intended for mass readership, cover illustrations appropriated movie-poster iconography and design even when no cinematic adaptation existed for a given novel or when a publishing house did not have the rights to use the movie studio's images.[2] For instance, a variation of the direct movie tie-in were those editions that depended on the public's recognition of an film version without using film art from the adaptation. A 1951 Bantam edition of Hemingway's *For Whom the Bell Tolls* capitalises on precisely such public recall; the cover by Mayan depicts a rugged brown-haired man looking pensively at an attractive blonde. George Lupoff models a consumer's response to the cover: 'That's not quite Gregory Peck as the American adventurer and Ingrid Bergman as the unlikely blonde, blue-eyed Spanish Republican guerrilla fighter from the 1943 film of Hemingway's novel, but they're close enough' (2001, 147). Close enough, that is, for readers reminded of the film version to be encouraged to purchase the novel.

Such illustrated covers would remain popular even for direct film-tie in versions, but by the mid-1950s film stills were overtaking illustrated covers for tie-ins (Crider 1979, 32–4). Publishers need not print a new edition to tap into this lucrative market. Piet Schreuders, in his superb survey of cover art, notes that dust jackets were often seen as a quick way to update current paperback covers with more pressingly current iconography, such as that provided by a movie tie-in. Schreuders notes two particular examples – Pocket Book's 1948 cover for *Chicken Every Sunday* and Bantam's 1949 *Great Gatsby* tie-in based on photography from the Alan Ladd film. These photographic stills were in sharp contrast to the prevailing covers in the 1940s, which were still typically drawn or painted (1981, 116) and established the precedent for film tie-in covers that followed.

Cross-Promotion Today

Since the earliest days of pictorial tie-ins, the publishing industry has adopted far more from the cinema than simply images for novel covers. The film industry's approach to marketing and promotion offers a productive model for the bookseller, not only because they have significantly greater marketing budgets than the publishers do (Bolonick 2001, 17), but because their tactics for promoting films are applicable to the marketing of texts: 'announcing the arrival of a new epic; making known its content and appeal; and carrying right through to the high street the facts about its availability to an audience' (Hyde 1977, 47).

The overlap between the industries is growing stronger, expanding to include ancillary texts and other literary tie-ins, such as audiobooks, in addition to the novel upon which the movie was based. The 1996 release of Ang Lee's adaptation of Austen's *Sense and Sensibility* inspired a surge in sales of the movie tie-in edition featuring photography from the film as well as the Penguin edition (without movie cross-promotion), Emma Thompson's screenplay of the film and the audiobook (Maryles 1996, 322). Such is the demand for such movie-related literature that even 'original scripts will often have simultaneous publication of a "novelization," the book of the film' (Giddings 2000, 22). Novelisation attests to the desire to concretise

---

2   While the text of classic novels is almost invariably in the public domain (as are the fine art images usually used on covers), publishers compete to buy the rights to the film still at auction. See Norman Oder's (1996) '"Sense"-ible tie-ins', *Publishers Weekly* 243(1) (1 January): 36.

the experience of watching the film; it makes the temporary and ephemeral permanent. It is a strong desire: Randall Larson's *Films to Books* documents more than 2,500 such film-based novels (1995).

To be sure, a film's success can also be enhanced by the mutual promotion of an early release of the tie-in novel; with film cover art being released, in some cases, months before the film version hits the theatre, studios hope to create a buzz about the film version with lovers of the novel (Maryles 2001, 19). But it is the publisher who benefits most from the cross-publicity offered by film versions. Film tie-ins have become so common, and are such an important promotion tool, that industry journal *Publishers Weekly* now features regular listings of novels with upcoming film versions. In addition to opportunities for cross-promotion, movie tie-in versions of classic novels offer the opportunity for higher pricing – Penguin Classic's *Pride and Prejudice* (Figure 9.2) lists for $8.00, while the movie tie-in version with Keira Knightley and Matthew MacFayden on the cover lists for $10.00. The cover change is not limited to iconography; while the interiors of the novels are exactly the same, Penguin followed the filmmaker's choice of title, replacing the 'and' of Austen's title with the ampersand of the movie, further blurring the line between the literary and the cinematic.

Such willingness to adopt the look (and in the case of the previous example, the title) of cinematic versions of novels illustrates the power of potential profit: it seems to be a truth universally acknowledged that 'when a movie is made of a classic or literary title, interest in that book picks up' (Pedersen 1993, 2), and most discussions in industry publications follow the maxim that all publicity is good publicity. When asked if there was a risk associated with production costs of movie tie-ins, Patrick Nolan, Trade Paperback Sales Director for Penguin Books in the US, noted that there was 'Not really a risk – with a hit there is only upside' (Nolan, 2004).

The Reader and the Starring Role

That movie tie-ins can be lucrative cross-promotion tools benefiting both studio and publishing house has been well determined. But the easy relationship between the two industries is complicated when one returns to the comments of the English undergrad cited at the opening of this piece. Film tie-ins seem like a winning prospect for publishing houses, but why do they inspire such strong reactions from the reading public? And why, even for the reader not already familiar with that novel, is that reaction often negative? To answer this question, one must look beyond sales figures to the experience of reading and further, to the experience of imagining a book.

The rise of phenomenology as a mode of literary (as well as philosophical) discourse parallels the rise of cinema. Stemming from Husserl's early twentieth-century organisation of experience as an incumbent for understanding the nature of one's reality, the reader response schools took up the cause of granting value to the subjective, albeit 'informed' (Fish 1970, 145) response to poetry, fiction and indeed film, as a site of meaning-making. Validating the personal rendering and reading of the novel meant validating one's mental iconography as well – the way that the individual interprets and constructs the narrative in the mind. Adaptation theory may propose criteria with which to judge an adaptation's relative fidelity to the events, tone or 'universe' of a novel, but it is less adequate at addressing why an actor may appear, to one reader, to embody precisely a favourite character while, to another reader, he appears utterly wrong. While, as a school of literary criticism, reader response stalled in the 1980s, it comes closest to offering a way to understand the intensely personal response to the cover of a novel.

The current favoured cover art for classic novels is paintings by old masters, and most depict individuals who are unidentifiable to today's reading public. Oxford World Classic's *Portrait of a Lady*, for example, uses a Henri Fantin-Latour's *Portrait of Sonia* on its cover. Is it an ostensible illustration of Isabel Archer? Or is it simply, as the title suggests, 'a' portrait of 'a lady', without a specific referent? 'No one,' writes Susan Sontag, 'takes an easel painting to be in any sense co-substantial with its subject' (1989, 155); perhaps no one but the subject of the painting herself. As a cover illustration, the image can be understood not as a portrait of the novel's character, but simply as a portrait of a contemporary woman; images like this thus take on a generic quality, standing as a filler image. These covers become, through their positioning as old masterworks in and among the public domain, a blank canvas, or a placeholder for the reader's mental imagining of the character.

Replace that placeholder with a discrete persona, identifiable as a specific character in the novel and, more importantly, identifiable as an individual living in the world *with* the reader, and the cover art becomes less a blank canvas and more of a restriction. When that actor's appearance or demeanour contrasts with the reader's mental image of a character, the result can be disappointment or even hostility. 'The interesting theoretical point to be made about evaluative descriptions,' writes Seymour Chatman, 'is that they invoke visual elaborations in the reader's mind' (1999, 442). The specification required by the visual rhetoric of the cinema risks contradicting the reader's 'visual elaborations', and in doing so alienating the viewer.

Even in situations when a 'real' character in a text does exist, the lines between readerly relation to the author or character and to a cinematic portrayal of that individual may become blurred. When Viking (a subsidiary imprint of Penguin Books) published a translation of Reinaldo Arenas's memoir *Before Night Falls* in 1993, they used an understated cover design featuring a black and white portrait of the author. When, in 2000, director Julian Schnabel filmed the biopic based on the book, Penguin printed a movie tie-in version with starring actor Javier Bardem on the cover (the cover duplicates the film poster). Collusion between the text and the film is further complicated with this cover, as the novel is an autobiography; unlike a novel in which characters are fictional, Arenas *did* exist. Further, photos of him exist. Placing an actor on the cover, an actor who depicted the author in the filmed version of his life, leaves the reader in the position of having to determine where Arenas *is* in the images.

At the heart of the problem is the difference between reading text and reading the image of a film. Both involve seeing – the taking in of information through vision, but the similarities seem to end there – at least to the literary critic: 'Narrative does not show,' writes Roland Barthes, 'the passion which may excite us in reading a novel is not that of a "vision" (in fact, we do not "see" anything). Rather it is that of meaning, that of a higher order of relation which also has its emotions, its hopes its dangers, its triumphs' (1977, 124). If 'meaning' excites, it is meaning as constructed by the reader; apprehension of the visual narrative represented in a film seems to be more immediate and require less construction. Under Barthes's schema, passion derived from 'meaning' as opposed to that derived from 'vision' is 'of a higher order', a value judgement that continues the privileging of the novel seemingly implicit in adaptation theory. George Bluestone similarly contrasts the direct perception required to understand a film with the 'screen of conceptual apprehension' required to understand language (1966, 20). It is reductive to imagine that images are not also filtered through the screen of 'conceptual apprehension', especially when the defining conceptualisations of actors' screen and off-screen persona are so intentionally and well crafted, but this bias undergirds much of readers' responses to the bowdlerisation of fiction through association with filmic adaptations.

That the adaptation is seen as a text's reduction to the visual, rather than an enrichment of the textual via the visual, is echoed in Virginia Woolf's objections in her scathing 1926 polemic against the cinematic adaptations of literary classics. Unlike the student buying *Pride and Prejudice* who objected to the cover before reading the novel, and thus before imagining the characters in her mind's eye, Woolf's reactions to film versions are shaped by her intimate familiarity with the characters brought about by the experience of reading. 'The result' of adaptation, she writes, 'are disastrous' to both the text and the film:

> The alliance is unnatural … The eye says 'Here is Anna Karenina,' a voluptuous lady in black velvet wearing pearls comes before us. But the brain says 'That is no more Anna Karenina than it is Queen Victoria'. For the brain knows Anna almost entirely by the inside of her mind – her charm, her passion, her despair. All the emphasis is laid by the cinema upon her teeth, her pearls, and her velvet (1926, 309).

Though Woolf is concerned with the fetishisation of the visual external as opposed to a depiction of the internal, the mental and ideational, her objection also raises the issue of the fidelity to the reader's experience of Anna rather than the novel's construction of her character. 'That is no more Anna Karenina than it is Queen Victoria' may also refer to the objection that the Anna Karenina on screen matches the viewer's conception of her no more than Queen Victoria would. At the time Woolf wrote this piece for *The New Republic*, at least four versions of Tolstoy's novel had been committed to film, and the title heroine had been played by Irén Varsányi, Lya Mara, Betty Nansen and Mariya Germanova; none was equal to the mental work done by Woolf's reading.

Actors are well aware of this relationship between reader and text and the potential to disappoint readers through the personification of a character on screen. Clark Gable was famously disinterested in the role of Rhett Butler in *Gone with the Wind* precisely because of this pressure. In his reflections printed in a souvenir programme for the film, he wrote, 'Miss Mitchell had etched Rhett into the minds of millions of people, each of whom knew exactly how Rhett would look and act. It would be impossible to satisfy them all. An actor would be lucky to please even the majority' (Dietz 1939, 13). His objections, along with Woolf's, have less to do with favouring the intrinsic nature of the novel than with concern over upsetting the intimate correspondence between reader and text. The subjective experience of the novel, and the complementary mental invention of the physical characteristics of its characters (if indeed that invention takes place), is defined by the various apprehensions of the minds of the individuals – while some shared 'intersubjectivity' (in Husserl's sense) makes it possible to have *some* shared vision of a character, there remains the potential for serious alienation.

It is this possible alienation that leads to *some* trepidation among publishers and booksellers regarding the ubiquity of movie tie-in versions of classic literary texts, despite the prospective monetary gains: 'One is uncomfortably reminded that today the novel is often regarded as no more than an adjunct to or advertising medium for the film' (Wagner 1975, 43). Wagner's discomfort is a sign of anxiety that the novel should be treated as if it were not primary at all; it also demonstrates the persistence sway of privileging the literary over the visual, a persistence perhaps not surprising in bookstore owners. Yet booksellers also face the displeasure of readers – Marcia Burch, Vice President at Penguin, notes that not all bookstores are excited to carry tie-in editions: 'They complain that it's junky-looking, not as up-market as their clientele' (cited in Pedersen 1993, 24). The objections tend to be rooted in the experience of book-buying for the reader, a stance exhibiting the cultural bias noted by Robert Stam: 'I think taking a book written in the nineteenth century and throwing a movie tie-in with the actors on the cover somehow cheapens the package' (Pedersen 1993, 24). These concerns demonstrate the booksellers' anxiety over loss of sales and loss of literaryness of their product because of its association with a film version. They reflect Robert Stam's notions that seniority ('the novel is no more than an adjunct ... for the film') and iconophoia ('actors on the cover ... cheapens the package') account for the critical pro-text/anti-film bias. They do not, however, address the concerns of readerly imagination with regard to the film imagery – the concern evidenced in Virginia Woolf's protest of *Anna Karenina* and Clark Gable's anxiety about playing Rhett Butler.

Selling a novel through a movie is thus a delicate business for reasons beyond the superficial concern of sales rates and symbiotic promotional tactics. The use of specific photographic images of actors portraying characters of beloved novels brings into question the role of the individual reader's agency in creating an imaginary diegesis for the story. Those biases towards fiction on display in critical or theoretical discussions of the subject may be mirrored in some readers' refusal of the movie tie-in. So personal for the reader is the creation of mental visions of characters, or even a lack of mental vision of characters, that to identify a novel's cast with concrete images – photographs, even – of modern-day actors and actresses is to risk losing a consumer. Still, the potential gain from sales to consumers attracted to these tie-in editions is persuasive enough to demand their production. To resolve this dilemma, publishers have a standard edition and the movie tie-in edition containing exactly the same pages between their covers (Nolan, 2004). But such is the power of the cover image that booksellers are compelled to carry both – if only so that undergraduates need not tear the covers from their novels.

Chapter 10

In Real Life: Book Covers in the Internet Bookstore

Alexis Weedon

University of Bedfordshire

Genette's description of the paratextual elements of books as the threshold or entrance hall has considerable metaphorical power (1997). Book covers can be seen as a doorway through which we glimpse the text. The illustrated front is an advertisement and a tease, partially revealing, partially concealing the content. It is the threshold between the public commercial arena where the book is for sale and the more intimate world of the text where the author speaks to us alone. In the bookshop or the library it is a place of negotiation and decision. The cover dallies with us – should we open the book? Should we take it and own it? Will it give us the enjoyment we seek? In particular it leads to browsing behaviour and is a site for the pleasures of choice and anticipation which is a prelude to the sale and consumption of a work.

Bookshop interior designers know the importance of browsing – it is articulated in their layouts. Libraries too, though in a different way, encourage reflective selection. There are physical cues within each of these spaces, not only in the signage, but also in the height and visibility of the shelving, the choice and position of furniture, the colours and textures of the flooring, the position of the escalators and stairways which tell us a story of how the space is organised, what it contains and the community it serves.

In marketing terms the book cover is used within this space to feature selected titles within the bookshop. It encourages customers to see what is on offer on the tables where books are arranged flat or upright so the cover can be seen; it shows what is new, and draws the customer further into the shop. Seen from afar is the cover, the object by which customers navigate their way through the space guided by signs. Bookshops have been designed to draw out customers' latent patterns of consumption, whether they have been mediated through television and advertising or the more traditional methods of word-of-mouth recommendation and reviews. On shelves books are arranged by association as well as by genre, author, lifestyle or by media.

Look through the door of a bookshop and you can see this. The curved frontage of Waterstone's in Cambridge opens onto their 3-for-2 offer table, books stacked so the browser looks down onto the cover of popular genres: fiction, biography, humour. To the right are bookcases labelled 'Richard and Judy' book club selections and 'Cambridge recommends' with face-out books displaying their covers and underneath cards filled in by staff recommending certain reads. To the left is an 'In the media' selection, again face out displaying covers featuring celebrity faces. The customer can look over the offer table to the shelves beyond and will be drawn in closer to the shelf through the signage, then the cover and then the recommendation on the card. In a larger shop like Borders face-out books are used on the back wall of alcoves of bookcases positioned to draw the customer in to the section. On the sides there are fewer face-out books but still some there to catch the eye after the initial lure. Of course it does depend on the genre: cookery has more turned-out books than law. On the sides of the alcoves there may be posters as in Figure 10.1 creating overt links between the book and other media – DVD, audiobook – or the book and other similar ones.

Figure. 10.1 In Borders' Cambridge store the DVD release is advertised next to the book and surrounded by titles the customer interested in Chevalier's novel might also like to read. Photograph taken September 2003 by Alexis Weedon

The layout of the bookshop also encourages browsing behaviour. Waterstones in Milton Keynes welcomes browsers with a chalkboard by the door listing times and dates of author signings, some of local interest. On the other side of the entrance is the desk display of the author's books, sometimes in a setting featuring posters of the book cover and of the author, the paraphernalia of celebrity reinforced by red silk ropes which keep the customers in line. Even from this entrance though the browser can look diagonally through the shop to the 'Costa coffee upstairs' sign by the escalator.

Genette's paratextual elements are evident in the physical space of the bookshop: from genre labels and written recommendations to authors' interviews and signings. The direction of customers' browsing is affected by the navigation of these texts. The online bookstore has to emulate this environment – and compete with it. People using online information have traditionally been task orientated, and facilitating the completion of the task does not always fulfil the customers' needs. In a study of an online grocery store Svensson *et al.* observe how designers have sought to add to the task in hand a 'general overall experience of browsing, with distinct emotional and affective features' (Svensson *et al.* 2000, 260). Designers have sought to aid navigation by adding pleasurable social experiences through chat rooms, games, quizzes, hypertext stories from Sainsbury's 'recipes, articles and ideas' to eBay's chat boards. More specifically they have introduced the idea of social navigation, letting the users help each other in various ways by posting recipes or making food recommendations, for example. Molesworth and Dengeri-Knott's study (2005) of the auction site eBay gives evidence that some users go to the site simply for the pleasure of the bidding. This is perhaps unsurprising as gambling is a recreational activity and highly profitable end of the entertainment market both online and off. Many games from Monopoly onwards include the excitement of bidding found in auction rooms. But what is different in the case of eBay is the element of risk and real financial commitment. From grocery shopping to auctions the online environment is a constructed space designed for customers to explore social and consuming pleasures through the shared interface of the computer terminal.

An analysis of the role of the book cover in browsing behaviour shows that there is much more browsing than the associative link made by the web text or by the poster advertisement. By structuring an online environment for browsing, some bookshop designers have created the stage and the props for a narrative. The processes of searching, choosing, engaging with other individuals though recommendations, lists and voting systems, leading finally to a selection and purchase (or bail out) form a sufficiently firm structure for narrative resolution. Of course digital narrativity does not have to be linear. There are multiple paths and users may go over and over the same circuit, reading and rereading recommendations and reviews to compare their choices. Internet bookshops have been particularly successful at remediating the old circuits of recommendation and review and allowing the personalising of customers' differing needs for news of recent publications, response to publishers' promotional activities and wish lists of aspirational purchases.

Yet there are significant differences in the way online publishers and bookshops have developed. Search 'girl pearl' on Ottakers' site and you get an uncrowded design with few thumbnails. This page presents like a magazine, with a columnist (Yossarian's diary), news (SciFi/Fantasy/Horror newsletter), quiz and readers opinions. Do the same search on HarperCollins and you are presented with a list more like a library catalogue (Figure 10.2). Follow the link and it leads you to a page which sidelines the thumbnails in a right-hand frame and centrally places the written word, which includes the blurb, reviews, author interviews (with a picture of the author) and other paratextual writings. This site tells you more about the author, her other books and critics' opinions of them than other online bookshops, but the structure is hierarchical and designed to supply information rather than create a browsing experience.

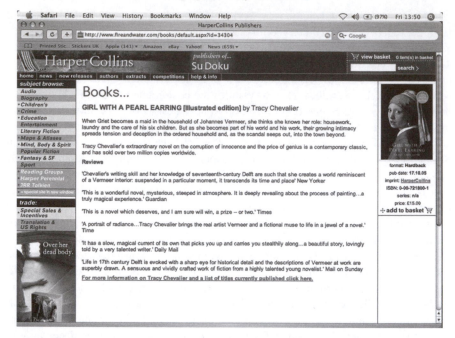

Figure 10.2 HarperCollins' online bookstore website © (2006) HarperCollins
           Publishers Ltd

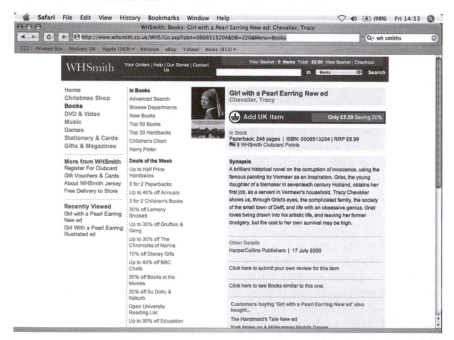

Figure. 10.3 WHSmith's online bookstore. Reprinted by permission of WHSmith's
            website

WHSmith (Figure 10.3) allows users to 'browse books similar to this one' 'submit your own review' and, for the curious, allows browsers to find out what other customers also bought. The 'similar books' link leads you to a page featuring thumbnail covers of works by Cecelia Ahern, Ben Elton and Nicole Richie amongst others. The selection is by genre, as the covers clearly and instantly communicate to the browser. 'Other customers' choices' have a different logic. Displayed as links to other pages, they show customers purchasing Margaret Atwood's *The Handmaid's Tale*, York notes on *A Midsummer Night's Dream*, Charlotte Bingham's *Nanny* and more York notes on Maya Angelou's *I Know Why the Caged Bird Sings*. In contrast Amazon.co.uk uses thumbnails to encourage social interaction between customers by placing them beside customers' recommended lists but not by 'also bought' links. However it places the synopsis, publisher's blurb or Amazon review all on the main page with customer reviews beneath.

What is interesting about the practice of WHSmith and Amazon.co.uk is the way it seeks to stimulate the construction of the browsing narrative through the web text. The book cover image – almost always a thumbnail scan of the front cover – works with the surrounding online text to foster browsing. You cannot read the publisher's blurb as you can in the bookshop. The blurb (or often the bookshop's own synopsis) is underneath. Separating the blurb from the book moves it to a critical distance away from the text. Humorous, ironic blurbs are replaced with descriptive synopses and links to or excerpts from newspaper reviews. In this way an essential component of the cover is lost. Personal recommendations are translated on the net into customer reviews, some designated as 'Top' reviewers or spotlight reviews. On Amazon lists of recommendations often cut across media. For example Cecily von Ziegesar's *Gossip Girl 2* page contains a quote from *Publishers Weekly* and a synopsis which reveals the marketing plans, presumably of US publisher Bloomsbury ('We will be publishing the series at regular intervals throughout 2003 with a high profile, energetic and suitably cutting-edge marketing campaign. Catty and engrossing, this series is spicy!'). Scrolling down to the customer reviews it has been commented upon by 'a student', DesignerDiva-alicja, who incidentally reviewed entire series. DesignerDiva-alicja posted her own 20-item recommended list which included Insider series (by Bloomsbury), TV shows and films from, *Absolutely Fabulous* to *Sex in the City*, *Romeo and Juliet* and the Collected edition of Audrey Hepburn's films. Browsing these lists the user is led by association, similarity of taste and interest and personal recommendation. There is a strong element of identification: do I have similar interests? If yes then I might try their recommendation. Identifying oneself as part of a group with shared interests 'those who bought …' encourages consumption. It also forms part of the inner narrative as the user moves from the task of searching and choosing a product to comparing and evaluating their requirements. Through interaction with the props and characters, the task aspect gives way to the story and the browser begins to interact with other customers. The browser takes pleasure in the connection with other fields of meaning – both social, through recommendation and other presences, and cultural, through reference to shared interests and understanding mediated by the media.

One frequently voiced criticism on buying online is that you can't handle the book, often articulated as a need to turn it over and read the back cover or look inside.

Physical handling is an important part of the gratification of browsing (if you don't believe me try going into a shop and not touching anything; it is much less pleasurable). Yet of course, shops do not want their stock soiled. While it is more common to be able to look in a book in a bookshop, it is not universal. The DVD+book combinations sold in British retailer Woolworths, for example, are cellophaned and security labelled and you cannot look inside. Borders online and Amazon have responded to this need to look inside with PDFs of part of the work. Graphics are attached to the thumbnail to signal that you can access some copyright material from the book. Click on the image and you get a different scan of the full-size cover and pages of the book which you can leaf through. Thanks to such images, online, as in the high street bookshop, the user can cross Genette's threshold. All the excerpts can be searched on Amazon and Google. It means that the prelims and first pages of the book are repeated and excerpted all over the Web, making Genette's virtual vestibule, a hall of mirrors.

Online the old distinctions between media and the hierarchy between media, for example book versus film, are of less importance than the association between them. In a store which sells a range of media such as Amazon or WHSmith the initial search is revealing. Take for example the title *Girl with a Pearl Earring* by Tracey Chevalier. The book was made into a film (Peter Webber, UK, 2003). When you search on Amazon.co.uk for 'girl pearl' in all media products relating to the title there is no distinction between the media form, whereas WHSmith visually separates the media by a blue line. However on both the size of the images can be misleading. The audio CD of the soundtrack is the biggest thumbnail yet the smallest on the shop shelf. The user has to read the text to differentiate between them. The audiobook and the paperback are particularly hard to tell apart any other way. Across all the online bookshops the cover image is an icon which does not show the media's physical form, though there are clues in that the image may be portrait or landscape (as with the audiobook on tape or CD). The only site I found which did graphically indicate the physical form of the book image was at bol.com. And it is not used as a button or link except to a larger version of the image or the copyright material on Amazon. In effect the cover image is not a threshold as it leads nowhere.

While Amazon and WHSmith online do not discriminate between media, the two images on the covers themselves show that the producers have a clear idea of the market and status of their product. The images used on the covers of *Girl with a Pearl Earring* are Vermeer's synonymous painting and a film still. The different cultural connotations of the images separate the book from the film. The painting has instantly recognisable cultural value and appears on nearly all the book editions. The 1999 HarperCollins edition has an illustration which includes a miniature of the Vermeer painting. This image also appears on the front cover of the millennium paperback, filling the whole cover, and on the HarperCollins audio cassette, audio CD and large-print edition. Plume Books' 2005 edition also uses this image though with distinguishing blue stripes. The front cover of the October 2005 HarperCollins hardback edition has the addition of a medallion like a hair ornament advertising the fact that it is a limited edition with new material and illustrations. On bol.com this thumbnail is accompanied by text citing the beauty of the film and of Vermeer's paintings as a reason to acquire the book, while Amazon quotes the publishers saying: 'To celebrate one million copies sold of this contemporary classic, this is a full colour, illustrated edition featuring nine Vermeer paintings integrated with the original text.' The association is clear: books and old masters are timeless works of art.

It is not surprising that the publishers want to make that link: the book is a fictional story about Vermeer's family and servant. However it has resonances within media theory. The early and key media theorist, Walter Benjamin, analysed *The Work of Art in the Age of Mechanical Reproduction*, raising the issue of the original versus the copy. One of the examples he takes is the reproduction of old master paintings printed in their thousands after the mechanisation of colour printing in the mid-nineteenth century. Distributed to a wide market and they became, he argued, familiar, every day, while only the original painting continued to inspire the awe in the viewer. Benjamin's definition of aura is particularly significant to media studies as he argued that film and other reproductive media could not capture it. As Bolter defined it, 'Aura can usually be understood as a psychological state, an attitude or feeling that the viewer experiences when contemplating a work of art' (2006, 26). Is the cover image of the painting therefore offering the reader something closer to an auratic experience when reading the book? In this respect the film/DVD cover falls along traditionally accepted lines in that it does not seek to do this, rather the cover image is a hypermediated form of the painting.

Given the absence of spatial demarcations between types of books in the online bookstore, book covers online come to signal genre in complex and important ways. Historical and revered paintings are frequently used on front covers of classic book series to denote cultural value as well as placing the titles in a specific historical era. Covers of historical fiction also sometimes use paintings or artefacts from the time to communicate the period of the tale. Similarly historical biographies feature images, often paintings, of their subject. Though not necessarily old masters, the use of old paintings in all three genres makes the interpretation of the front cover of Chevalier's novel equivocal, while making it evident that the painting is the original inspiration of the novel.

The DVD cover uses a film still, though not one which is an actual image from the film. The still is a partial reconstruction of the painting by Vermeer and an image which unequivocally states the film's genre, a historical romance. It also reflects Chevalier's narrative interpretation of the painting and captures an intimate moment between the painter and his model. It projects a simplified and not wholly accurate interpretation of the relationship between the protagonists at the key moment of the film. (For while the film plays upon the power relations within the household, the still image lacks the complex and dark undertones of the narrative at the moment when the character of Vermeer has just inserted his wife's pearl earring into the maid's newly pierced ear.) The DVD+book combination uses the film still within a yellow frame and with additional stickers of approval in terms of awards and nominations (nominated for ten BAFTAs and three Academy Awards including Best Actress and Best British Film). These are added endorsements for the bookshop browser, though these cover medallions are not legible on website thumbnails, and can only be seen on the enlarged image. The cover makes overt links between the book and film, with simple graphics on the front and back cover representing an open book and piece of film. In fact the DVD+book combo is marketed to the consumer as both a film viewer and reader. It raises and postpones a common question: which to read/view first? Buy both, then decide. Iconographically however the book is signalled as the DVD add-on as the book of the DVD+book combination uses the film image on the front cover – unlike all the other book editions which have used Vermeer's painting. It is an indicator of the shift in a cultural attitude to books that we can no longer point to the printed text as being the first encountered or necessarily the original. The various media forms of the work are all copies and for consumers there may be no 'original' narrative that is adapted to other media. They may have come to the work by watching the film, reading the book or playing the video game first and each subsequent encounter is informed by their previous experience. The online environment of the bookshop is a critical place where the boundaries between media have been eroded, but it is not the only place. Producers are now designing their products to combine the multiple copyrightable properties of a creative work – the book, film, audiobook, film music – and merchandise, collectables, holiday tours and so on.

To explain the ways in which the internet shop creates browsing pleasures a second metaphor is useful: Brenda Laurel's conceptualisation of *Computers as Theatre* (1993). The metaphor draws a comparison between the staged space and the virtual. Put simply: the screen is the stage, the user an actor or protagonist and the icons are the stage props. This metaphor adds in the element of narrative as a story is created by the interaction between the protagonist and the stage props. Laurel's (1990) concept of the 'narrative interface' moves away from the Aristotelian definition of narrative and proposes instead that narratives come into being on the screen, through the users' interaction with icons linking to hypertextual objects. It is a concept that goes beyond the literary definition of narrative of Genette's work. In effect there is no narrative voice other than the mind of the user who creates a story from moving round the screen and engaging with the icons; nor is there a separation of the world of the narrative and the narratee. Laurel's later amendment of her argument (1993) added that the story had to be written into the computer system's design. Such 'narrative frames' exist in many real-life and online games, from paintballing to Invaders, where a narrative is set up which participants then enact with varying degrees of choice depending on the rules. However this rather different inflection raises issues of transgressive play and resistance which have long been a feature of the online environment and hacker culture and are inimical to commercial sites. Laurel famously cited *Star Trek*'s Holodeck as the most realised representation of a virtual narrative. (The Holodeck is a computer-generated virtual world in which participants can interact with story characters within 'safety protocols'.) This has been taken up and contested by games theorists such as Janet Murray, Henry Jenkins and Marie-Laurie Ryan (Murray 1998; Cassell and Jenkins 2000; Ryan *Narrative* 2001). Indeed as the TV series itself showed, reality has a dangerous way of circumventing the safety protocols as fantasies intrude into real life.

Ryan's work on narrative in games moves the notion several steps on. She argues that narrative is not tied to any specific medium or form such as the novel; it is a mental representation 'of a world (setting) situated in time, populated by individuals (characters), who participate in actions and happenings (events, plot) and undergo change' (Ryan 'Beyond Myth' 2001). Game play is one such mental representation which creates different narratives within a structured and delimited space. The puzzle and challenge is central to the pleasure of gaming, but also important is the way the narrative is self-determined. How close is this to the experience of the online browser? I think it helps us understand the attraction of net surfing and the enjoyment of aspirational consumerism, for browsing encompasses the pleasures of seeking and finding, of anticipation and reward and even indulgence. However gaming is an intentional, consciously determined and directed exercise, while browsing is a liminal, reflective pleasure. It is this liminality which keeps the user on site, and the customer in the shop as they create their own narrative through pleasurable associative links and social connection.

PART 4
Translating Covers: Moving Audiences and the Marketing of Books

Chapter 11

Cover Charge: Selling Sex and Survival in Lesbian Pulp Fiction

Melissa Sky
Appleby College, Ontario

Lesbian pulp fiction novels were some of the most lucrative texts to emerge from the American, mid-century Golden Age of the paperback, due largely to their sensational cover art, which continues to circulate as retro kitsch on contemporary consumer items. This chapter traces the fascinating cover and reception history of the most successful and beloved star author of the genre: Ann Bannon. The chapter is structured in four key sections. 'DisCovering Lesbianism' introduces the history and publishing context of Bannon's five-book 'Beebo Brinker Chronicles' series. I also analyse the original, Fawcett editions in relation to their small but loyal lesbian audience, focusing on their status as what Joan Nestle, co-founder of the Lesbian Herstory Archives, calls 'survival literature' (cited in *Queer Covers*, 1993). Gay women learned to recognise these covers iconographically and to read them against the grain of the negativity that censorship required. 'UnCovering Lesbianism' analyses the 1950s and 1960s Fawcett originals in relation to their production history as sexploitation. Produced largely by and for heterosexual men, these covers promise and deliver titillation, a kind of forbidden peek at the twilight world of deviant women. The covers also reflect contemporary confusion regarding lesbianism. Consequently, they seek to uncover the lesbian in the sense of undressing her for kicks, but also to uncover her in the sense of illuminating her mystery. 'ReCovering Lesbianism' analyses the 1980s Naiad reprints and how they reflect a second-wave feminist ideology. Specifically, I argue that the covers centre on a feminist ambivalence towards the relationship between sex and power as it is articulated through butch-femme relationships. Finally, 'Covering Lesbianism' analyses the recent Cleis reprints.[1] I focus on their status as postmodern camp, for they are presented as a playful cover tune of the originals. As part of a hip marketing scheme of self-conscious tackiness, Cleis promotes them as an amusing kind of literary

---

1   The Fawcett, Naiad and Cleis reprints are not the only ones available. Bannon's novel *I am a Woman* was also reprinted in hardcover by Arno Press in 1975 for a series called 'Homosexuality: Lesbians and Gay Men in Society, History and Literature' and the series was reprinted in an omnibus edition (omitting *Journey to a Woman*) by The Quality Paperback Book Club in 1995 for a series entitled 'Triangle Classics: Illuminating the Gay and Lesbian Experience'. English, Dutch and Italian editions of her texts have also been produced throughout the years. I limit my analysis to the covers of the three major, American editions, because I focus on the cover art; and the Arno and QPB editions, while interesting for their contribution to improving Bannon's series' literary status, have never had the popularity of the other editions for collectors because they do not have compelling covers.

slumming, cashing in on the pulps' tawdriness, even as they formally apologise for it in new introductions and prominently feature positive reviews from prestigious queer writers and publications on the back covers.

DisCovering Lesbianism

The history of pulp fiction novels begins during World War II when American soldiers received small, paperback Armed Services Editions of literary reprints. The return of demobilised forces created a paperback explosion in the publishing industry because the soldiers had become accustomed to cheap, disposable books. Literary tastes also expanded as women's lives had become more diverse during the war years and they sought a reflection of that shift in literature. Jaye Zimet, in her anthology of lesbian pulp cover art, *Strange Sisters*, points out that while the drive to 'normalcy' after the war created a big business market for traditional romance novels, the radical counter-culture was also creating a market for books about sex, drugs and criminal activity (Zimet 1999, 19). The lesbian pulps fit into both of these trends, making them extremely popular. In 1957, the 'Roth' decision in the US Supreme Court created a less restrictive definition of obscenity and this created opportunity for even more sensational literature. By the 1960s, the newly relaxed censorship laws, in conjunction with the sexual revolution, allowed many publishing houses to produce what was effectively soft-core pornography in paperback. Many of theses works were sensational stories of lesbianism. These novels flooded the presses and sold thousands of copies in bookstores, drugstores, supermarkets and train stations (Weir and Wilson 1992, 98–9).

The history of lesbian pulp fiction begins with Tereska Torres's 1950 semi-autobiographical novel about French women soldiers in London during World War II entitled *Women's Barracks*. Its publication created an uproar. The US House of Representatives centred much of their 1952 Committee on Current Pornographic Materials on this text. During the five days of hearings, paperbacks were routinely lambasted because of their objectionable content, lurid covers and wide availability in public places. The Committee's majority report states that *Women's Barracks* is a prime example of 'the so-called pocket-sized books, which originally started out as cheap reprints of standard works' but 'have largely degenerated into media for the dissemination of artful appeals to sensuality, immorality, filth, perversion and degeneracy' (United States 1952, 3). The publicity surrounding the hearings boosted sales and many publishing houses attempted to cash in on the success of the lesbian theme.

Fawcett was one of the most influential of these companies. They published many lesbian pulps as part of the 'Gold Medal' imprint. Their distribution company, Signet, limited the number of reprints from hardcovers, so Fawcett began to publish original material under the name 'Paperback Original' (Zimet 1999, 19). This move created lucrative opportunities for many new writers. Another unique feature of Fawcett was its commitment to publishing relatively authentic and well-written lesbian stories. While most of the lesbian pulps were written by heterosexual men under feminine pseudonyms, most Gold Medal books were written by women, many of whom were lesbian. The Paperback Original line allowed out lesbian writers to publish stories that hardcover publishing companies would never have approved because they were too controversial. Although this publishing boom provided a new opportunity to write openly about lesbianism, authors could not write freely. Susan Stryker, in her anthology, *Queer Pulp*, points to the effect of the congressional investigation's report on the paperback publishing industry:

> The report created a climate of fear in the publishing industry by threatening fines and jail terms for those who refused to embrace the Committee's vision of morality. This resulted in a general toning-down of sexual content in paperbacks, particularly in their cover art, and a greater emphasis on stories that drove home the generally tragic consequences of straying from the straight and narrow path (2001, 51).

While *Women's Barracks* inaugurated the lesbian pulp genre, Fawcett's first lesbian pulp, Marijane Meaker's instant bestseller, *Spring Fire*, really inspired the craze.[2] Its publication history demonstrates the degree of censorship involved in lesbian pulps, for although it was a sympathetic portrayal, Meaker was told from the beginning by her editor, Dick Carroll, that it could not have a happy ending otherwise the post office might seize it as obscene (Zimet 1999, 20). Consequently, one woman goes insane and the other woman reverts to heterosexuality. This established an important convention of the genre. The lesbian generally had three options in the end: die, go insane or marry a man. Meaker, at a 2004 queer publisher's talk, 'Doyennes of Desire', elaborated on her response to this convention, stating,

> I was so glad to get published, I didn't care. And the people who wrote me didn't seem to care either. They were so glad that finally in a paperback there was something about them. Ok, it wasn't a happy ending, but in the 50s there weren't a lot of happy endings to gay life. Your parents disowned you. Friends didn't want anything to do with you (Bannon and Meaker 2004).

This authorial lack of choice also played out in the cover art. Authors had no say in their titles or what might appear on the covers of their novels. After reading *Spring Fire*, the most subsequently popular lesbian pulp writer, Ann Bannon, wrote to Marijane Meaker to praise her on her novel and Meaker encouraged Bannon to send in a manuscript for the same line. In 1957, Bannon followed Meaker's advice and published her first lesbian pulp, *Odd Girl Out*. She admits now that she was 'dismayed' (Bannon and Davis 2004) with its original cover art by Barye Phillips: 'They look like 1930s Nancy Drew covers. I remember saying to Dick [Carroll, her editor], is there something that we could do about this? They look so pre-World War II and this is cutting-edge 1950 whatever' (Bannon and Meaker 2004). Bannon describes the covers to her five-book 'Beebo Brinker Chronicles' series as ranging 'from peculiar to surreal', adding, 'those of you who can recall that original cover must have wondered if the editors had read the book – as indeed, the cover artists seldom did' (Foreword 1999, 10). Nowhere was this more apparent than in the original cover for *Beebo Brinker*. She describes her incredulity at the discrepancy between her vision of her butch dyke protagonist and the cover artist, Robert McGinnis's, rendition:

---

2   Following established conventions in the scholarship, I utilise Marijane Meaker's real name rather than the pseudonyms she used for her lesbian texts (Vin Packer, Ann Aldrich), but I utilise the pseudonym Ann Bannon when discussing Ann Thayer/Weldy's texts.

> I studied the cover. It was really the only time I found myself in *The Twilight Zone* over one of my own books. There gazing back at me was a skinny, scared, adolescent girl with a page boy bob, wearing brown broughams and white bobby socks—a fusty fashion disaster … As covers went, it was a megabomb (Foreword 1999, 11).

Although Bannon admits that McGinnis was 'probably the very finest cover artists of that era' (Bannon and Davis 2004), the cover bears little resemblance to the content, as indeed few lesbian pulp covers did.

Most lesbian pulp covers did, however, bear a striking resemblance to each other. Zimet clarifies how on most of the lesbian pulp covers, 'the style of painting was drawn from the dimestore pulp digest magazines that the paperback was fast replacing. In fact, many of the paperback illustrators got their start doing work for the pulp mags. They were done in a hyperrealistic style and featured curvaceous women, scantily clad, whose overt sexuality dripped off the cover' (1999, 22). This highly stylised iconography helped isolated lesbians across the country to identify paperbacks that might offer some hope that they were not struggling alone with their difference. In the foreword to Zimet's anthology, Bannon discusses this lesbian manner of reading the covers:

> Despite all the care devoted to developing cover art that would activate male gonads, women learned to recognize what was a nascent literature of their own by reading the covers iconically. If there was a solitary woman on the cover, provocatively dressed, and the title conveyed her rejection by society or her self-loathing, it was a lesbian book. If there were two women on the cover, and they were touching each other … [e]ven if they were just looking at each other; even if they were simply in proximity to one another; even if they were merely on the same cover together, it was reason to hope you had found a lesbian book (1999, 12–13).

Formulaic conventions also extended to the titles, which often used such telltale terms as odd, strange, twilight, shadows and so on. In fact, these kinds of terms figure highly on the back covers of the original editions of Bannon's novels and sometimes as blurbs on the front covers as well. The cover copy for *Beebo Brinker*, for instance, reads 'Lost, lonely, boyishly appealing—this is Beebo Brinker—who never really knew what she wanted—until she came to Greenwich Village and found the love that smoulders in the shadows of the twilight world.' Such telltale visual and verbal conventions mark the genre.

The importance of this literature to the sustenance of pre-Stonewall, American lesbians can hardly be overstated. Diane Hamer has argued that 'Bannon's novels did not merely reflect the reality of being a lesbian as she knew it in the 1950s, but also helped to produce one' (1990, 51) and she points in particular to Bannon's fan mail as evidence of her influence: 'The fictional fantasy world Bannon created through her novels was not separate from, but formed part of the reality of being a lesbian in the 1950s. Bannon herself was swamped with requests for help and advice about lesbianism from isolated women desperate for information' (Hamer 1990, 51). Bannon took seriously this role as an adviser on how to survive as a lesbian in a hostile culture. She claims of the letters she received:

The major message from the majority of them was … 'If I hadn't found your book, I was ready to kill myself. I really thought I was unique. I thought there were no other women in the world who loved women. I didn't know how to handle it. I haven't been able to reach out to anybody. I know all too well that my family will either disown me or take after me with an axe' (Bannon and Meaker, 2004).

Despite their highly constrained nature both in terms of the text and the cover, it is no exaggeration to claim that Bannon's novels literally sustained lesbian lives. As Bannon herself puts it, 'Despite all their editorially imposed quirks, the covers provided links among members of a wide-flung and incohesive community; a community that did not even think of itself as one and that, therefore, valued all the more any connection with others whose experience paralleled their own' (Foreword 1999, 13).

UnCovering Lesbianism

Lesbian pulp fiction was initially published as a lucrative form of sexploitation. The original Fawcett covers for Bannon's 'Beebo Brinker Chronicles' series were, like all lesbian pulp covers of the era, produced by and for heterosexual men. Fawcett did, however, appeal to the texts' small but devoted lesbian audience by promoting Bannon as an author, a rare move, by identifying her previous works on the covers of her newer ones. Nonetheless, the motive for producing these texts was purely economic. Bannon herself recognised that if 'authors were the last people consulted by the editors about pulp fiction covers', it was because 'we knew what our characters looked like and wanted to see them materialise on our book covers. We cared intensely about the effect the cover designs would have on the readership. The editors, however, knew something more practical: how to move their inventory' (Foreword 1999, 10). As the cliché goes: sex sells, and the covers of most lesbian pulps exploited it to the fullest extent the publishers dared. It is important to remember, as Stryker notes, that 'before the sexual revolution of the 1960s and the explosion of soft- and hard-core pornographic magazines that came in its wake, paperback books were pretty much the only game in town when it came to explicit portrayals of sexuality in the mass media' (8). Therefore, while lesbians may have approached them differently, from the publishers' standpoint, lesbian pulps were simply sensational commodities.

Bannon's Fawcett covers, however, are actually far more restrained than most in the genre. The covers of Bannon's *I am a Woman* and *Journey to a Woman* reveal a fair amount of skin, but her other pulps are only sexualised in a highly abstract manner. While there are several anthologies that showcase lesbian pulp covers, few scholars have scrutinised them. Michele Aina Barale's article 'Queer Urbanities', however, has illustrated the radical, sexual symbolism of the original *Beebo Brinker* cover, focusing on the cover artist's choice to switch the colour of the protagonist's socks from white to pink (2000, 211). Pink is a toned down version of red, which is often used to symbolise desire, and pink is also linked to left-wing politics, so the cover, despite its fairly demure depiction of Beebo, nevertheless suggests her potential to become a fiery sexual deviant, which is why 'there is a fire hydrant nearby … It seems to suggest that should pink intensify—to a flaming red, for instance—municipal authority has the matter under control' (Barale, 213).

All of the Fawcett covers seek to uncover the lesbian both in the sense of undressing her for prurient purposes and also uncovering her in the sense of demystifying her enigma. Mainstream fifties American culture promoted conflicting views on lesbianism and the cover art reflects these indeterminate discourses. The covers seem to attempt to answer a number of questions about lesbianism that were circulating at the time: are they dangerous? Are they really women? Are they easily identifiable or might lesbianism lurk in any given woman?

The cover art on the first novel in the series, *Odd Girl Out*, centres on a depiction of the relative danger of lesbianism. The original Fawcett cover painting portrays an apparently distraught brunette woman lying face down in front of what appears to be a cave, her hand to her face. A blonde woman is leaning over her, one hand on the brunette's shoulder and one on the other side of her body, so that the blonde's entire upper body is directly over the brunette's body. Whether she is comforting her or pushing her down, however, is difficult to ascertain with certainty, since both their eyes are downcast, making it difficult to read their expressions. If the blonde was a man, it would look more like he was about to take the brunette from behind, perhaps non-consensually. The fact that we cannot read the blonde's face or pose as either loving or menacing reflects the social uncertainty as to whether lesbianism is about love or whether it is a kind of moral evil. Some of the ambiguity surrounding the two women's postures and expressions is cleared up, however, in the new cover painting Barye Phillips created for the third printing. Although even less of the blonde's face is showing, her gesture is more clearly one of consolation for the more obviously upset brunette. This new painting, nevertheless, retains the sense of ambiguity about lesbians since their poses seem less menacing, but the background becomes more unmistakably ominous.

The backgrounds of both of the Fawcett covers for *Odd Girl Out* represent the danger of lesbian relationships, for in both the setting includes a chasm and precipice. In the cover for the first and second printings, the two women are positioned just outside the mouth of a cave and the brunette is lying on top of a small slope. The cave represents the swirling vortex of their illicit relationship, popularly conceived of as a strange and dark passion which threatens to suck women into an abyss where they may be lost forever. The slope similarly symbolises how the women risk falling to some unseen peril. Although they are shown in nature, the slope is an odd, teal colour, representing the two women's purportedly unnatural love. The cover for the third printing updates the hairdos of the women and takes on a more abstract, modern look, but otherwise retains the key elements of the original. Although they no longer look like a cave and grassy slope, the chasm and precipice remain. The cave, for example, becomes an abstract, roughly painted, black hole fringed with fiery red and pink. The brushstrokes are discernible and overall the new elements evoke an increased sense of a boding threat. Both Fawcett covers thus appear conflicted as to the relative danger of lesbianism, for even though the third edition cover clarifies the harmless nature of the blonde's pose, it moves the threat into the background as a more theoretical, abstract peril looming over the pair.

All the covers for Bannon's second novel, *I am a Woman*, centre, to varying degrees, on one key issue: are lesbians, as Bannon's title asserts, really women? The original, Fawcett cover for this novel places a new emphasis on factuality. The title itself contains an affirmation of gender and the blurb that is contained within it affirms sexuality as well: 'I am a woman in love with a woman – must society reject me?' In addition, the choice to use a photograph on the cover of one of Bannon's novels for the first time creates a sense of realism and authority. Certainly, the woman depicted on the cover is conventionally feminine and the emphasis on her overwhelming cleavage, the visible symbol of womanhood, reinforces the cover's central concern (an emphasis which is repeated on the cover of the Cleis edition of *I am a Woman*). Moreover, the original cover suggests that the woman depicted not only looks feminine, but also speaks and acts in a traditionally feminine manner. The request that forms the book's blurb and the facial expression of the woman on the cover implore the reader. She literally looks up to the reader with a vulnerable expression and virtually begs for understanding. The blurb stresses love, conventionally appropriate for females, over the lust implicit in many other lesbian pulp fiction titles.

Despite these qualities, the femininity of the lesbian as she is presented on the cover remains unstable. It is a shaky representation, as even the title suggests, for the font is wobbly, signifying uncertainty, and the spacing creates doubt as well for a line break occurs between 'I am a' and 'woman'. Moreover, while the title contains an affirmation, it is contained within a sentence that is ultimately interrogative. It directly addresses the reader with a question. If the entire cover is questioning, it is because society is perplexed about the intersections of sexuality and gender, particularly the enigma of femme lesbians who appear to fulfil conventional gender roles, yet deeply undermine them. The ample décolletage of the cover model, for example, invites male attention, and yet the woman's declaration of same-sex desire subverts this invitation. Her breasts are not available for the traditional purposes of heterosexual pleasure or maternal utility. If, under heteropatriarchy, womanhood is defined by relationships to men and their offspring, how can this person, who so clearly bears the markers of womanhood, be considered a woman? This is the unsettling question this cover asks, questions which contemporary sexological theories posed but were unable to adequately answer.

In both the Fawcett and the Naiad editions, there is a subtle sense that lesbians may not only retain their femininity despite their sexual orientation and the predominant discourse of lesbian masculinity, but that they may in fact be extraordinarily gendered. The feminist press Naiad changed the presentation of the title, omitting the interrogative blurb, a political move in keeping with the lesbian feminist emphasis on lesbianism as a distinctly womanly phenomenon. It erases the original title's interrogation of lesbian womanhood and replaces it with a strong affirmation of such: *I am a Woman*. This strategic move reinforces lesbian feminist ideology as espoused by theorists such as Adrienne Rich, who argues for 'lesbian experience as being, like motherhood, a profoundly *female* experience' (1984, 418). The original cover contains this implication in the way that it stresses not only the womanhood of the lesbian speaking but also of her partner, so rather than consisting of two unsexed females, lesbianism might be womanhood squared. This is suggested as well in the Naiad edition in which the title appears between two kissing women's throats. This placement of the affirmation of gender in the intimate space between two female lovers implies that their homosexuality does not make them any less female, but perhaps even more so. Nevertheless, the unsettling effect of a feminine woman who does not fit into mainstream conceptions of lesbians as failed women, as mannish members of a third sex, is highlighted throughout the original cover and the issue of lesbian gender roles is addressed in all three major reprints.

In some ways, all the Fawcett covers are concerned with discerning how threatening lesbianism is to the deeply heteropatriarchal society of 1950s and early 1960s America, for their interest in the relative femininity of lesbians betrays how much lesbianism destabilises the conventional gender roles upon which heteropatriarchy subsists. Another way the threat is assessed is by attempting to understand the prevalence of female homosexuality. The Fawcett covers for *Women in the Shadows* and *Journey to a Woman* address this concern. On the original cover of *Women in the Shadows* a large silhouette of a female head looks directly to the left. Contained within this shadow is a photograph of another woman's head looking to the right. Based on the shape of the hair and nose, it appears to be the same woman. The photographic woman remains in shadow, for there are shadows under her eyes and half her face is obscured by shadow as well. Her brow is furrowed and she is frowning, contributing to the overall sense of darkness on the cover (despite its luridly bright pink background). The fact that homosexuality was considered a mental illness is played out on the cover as the woman is shown with two heads looking in different directions, which intimates mental dissolution or a psychic split. The photographic woman appears creepy, perhaps haunted, or paranoid since she is literally looking over her shoulder. This regressive look, however, given the book's topic, may represent the woman's lesbianism, because in the psychological literature of the era, particularly the popular understanding of Freud's work, female homosexuality was considered a kind of arrested development. Moreover, the depiction of the photographic woman contained within the female silhouette could represent the potential lesbian lurking in all women. In this scenario, the silhouetted woman is a 'normal', heterosexual woman heading in the 'right', *straight*forward direction. She is depicted as a shadow because in mid-century America that is all women were expected to be, and so the photographic woman is the colourful, desiring woman trapped inside the ideal. This sense of repression is furthered by the placement of the cover copy to the left of the silhouetted woman's highly emphasised throat, where it acknowledges what she cannot say: 'Their dark and/troubled loves could/flourish only in secret.'

The Fawcett cover of *Journey to a Woman* also suggests a concern with the prevalence of lesbianism, and like the cover of *Women in the Shadows*, it depicts a partially obscured and apparently psychically split woman. The background is a blurry fog of smoke, which could represent the cultural confusion over lesbian sexuality, especially as it relates to this novel, which depicts a married mother abandoning her children and divorcing her all-American husband to find her long-lost lesbian love. This narrative undermines the widely held belief that lesbians just need to find the right man. The fog may represent the confusion lesbians were purported to suffer from, their misunderstanding of their life's role and purpose. The smoke may also signal that smouldering passion which threatens to consume her and her family, tying the cover back into the general theme of danger which unifies all the Fawcett jackets. Indeed, the woman appears aware of the threat of her desire, for she is naked and clutching herself in a protective pose, her eyes alarmed. This cover brings together all the themes of the original covers for it validates the fear surrounding lesbianism by inferring that lesbianism is indeed a real and present peril. It may happen even in the most unsuspected of places, in women who appear thoroughly, safely ensconced in heteropatriarchy and their traditional roles as wives and mothers. Yet the depiction remains ambiguous as well, the cultural confusion persists, for the woman appears both vulnerable and threatening. Mid-century America simply could not make up its mind as to whether lesbianism was a titillating and relatively harmless deviation or a serious risk to the social structure.

ReCovering Lesbianism

Most lesbian pulp fiction died out when the sexual revolution occurred and pictorial forms of pornography became more available, undercutting the market for sexploitation novels, but Bannon's books were cherished, collected and shared by countless lesbians until two decades later, in 1983, when Naiad Press reprinted them. Naiad Press was founded by Barbara Grier and her partner Donna McBride in 1973, and it quickly became the leading publisher of lesbian literature. Grier had previously worked on the Daughters of Bilitis's (DOB) lesbian periodical, *The Ladder*. The DOB was a homophile organisation that had always had a conservative, assimilationist ideology under the leadership of its original founders, Phyllis Lyon and Del Martin, until Grier and others brought to it a more lesbian feminist agenda. Grier became editor of *The Ladder* in 1968 and eventually she was part of a coup which usurped the subscription list from the DOB and revamped the magazine to focus on women's issues and not solely lesbian issues. Grier's lesbian feminist background informs Naiad Press; from the very beginning, it was created to be a press with an activist agenda, and not merely a commercial endeavour. Naiad Press republished Bannon's series as part of its mission to recover lost female, particularly lesbian, artists. The back covers of these editions demonstrate this aim, for they reveal a new stress on the author and her words. Each text in the series has a direct quotation from that novel as its back cover and there is a small photograph of the author, all part of the publisher's objective to make the author's work and lesbianism more visible and honoured. Given this lesbian feminist political background, one would assume that in Naiad's editions lesbianism would move out of the shadows and into the sunlight, that it would no longer be associated with danger, and yet the Naiad covers retain, to a certain degree, these conventional associations, because they preserve the shadows iconography, and centre on a feminist ambivalence toward the risky relationship between sex and power.

All of the covers of Naiad's editions of Bannon's five-book series depict blue female silhouettes on a white background, thus maintaining the lesbian pulp association between lesbianism and shadows. According to *The Penguin Dictionary of Symbols*, shadows are 'the very image of fleeting, unreal and mutable things' (Chevalier and Gheerbrant 1996, 868), which may explain the association, since lesbianism was popularly believed to be merely a phase or a pale imitation of heterosexuality. In general, shadows may connote danger and mystery, but the use of silhouettes, in particular, on these covers, obscures the individuality of the women depicted, allowing for greater reader identification. This invitation to identification is important in a lesbian feminist reprint, for lesbians have a long history of cultural invisibility and have hungrily sought a reflection of themselves in literature. Naiad Press was always envisioned as a press created by and for lesbians. Its focus was fundamentally about lesbian identification, about reclaiming and celebrating lesbian identity. The use of silhouettes also suggests that lesbianism may be a universal phenomenon, since it erases all features that might identify a time or place. Affirming the historical and global presence of lesbians would also be in accordance with lesbian feminist objectives.

The association between lesbianism and danger remains, however, for the cover art betrays a feminist ambivalence towards the kinds of non-egalitarian relationships depicted in Bannon's series. Bannon was writing in the pre-Stonewall and pre-Women's Liberation era, and her stories reflect the Greenwich Village working-class bar scene. Butch-femme relationships are central to the series, a type of relationship that was misunderstood and denounced by mainstream society, homophile associations like the DOB and later by the second-wave feminist movement. Politicised lesbians during the 1970s and 1980s often adopted an androgynous aesthetic and argued that those lesbians who chose a butch-femme aesthetic were engaged in a form of oppressive heterosexual imitation that was contrary to lesbian feminism. Writing before the second wave of feminism, Bannon does not advocate this position, but she does not shy away from showing both the pleasure and the pain of such role-playing either. The Naiad covers reveal a similar love-hate relationship with it. The cover for the first novel in the series, *Odd Girl Out*, depicts an egalitarian relationship, while the covers for the ensuing books in the series present increasing levels of hierarchy and role-playing.

The Naiad cover of *Odd Girl Out* presents the silhouette of two women kissing (Figure 11.1). They are centred on the cover and shown in profile. Their pose suggests an egalitarian relationship, for they face each other directly and echo each other's position. They both have long hair, which further suggests that they are not engaged in the kinds of clear-cut butch/femme role-playing so pervasive in Bannon's texts. This depiction is rather modest with its censoring blue curve along the bottom, which obscures the lovers from below the belt. The rounded back of the woman on the right further distances this depiction from previous depictions of lesbianism on pulp covers, for she is not posing in the typical arched back fashion popular in heterosexual male pornography. This pose and representation are meant to appear more realistic, since this time the books were aimed at lesbian readers, rather than straight men. Nevertheless, while it portrays an embrace between women, which is always provocative, I find that the distance and empty white space in this depiction create an overly clinical and cold impression when compared to the covers that follow it.

The Naiad covers for the next three novels in Bannon's series display increasing levels of power play in the relationships, and, I would argue, an increasing level of discomfort with this imbalance. The next book in the series, *I am a Woman*, depicts two women's heads and necks in profile as they kiss, but this time the kiss is not direct.

Figure 11.1 The Naiad edition of *Odd Girl Out*

While the women on the left approaches her lover in a straightforward fashion, the woman on the right's face is angled up. This cover thus begins to introduce hierarchy as the woman on the left takes up more space on the cover and the woman on the right avoids a direct advance. This cover's effect is more powerful and intimate, which is an achievement given that the pose allows for a reading in which there may be an asymmetrical attraction. While *Odd Girl Out*'s cover depicts a moment of reciprocal pleasure, *I am a Woman*'s cover focuses more on one woman giving and one woman receiving.

The Naiad cover of *Women in the Shadows* continues to showcase increasingly hierarchical relationships. Once again, there are two women kissing in profile, and once again, the woman on the left, her hair wild and unruly, is taking up more cover space and initiating a direct kiss, while the woman on the right is slightly angled. Once again the angled position of the woman on the right is ambiguous. Is she pulling back, and if so, why? Is the woman on the left 'too much'? Too aggressive? The silhouettes permit such a reading even as they permit a more romantic reading. This cover asks the question second-wave feminists struggled with in regards to lesbian relationships, particularly of the sort Bannon describes: why would two

Figure 11.2 The Naiad edition of *Journey to a Woman*

women who are, or should be, equals treat each other in any other fashion? Are power differentials in a sexual relationship dangerous? Is danger itself sexy?

The cover for *Journey to a Woman* also asks these questions and provides ambivalent answers (Figure 11.2). It, more than any of the Naiad covers, examines an obviously butch-femme relationship. An uneasiness with this type of relationship is suggested by their positioning with each other and on the page itself. The femme is shorter and her head is tilted so far back to kiss the other woman that it is practically horizontal. Her position is anything but comfortable and this insinuates a power imbalance between the two women. This cover implies the lesbian feminist belief that butch-femme relationships perpetuate oppressive patriarchal power dynamics, that the butch is sexist and male-identified, while the femme suffers from an unliberated, false consciousness that keeps her enslaved in conventional, feminine roles. The two women's relationship is further intimated as unbalanced by their placement on the cover. The two women are not centred on the cover even though it leaves a strange, sizeable patch of empty white space to the left of the femme's body. Therefore, while the Naiad covers are affirming lesbianism, they contain a wariness about the potentially unequal power dynamics in lesbian, particularly butch-femme, relationships.

The cover of *Beebo Brinker* is distinct from all the others in several ways (Figure 11.3). While the previous covers all infer a preference for egalitarian sexual correspondence,

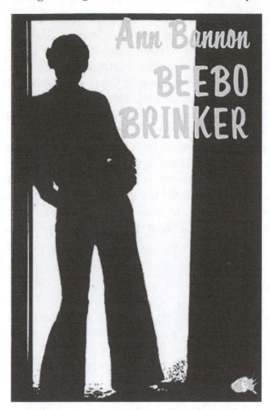

Figure 11.3 The Naiad edition of *Beebo Brinker*

this cover displays the appeal of sexual difference and authority. This is the only one in this series to portray a lone woman on the cover. Her pose is so clearly that of a butch lesbian that there is no need to depict her with another woman in an embrace as all the other covers do. There is not even any indication in the title itself as to the topic of the novel or the sexuality of the woman shown, because it is so unmistakably queer. This is also the first full-length depiction and the first illustration to suggest a time and space, for the woman is shown wearing bell-bottom trousers and leaning in a doorway. The choice to present her in contemporary clothing, rather than apparel accurate to the time period in which the novel is set, reinforces that the butch lesbian continues to be something to be contended with. The woman's positioning in a doorway symbolises her liminality as a person who straddles the gender binary. It also reinforces the need to contend with her, for in the cover's imagined world, if you wanted to enter or leave, you would have to encounter her, to ask her to move or brush past her. She takes up space. She stands casually, but firmly, and demands attention. Moreover, she is the first woman to be shown facing the reader head on. She is not the passive object of the gaze. Surprisingly, this depiction of a strong, butch lesbian has little of the ambivalence of previous illustrations. She is powerful but non-threatening, as her pose implies strength in reserve.

Feminism, as a struggle to redistribute and/or transform power in social relations, is understandably uncertain how to approach women who claim power, particularly when it looks so much like the power of the men most feminists identify as the enemy. The woman on the cover of Naiad's edition of *Beebo Brinker* is, I would argue, the epitome of what many, if not most, lesbians find sexy, precisely because it is different, courageous and requires strength to pull off in a hostile world. There is a reason why the series has retrospectively been dubbed 'The Beebo Brinker Chronicles' despite the fact that it is the femme, Laura Landon, who appears in each novel (and Bannon's only other book, *The Marriage* as well). That reason is the incredible subcultural status butch lesbians currently enjoy and the provocative response they have always drawn, either intensely positive or negative, within and outside of lesbian subculture. These portrayals suggest that the butch alone may exude a kind of power that is alluring, but in context with her partner, in the middle novels, it becomes apparent that for her to be more powerful, someone has to be weaker. Consequently, the feminist press Naiad's covers all struggle in a typically ambivalent second-wave fashion with how power may be sexy but risky and politically suspect.

Covering Lesbianism

Between 2001 and 2003, Cleis Press reprinted Ann Bannon's series with new introductions by Bannon. Cleis Press is a predominantly queer press. Its website states that, 'Cleis Press publishes provocative, intelligent books in the areas of sexuality, gay and lesbian studies, erotica, fiction, gender studies, and human rights' (Cleis Press 2005). A linked interview with the founders states:

> Cleis Press, the largest independent queer publishing company in the United States, celebrates its 25th anniversary this year. Among many lesbian, feminist, and gay presses that emerged in the 1970s and 1980s, Cleis is the only press that is still run by its founders (Marler, 2005).

In the interview, when asked if they are a feminist press, Felice Newman answers affirmatively, but briefly and with qualification, saying only: 'As long as the definition of feminism keeps changing to include us, then I'm very happy to call myself a feminist.' When asked if they are a lesbian press, in contrast, both founders answer at length, beginning with Frederique Delacoste, who responds, 'We are a queer press, and I enjoy that point of view—living/thinking outside of the box. Our core audience was and possibly still is lesbians, but we have a large gay audience and a lot of queer or straight people read us and feel reflected in the work we do.' Newman is more comfortable with the label lesbian, but with a more modern, broadened definition which acknowledges 'that lesbians may have sex with men, they may be quite transgressive and fluid in their sexuality and gender'. I draw out this distinction to differentiate the queer focus of Cleis Press from Naiad Press's more lesbian feminist slant because their differing ideological backgrounds help to explain the sorts of covers they produced for Bannon's series.

The Cleis covers for Bannon's 'Beebo Brinker Chronicles' recycle the original mid-century covers for lesbian pulp fiction (though never Bannon's original covers), and thus return to an emphasis on the pulps' representation of forbidden desire.

Cleis is committed to publishing 'the most ground breaking sex guides' (Marler 2005) and is largely understood to be 'a press that supports itself financially with the sex books, but that also publishes "serious" books' (Marler 2005). Cleis promotes the books on the back covers with favourable reviews from sex-radical sources such as *On Our Backs* and the erotica writer Dorothy Allison. The front covers, like the originals, sell sex very blatantly. The women on the covers are either in various states of undress, or their lusty gazes reveal that they are fantasising about being in such states. While lesbian feminism may be ambivalent towards sexuality in general, and the relationship between power and sexuality in particular, queer theory celebrates transgressive desire. The sensational iconography of mid-century pulp covers is reproduced here for the pleasure of a hip, postmodern audience. They function like self-conscious, playful cover tunes of the originals and thus constitute a classic example of camp sensibility.

In her analysis of lesbian pulp covers, 'Forbidden Love: Pulp as Lesbian History', Amy Villarejo argues that lesbian pulps are not camp: 'Aligned with but not equivalent to camp and kitsch, pulp seems to secure at minimum some mode of circulating and transforming abjection, bad taste, outrageousness, criminality, and despair, but it does so, historically at least, at the level of the cover' (1999, 320). A careful comparison to Susan Sontag's groundbreaking analysis, *Notes On Camp*, however, reveals how lesbian pulp covers do indeed display a camp sensibility. First of all, the Cleis covers reproduce the conventional, highly stylised iconography of the original covers of lesbian pulp. What appears on the cover of any given text in Bannon's series has no specific relationship to that text, only to the genre itself. The Cleis edition of *Beebo Brinker*, for example, has no butch depicted on the cover, despite the fact that the protagonist and namesake of the novel is a butch lesbian. The original covers that Cleis reuses within their covers have no relation whatsoever to the Bannon texts they are used for. The original cover art that appears on the Cleis edition of *Women in the Shadows*, for example, is from two different mid-century pulps. The butch woman smoking a cigarette while eyeing an undressing femme is formerly from Kay Addams's 1960 novel *Warped Desire*, a book whose copy promises that the novel 'boldly probes the problem of the frigid woman, forced by her own desperation into unnatural paths!' This illustration also appears two years later, in 1962, on the cover of Richard Villanova's *Her Woman*, whose copy describes how its lesbian protagonist 'began the search for a man, any man, who could satisfy ... and SAVE HER!' Neither frigidity nor heterosexual conversion feature in *Women in the Shadows*. Clearly, the Cleis reprints emphasise the genre of lesbian pulp fiction over the content of Bannon's specific novels. Where changes occur to the original art, they are generic reinforcements, not references to individual storylines. Other than changes to the backgrounds, sizing and flipping the side of the page on which a given female appears, all the changes to the originals involve adding shadows or smoke. The cover for *Women in the Shadows*, for instance, creates a cloud of smoke wafting from the butch's cigarette and adds a shadow to the left of the femme. These changes are not necessarily allusions to the title, however, since the cover for *Beebo Brinker* casts a shadow over the face of femme as well. These changes reflect the lesbian pulp association between lesbianism and shadows, not anything in Bannon's novels in and of themselves. This emphasis on style over content is a camp quality. As Sontag describes it, 'to emphasize style is to slight content, or to introduce an attitude which is neutral with respect to content' (1966, 279) and camp 'incarnates a victory of 'style' over 'content' (1966, 289). This emphasis on style over content is reinforced on the back covers of the Cleis editions as well in that the first and largest quotation on the back covers of three of the five texts is one from the Chicago Free Press, which comments on the texts' genre, rather than the texts themselves: 'Sex. Sleaze. Depravity. Oh, the twisted passions of the twilight world of lesbian pulp fiction.'

The heavy stylisation present on the original and the Cleis covers is campy because it functions as a kind of 'badge of identity' (Sontag 1966, 277). The representations on the covers foster a community of those in the know (then and now). Sontag claims that, 'to camp is a mode of seduction – one which employs flamboyant mannerisms susceptible of a double interpretation; gestures full of duplicity, with a witty meaning for cognoscenti and another, more impersonal, for outsiders' (283). These covers do nothing if not seduce through ostentatious displays, but they do remain strangely ambiguous at the same time. A quick, superficial glance at the covers of the Cleis editions of *Beebo Brinker* or *Journey to a Woman*, for example, would only reveal one woman looking at another woman. You must know how to recognise that telling depiction of the look to identify the genre. Zimet, in her work on lesbian pulp covers, comments on the significance of this gaze: 'Is she or isn't she? Just follow her gaze' (103). Thus, while the lesbian pulps were mass produced and highly formulaic in their visual and written representations, they nevertheless remain sufficiently cryptic to qualify as part of Sontag's definition of camp as 'esoteric – something of a private code' (277). This private code was one lesbians learned to read early on as discussed in the 'DisCovering Lesbianism' section. Indeed camp has a special relationship to homosexuals. Sontag explains that, 'while it's not true that Camp taste *is* homosexual taste, there is no doubt a peculiar affinity and overlap', for 'homosexuals, by and large, constitute the vanguard – and the most articulate audience – of Camp' (291). From the 1950s to today, the iconography of lesbian pulp fiction has functioned as a kind of fun house mirror in which queer women have found an often ludicrously distorted reflection of themselves.

The distortions in the image of lesbianism present in lesbian pulp iconography are part of its campy, postmodern appeal, for 'the essence of Camp is its love of the unnatural: of artifice and exaggeration' (Sontag 1966, 277). Pulp fiction has become popular with readers today for a variety of reasons. Villarejo conjectures that because it is 'easily commodified … pulp has entered the mainstream at alarming speed as the new postmodern buzzword' (320). Postmodern taste, like camp taste, privileges the marginal, the outrageous; they both suspend traditional aesthetic judgements. Sontag writes of camp, 'Camp taste turns its back on the good-bad axis of ordinary aesthetic judgment. Camp doesn't reverse things. It doesn't argue that the good is bad, or the bad is good. What it does is to offer for art (and life) a different – a supplementary – set of standards' (1966, 288). The Cleis editions contain seemingly contradictory representations of the worth of Bannon's novels. On the back covers, they are described by the Chicago Free Press as 'sleaze' and author Joan Nestle admits they were 'called trash by the literary world and pornography by the commercial world'. Alongside admissions of their trashy status, however, are claims that they are significant, even canonical. A review from the *San Francisco Bay Guardian* calls them 'legends' and on each back cover Cleis promotes the series as 'the classic 1950s love stories from the Queen of Lesbian Pulp Fiction'. French feminist Hélène Cixous contributes most to their prestige in her powerful recommendation of *Women in the Shadows*, going so far as to assert that, 'in its proper historical context, WOMEN IN THE SHADOWS is a masterpiece'. The back covers demonstrate that Cleis is simultaneously invested in the series as trash and canonical material. This is a campy aesthetic evaluation since, as Sontag argues, 'there exists, indeed, a good taste of bad taste' (1996, 292), and this is precisely how Cleis promotes the series. Cleis markets Bannon's texts as an amusing form of literary slumming, even as they simultaneously proclaim the series' literary and historical importance.

The fact that Cleis sells Bannon's novels with these kitschy, retro covers reveals that they believe our contemporary queer community is ready to appreciate and enjoy their camp qualities. Lesbian pulp fiction came to exist during a particularly grim period in American gay history, so to reproduce some of its most extreme elements risks invoking trauma as much as pleasure, but Cleis rightly recognised that the contemporary queer American culture is distanced enough from that past to laugh at it. This distance is critical to camp sensibility, for as Sontag explains, 'The relation between boredom and Camp taste cannot be overestimated. Camp taste is by its nature possible only in affluent societies, in societies or circles capable of experiencing the psychopathology of affluence' (1996, 291). For all their continuing oppression, American homosexuals today are among the most privileged in world history. The Cleis covers of Bannon's novels replicate the conventional aesthetic style of the original, mid-century lesbian pulp covers, but do so in an ironic fashion that speaks to the progress the struggle for gay rights has made.

Lesbian pulp fiction was originally produced as a throwaway commodity that sold deviant sexuality to heterosexual men, but it was seized upon and treasured as a form of survival literature by lesbians. Ann Bannon's five-book 'Beebo Brinker Chronicles', in particular, has been kept in print by gay publishers ever since its original publication by Fawcett in the 1950s and early 1960s. The front covers of all three of the major editions have profoundly reflected their historical and publishing context. The Fawcett editions reveal mainstream confusion and fear regarding lesbianism and its threat to heteropatriarchy. The Naiad editions reveal a lesbian feminist ambivalence to non-egalitarian or butch-femme relationships and the Cleis editions function as a form of sexy, queer camp. It is rather remarkable that texts which were originally published as mere sleaze became international bestsellers, hot collectors' items and classics of the lesbian canon. Their evolving cover art has illustrated the shifting landscape of fear and desire the lesbian evokes in depictions of her that are almost unrecognisable from one representation to the next, making the covers themselves 'strange sisters' indeed.

Chapter 12

Addressing 'Young Adults'?
The Case of Francesca Lia Block

Chris Richards
London Metropolitan University

Addressing 'Young Adults'?

Looking at, handling and reading the early 1990s paperback editions of Francesca Lia Block's Weetzie Bat novels is suggestive of the 'young adult' publishing strategy of that period. They are insubstantial and lightweight.[1] Of course, I'm describing physical characteristics but these are commonly elided with 'accessibility'. This is 'easy reading' for young people seen as unlikely to pick up and stay with 'thicker' books. Amidst the proliferation of both older visual and new media, reading is often seen as embattled. A consequent decline in habits of attention, concentration, reflection, thought and imagination are together taken to constitute a kind of cognitive erosion. Though such anxieties about declining print literacy are usually invoked in relation to boys, these titles – *Weetzie Bat*, *Witch Baby*, *Cherokee Bat and the Goat Guys*, *Missing Angel Juan* and *Baby Bebop* – seemingly address young teenage girls. These are not 'tough' books explicitly challenging readers to prove they can take 'it' – realism, violence, death, conflict (though these figure in all of them). To the contrary, they are 'fantasy', and with their highly stylised cover art, are thus implicitly 'girly' books.

In 1998, HarperCollins repositioned Francesca Lia Block's Weetzie Bat novels as no longer for 'Reluctant Young Adult Readers', but as tales of youthful 'hip' life equally of interest to adult readers.[2] Collecting the five novels together as *Dangerous Angels* (1998) was, at that time, represented as 'an unusual move in children's

---

1   The mid-1990s paperbacks (Harper Trophy) are seven inches (17.8 cm) high, four and a quarter inches (10.8 cm) wide, with spines no more than one-quarter of an inch (0.7 cm) thick. Each volume has fewer than 140 pages.

2   Francesca Lia Block's writing appeared first as fiction marketed for a readership defined variously as 'Junior', 'Juvenile' and as 'Young Adult'. From 1989 to 1997, her books are clearly located in the Junior/Young Adult market with a majority of the paperback editions – and some hardbacks – carrying the full record of her American Library Association Awards in the categories of 'Books for Young Adults' and 'Books for Reluctant Young Adult Readers'. From 1998 to the present, her books no longer carry references to American Library Association Awards and are not published in imprints explicitly associated with the 'Junior' or 'Young Adult' market. Six short novels from the first publishing phase have been reissued in the second – five of them in the collection *Dangerous Angels* (1998) and *The Hanged Man* in 1999 (first published 1994).

publishing' (di Marzo 1998). Cindi di Marzo's report, in *Publishers Weekly*, traces the 'crossover' strategy:

> The ultimate aim of this repackaging effort is to achieve the kind of crossover to adult readers that [Block's editor] initially hoped for ... The collection is being released in paperback only, and Harper hopes that the large trim size, provocative cover art and increased page count will make it stand out on shelves, both adult and YA (di Marzo 1998).[3]

Sales of Block's novels, which prior to 1998 carry their American Library Association (ALA) endorsements, are largely attributed to 'schools, libraries and children's bookstores'. But a 'readership' of a different kind is addressed by the new collected edition. Reporting comments made by Block's current editor, Joanna Cotler, di Marzo sketches the intended audience as composed both of '20-somethings' and 'Gen Xers' [born 1966–79]. These loose generational categories blur into each other but the implication is clearly that interest in Block's writing can be elicited from those well beyond their 'teens' and even into their thirties.

The 'repackaging' strategy included both entirely new cover art and a repositioning of both the novels and their author – as an emergent 'celebrity' – in contexts likely to draw a younger adult, rather than 'young adult', audience:

> To achieve a cover image that would appeal to adult readers and give a sense of Weetzie's realm, Cotler worked closely with Block. The paperback editions had been reissued once before, in single volumes with bold, earthy artwork by Caldecott Medalist David Diaz [the mid-1990s Harper Trophy editions referred to above] that seems the antithesis of New York-based fashion photographer Suza Scalora's image of a delicate, otherworldly being with white-blond hair, body hugging strapless dress and pale purple wings (di Marzo 1998).

Harper's plans to focus attention on Block and her books include readers' group guides for adults, speaking engagements at colleges, Internet promotions and a party in Los Angeles to coincide with publication of the autumn book [*I was a Teenage Fairy*] (di Marzo 1998).

This strategy needs to be understood in the context of wider patterns in marketing. Obviously it is profitable to sell to a broadly defined audience but here it is the particular currency of 'youth' – and how 'youth' is constructed – that is of particular interest. Jonathan Reynolds (of the Oxford Institute of Retail Management at Templeton College), rehearsing current marketing discourse (on BBC Radio 4, *You and Yours*, 31 March 2004), remarked of IKEA that it is aimed at 'young people of all ages'. Clearly that formulation has wider currency. Block, like IKEA, but with considerably more circumscribed success, has been 'revamped' for a similarly fluid audience.

Indeed, pursuing a related argument, David Buckingham has suggested that:

> ✳ 'Youth' has become an extremely elastic category, that seems to extend ever further upwards. In their shared enthusiasm for Britpop, Nike sportswear, Nintendo or *South Park*, for example, ten-year-olds and forty-year-olds can be seen as members of a 'youth' market that is quite self-consciously distinct from a 'family' market. In this environment, 'youth'

---

3   *Dangerous Angels* is 478 pages long, eight inches high (20.2 cm), five and a quarter inches wide (13.4 cm) and has a spine one and a quarter inches thick (3 cm).

has come to be perceived as a kind of lifestyle choice, defined by its relationship to specific brands and commodities, and also available to those who fall well outside its biological limits (which are fluid in any case). In 'youth television' and now in the marketing of popular music, 'youth' possesses a symbolic significance that can refer to fantasy identities as much as to material possibilities – a phenomenon which itself can only help to widen the audience, and hence to enhance its market value (Buckingham 2000, 99).

The emphasis on fantasy identities here suggests that 'youth' is claimed as a feature of lifestyle almost in active denial of circumscribed age phases. In this sense, 'youth' can be bought – or at least the feeling of continuing participation in youth is made available through consumption of appropriately inscribed commodities. I want to develop the argument that youth is now more a lifestyle than an age phase somewhat further.

But another kind of shift also needs to be noted here. Even as an age phase 'youth' is not so clearly delimited as it once was (Griffin 2001). It can be argued that a young adult lifestyle is, in addition to its construction through consumption, grounded in the extension of 'adolescence' or 'youth' – as lived – beyond 18 into people's twenties. The relative weakening of boundary-marking events (such as marriage, permanent relocation outside parental homes and entry into full employment) allows 'youth' to persist (on 'post-adolescence', see Ball, Maguire and Macrae 2000). In this respect, it could be argued that the *Weetzie Bat* books' 'second-wave' marketing also addresses a newly constituted audience of readers living their 'youth' well into adulthood and, further, contributes at the level of commodity packaging to the apparent lack of any clearly defined upper boundary to 'adolescence'.

But to what kind of youthful lifestyle are readers invited by Block's repackaged novels? There are three issues to consider here: gender, place and music. In Buckingham's comments the version of 'youth' in which 10- to 40-year-olds might locate themselves seems distinctively male. The differentiation from the 'family' market to which he draws attention is implicitly also a gendered differentiation. Britpop, Nike, Nintendo and *South Park*, though by no means exclusively male, do together evoke a masculine identification. Other, more markedly female markets, equally distinct from the family market, could be suggested – perhaps chick-lit, the White Stripes, Sleater-Kinney, *Friends*, *The O.C.*, *Glamour* (and so on) might compose the resources for one such alternative. The cover of *Dangerous Angels*, with its image of 'a delicate, otherworldly being with white-blond hair, body hugging strapless dress and pale purple wings', places the collection, if imprecisely, alongside genres understood to address female readers – fantasy, fairy stories, romance. Implicitly, the readers the repackaged edition seeks to draw in are women.

Though 'lifestyles' might be understood as only loosely anchored in terms of age, it is more difficult to detach them from ways of living already differentiated by gender and class or ethnicity. Giddens (1991), who has played a significant part in extending the concept of lifestyles, nevertheless stresses that they are constituted through *constrained* choices. Thus though he emphasises that a lifestyle gives 'material form to a particular narrative of self-identity', the construction of particular lifestyles also depends upon the characteristics of specific settings. Indeed, his concern is specifically with the sense of options in *non-traditional* cultures:

> Lifestyle is not a term which has much applicability to traditional cultures, because it implies choice within a plurality of possible options, and is 'adopted' rather than 'handed down'. Lifestyles are routinised practices, the routines incorporated into habits of dress, eating, modes of acting and favoured milieux for encountering others; but the routines followed are reflexively open to change in the light of the mobile nature of self-identity ... choices ... are decisions not only about how to act but who to be ... the more post-traditional the settings in which an individual moves, the more lifestyle concerns the very core of self-identity, its making and remaking (Giddens 1991: 81).

It is only in a particular kind of milieu, in other words, that 'lifestyle' has the attributes Giddens suggests.[4] Throughout Block's publishing history, but especially since 1998, her residence in, and identification with, Los Angeles has been reiterated on the covers of all her books. This is crucial. Place is central to the lifestyle evoked in *Dangerous Angels*. Los Angeles is widely represented as a global or 'postmodern' city (see Harvey 1989, 299–300; Susina 2002). California, but especially Los Angeles, has long had a currency in popular discourse as the antithesis of tradition, a place where the future happens first. Mike Davis, in *City of Quartz*, refers to 'Southern California's unsure boundary between reality and science fiction' (Davis 1990, 41). The reiteration of Block's place of residence, however understated, implies an equation between her writing and the city itself: shifting between reality and fantasy, between the present and the future, and in an indeterminate space between genres.

However, if Block's writing was offered as representing Los Angeles and thus subject to realist expectations, it must be judged as extremely circumscribed – with a predominantly white ensemble of characters living without the need to work in any routine way – though Weetzie initially works as a waitress. Susina, in 'The Rebirth of the Postmodern Flaneur: Notes on the Postmodern Landscape of Francesca Lia Block's Weetzie Bat' (2002), refers to the criticism that Block's characters live in 'a consumeristic paradise ... [and] rarely look beyond the confines of their own richly-appointed magic kingdom of wealthy white upper-class privilege' (Susina 2002, 198). Indeed, in terms of social range, the novels give much less than either, for example, Raymond Chandler or *Angel*, the dystopian Buffy spin-off where elite lawyers and 'brothers' from the hood mingle with the more usual vampires and demons.

But the identification with Los Angeles achieves something other than representational authenticity. The kind of non-traditional lifestyle, sketched by Giddens, is explored in a genre that is neither realism nor science fiction. Across the five novels the layered accumulation of crises and (partial) reconciliations produces a 'family' lifestyle in implicit defiance of new right politics and Christian fundamentalism.[5] 'Family values' here do not privilege biological paternity, heterosexuality or monoculturalism. Consistent with its repeated allusions to

---

4   This emphasis on the particularity of the milieu in which such a lifestyle might thrive is taken considerably further in a powerful critique of Giddens – see Skeggs 2004.

5   There are numerous challenges to Block's novels particularly from organisations seeking to challenge their availability in schools. See, for example missionamerica.com and PABBIS (Parents Against Bad Books in Schools), <http://www.pabbis.com/>. By contrast her work is enthusiastically endorsed by, for example, Gay and Lesbian Educators of British Columbia – <http://www.galebc.org>.

Lost Horizon, 'Los Angeles' (or 'Shangri-L.A.') is where such a way of living can be sustained against tradition; but where tradition has no place there is, necessarily, instability. This is not an indulgent fantasy or a simple celebration. Block's narratives repeatedly suggest uncertain, precarious, outcomes. In this respect, her writing does hint at the more sombre themes explored in, for example, *Mulholland Drive* (David Lynch, 2001). As Jack Zipes suggests:

> Hollywood as a symbol is a utopian fairy-tale destination, a place where the good-fairy as destiny waits to transform unknown talents into stars, where fortunes are made, where, like the enchanted forest, something special happens that brings genuine happiness to the true in heart. But Hollywood … is also a hard and cruel place. The people who first built up Hollywood always knew it, and everyone who works in entertainment in Hollywood today knows it too (Zipes 1997, 2).

The third aspect of the *Dangerous Angels* lifestyle I want to emphasise here foregrounds music. Simon Frith has argued that 'youth' is almost constituted in music:

> It is a sociological truism that people's heaviest personal investment in popular music is when they are teenagers and young adults – music then ties into a particular kind of emotional turbulence, when issues of individual identity and social place, the control of public and private feelings, are at a premium. People do use music less, and less intently, as they grow up; the most significant pop songs for all generations (not just for rock generations) are those they heard as adolescents. What this suggests, though, is not just that young people need music, but that 'youth' itself is defined by music … youth music is socially important not because it reflects youth experience (authentically or not), but because it defines for us what 'youthfulness' is. I remember concluding, in my original sociological research in the early 1970s, that those young people who, for whatever reasons, took no interest in pop music were not really 'young' (Frith 1987, 142–3).

There are numerous references within Block's novels to music. But what I want to examine here is how 'music' enters into the marketing of *Dangerous Angels*. Consistent with Frith, music appears to function here to further attract a wider audience wishing to identify with a youthful lifestyle. For though adults have been almost defined by their exclusion from and often intolerance of young people's music, music as the locus of 'youth' also has a continuing and contradictory resonance. As Christine Griffin observes, in *Representations of Youth*:

> Youth/adolescence remains a powerful cultural and ideological category through which adult society constructs a specific age stage as simultaneously strange and familiar. Youth/adolescence remains the focus of adult fears and pity, of voyeurism and longing (Griffin 1993, 23).

In an article in *Publishers Weekly* (October 1999) Shannon Maughan comments:

> More than ever before, teens are the target audience for retailers, clothing companies and myriad television shows, films, pop music acts and magazines. Where do books fit into the picture? Children's book publishers have long been aware of the needs of teen readers, and created the young adult genre of literature for them more than 20 years ago … As 2000 approaches, and adolescents face not only more demands on their time but more

entertainment choices than ever, getting word to them about books has never been more important. Happily the current willingness of the culture at large to embrace all things teen is providing a variety of new opportunities for publishers to promote their titles.

This suggests, again, that the 'crossover' strategy involves repositioning books as commodities equal to those generated by other media and as flexible in their modes of address. *Dangerous Angels*, on the front cover, carries one word of endorsement from the *New York Times Book Review*: 'Transcendent'. The back cover situates the text:

> Love is a dangerous angel … Francesca Lia Block's luminous saga of interwoven lives will send the senses into wild overdrive. These post-modern fairy tales chronicle the thin line between fear and desire, pain and pleasure, cutting loose and holding on in a world where everyone is vulnerable to the most beautiful and dangerous angel of all: love.

Further critical endorsement is cited from the US music magazine *Spin*: 'A sensualist's paradise …'. And the biographical note follows this through by further locating her not as a writer for children and young people but as a 'cool' figure:

> In addition to *The Weetzie Bat* Books, Francesca Lia Block is the acclaimed author of *Girl Goddess #9* and *The Hanged Man* as well as the fantasy novels *Ecstasia* and *Primavera*. She has written features for *Spin* magazine and was named one of *Buzz* magazine's 'Coolest People in L.A.' where she currently resides.

The repositioning of these five novels is furthered by the review sources immediately inside the front cover: *The Village Voice*, *Spin*, *The New York Times Book Review* and *Publishers Weekly*. *The Village Voice* is cited thus:

> Magic is everywhere in Block's lyrical and resonant fables, which always point back to the primacy of family, friends, love, location, food, and music. At once modern and mythic, her series deserves as much space as it can command of daydream nation's shrinking bookshelves.

The selection of reviewers' comments cues a readership defined more by what it knows of music and music journalism rather than of literary antecedents or parallels for Block's writing.[6] Thus the cultural map invoked in reviews includes Sonic Youth (*Daydream Nation*) and reference to broad, arguably 'non-literary' genres – fairy tale, myth, folklore, fable. There is very little literary reference, either to possible comparisons – perhaps Armistead Maupin's *Tales of the City* (six novels set in San Francisco in much the same period) – or to influences, acknowledged elsewhere, such as Isabel Allende's *The House of the Spirits* or Gabriel Garcia Marquez's *One Hundred Years of Solitude*. Association with named authors is rare; the only such reference serves more to situate her in terms of place: 'Ms Block writes about the real Los Angeles better than anybody since Raymond Chandler' [*The New York Times* cited with reference to *Cherokee Bat and the Goat Guys* in *Dangerous Angels*]. Despite the orthodox 'literary' authority of

---

6   A study of the reception of Block's writing is beyond the scope of this chapter, but it is worth noting that in internet exchanges among contributors to <http://groups.yahoo.com/group/witchbaby> music figures prominently in their self-identifications.

some of these critical sources, the novels are thus placed as addressing an audience not primarily defined as a readership at all. Perhaps, in the case of *The Village Voice*'s reference to 'shrinking bookshelves', there is also a lingering hint of anxiety at an implicit decline in active literacy – with Block thus hailed as, in an ironic echo of the ALA awards in the Reluctant Young Adult Reader category, again able to 'win over' a non-literary audience in whose lifestyle literature has a diminishing presence. But buying and reading *Dangerous Angels*, and having it around is also in its 'repackaging', made acceptable, even desirable, within such a lifestyle.

To conclude this introductory discussion, I want to emphasise that 'young adult' fiction now appears to be split between those novels written for inclusion within the school curriculum, or at least in school libraries, and a wider, more commercially visible market in young adult fiction relatively unconstrained by the regulatory concerns apparent in the educational context (Reid and Hutchinson 1994). In educational discourses, there is an uneasy mix of encouragement *to read* with moral anxiety at *what is being read* – consumed in private, contained, less leaky even than listening to music on a personal stereo.[7] Such discourses, attempting to fix 'young adult' fiction in place, are not entirely absent from the wider book trade but they do appear to be increasingly marginal to other marketing imperatives. 'Young adult' fiction is thus separating into two differently orientated genres, one implicitly sustaining a contract with education and the other hailing 'young people of all ages'.

It is worth recalling Fredric Jameson's discussion of genre here. He argues that genres are 'essentially literary *institutions*, or social contracts between a writer and a specific public, whose function is to specify the proper use of a particular cultural artefact' (Jameson 1981, 106). As I have suggested, 'young adult' fiction appears to be stretched between two versions of the specific public it addresses. It is increasingly destabilised by the consequent tensions between the implicit contracts entered into by authors. In a sense, the repositioning of Block's Weetzie Bat novels suggests an intensified commodification, propelling her work beyond the more 'protected' domain of writing 'for schools'. Jameson's essay comments on the emergence of a market in books:

> The generic contract and institution itself ... along with so many other institutions and traditional practices, falls casualty to the gradual penetration of a market system and a money economy. With the elimination of an institutionalized social status for the cultural producer and the opening of the work of art itself to commodification, the older generic specifications are transformed into a brand-name system against which any authentic artistic expression must necessarily struggle (Jameson, 1981: 107).

---

7   Jack Zipes comments, in 1983, 'The major difficulty facing the emancipatory fairy tales ... lies in the system of distribution, circulation, and the use of the tales, and all this is dependent on the educational views of teachers, librarians, parents and those adults who work with children in community centres' ('The Liberating Potential of the Fantastic in Contemporary Fairy Tales for Children', in Zipes 1991, 191). Arguably, market imperatives might now be seen as making more 'unusual, forward-looking, fantastic projections' (Zipes's words) more widely available.

Though Jameson refers here to a much earlier moment in the history of publishing, there is a parallel with the attempt to place Block in the wider fiction market, beyond schools. Block's writing is repositioned *within* the market system, between differently orientated genres. Rather than pursue issues of artistic 'authenticity' here I want to discuss further how her work is reinflected in its address to 'specific publics'.

Weetzie Bat and *Dangerous Angels*

I want to focus now on the characteristics of Block's writing with one particular concern in mind – why were her novels seen as so amenable to the 'repackaging' strategy I have outlined? *Weetzie Bat*, about which I comment in some detail below, introduces Weetzie, just out of high school, and her gay friend Dirk. Together they long for stable relationships and a place to live. Granted their wishes by a genie, they begin to establish a household to which friends, lovers and children are added as the novel progresses. *Witch Baby* focuses on Weetzie's 'adopted' daughter and her confusion about who she is and with whom she belongs. Witch Baby's troublesome behaviour provokes various crises – at least provisionally resolved by open acknowledgement of her origins and by her explicit inclusion in the Weetzie Bat household. *Cherokee Bat and the Goat Guys* traces the emergence of sexual relationships among the children – now teenagers – and their struggles to form a successful rock band. With all of the parental figures absent, Coyote, a Native American friend, is called upon to use magic to help them. Eventually Coyote intervenes to curtail the power each member of the band has taken from various animals. *Missing Angel Juan* is set in New York. Witch Baby goes to find Angel Juan, who has left her. There she meets, and is accompanied by, the ghost of Weetzie's father, Charlie Bat. She also encounters a threatening, uncannily 'white' mannequin known as Cake. *Baby Be-Bop* returns to Dirk's adolescence and to his feelings about being gay. After being beaten up, he encounters the ghosts of his great-grandmother and of his father and has long conversations with them about his family's past.

Weetzie Bat, Block's first novel, is an initially unsettling mix of whimsical word play, improbably named characters (Weetzie Bat herself, My Secret Agent Lover Man, Duck, Dirk ...) and fairy tale elements – three wishes and a genie, witches – with (though not explicit) somewhat regretted one-night stands, gay sex, sex between Weetzie and her two gay friends (and thus indeterminate paternity) and AIDS. The novel evokes a Los Angeles/Hollywood scene, full of references to bars and clubs, to popular music and to film stars from previous generations. As the novel sequence continues Weetzie herself recedes into the background and the four further novels focus much more on the teenage characters, rather than shifting with characters ageing beyond 'youth' into adult life.

The first edition of *Weetzie Bat* was published as a Charlotte Zolotow book (*Witch Baby* and *Cherokee Bat and the Goat Guys* are also identified with Charlotte Zolotow), thus associating it with a long established writer for children, who had also had a lengthy career (born 1915, at Harpers from 1938) as an editor of books for children and young people. On the back cover of *Weetzie Bat* (Harper and Row

Junior Books, 1989) the quotation from the text, inviting the reader in, is seemingly addressed to a very young audience:

> Weetzie and My Secret Agent Lover Man and Dirk and Duck and Cherokee and Witch Baby and Slinkster Dog and Go-Go Girl and the puppies Pee Wee, Wee Wee, Teenie Wee, Tiki Tee, and Tee Pee were driving down Hollywood Boulevard on their way to the Tick Tock Tea Room for Turkey platters.

But the opening chapter of *Weetzie Bat* begins with this:

> The reason Weetzie Bat hated high school was because no one understood. They didn't even realize where they were living. They didn't care that Marilyn's prints were practically in their backyard at Graumann's; that you could buy tomahawks and plastic palm tree wallets at Farmer's Market, and the wildest, cheapest cheese and bean and hot dog and pastrami burritos at Oki Dogs; that the waitresses wore skates at the Jetson-style Tiny Naylor's; that there was a fountain that turned tropical soda-pop colors, and a canyon where Jim Morrison and Houdini used to live, and all-night potato knishes at Canter's, and not too far away was Venice, with columns, and canals, even, like the real Venice but maybe cooler because of the surfers. There was no one who cared. Until Dirk (Block 1989, 3–4).

Dirk, wearing his hair in 'a shoe-polish-black Mohawk' and driving 'a red '55 Pontiac', becomes Weetzie's best friend and the only girl to whom he gives any attention. They go out clubbing together, 'slamming around the pit below the stage', and afterwards 'sweaty and shaky', they eat burritos at 'Oki Dogs' (Block 1989, 5–6).

A further shift, assuming that expectations of heterosexual romance are in play here, occurs when Dirk reveals to Weetzie that he is gay, at the end of this first short chapter. This is not a revelation deferred until late in the narrative. Their subsequent activities involve sexual cruising – or 'Duck Hunting' as it is called in Block's characteristically playful, and sometimes unsettling, rhythmic listing of potential erotic attractions. Thus the second chapter opens:

> There were many kinds of Ducks – Buff Ducks, Skinny Ducks, Surf Ducks, Punk-Rock Ducks, Wild Ducks, Shy Ducks, Fierce Ducks, Cuddly Ducks, Sleek, Chic G.Q. Ducks, Rockabilly Ducks with creepers and ducktails, Rasta Ducks with dreads, Dancing Ducks, and Skate-Date Ducks, Ducks in Duckmobiles racing around the city (Block 1989, 10).

Weetzie and Dirk seek out the 'Ducks' of 'their respective dreams'. Weetzie goes off, drunk, for a one-night stand with the bald, tattooed singer fronting a band and finds herself held down and handcuffed in his basement. Waking the next morning 'wincing, still drunk', she calls Dirk. Comparing their sexual (mis)adventures, over bagels at Canter's, 'a cart of pickles' is 'wheeled by, the green rubbery pickles bobbing', eliciting a regretful exclamation from Dirk: 'Oh, God, that's all I need to see after last night' (Block 1989, 12–13).

Between the extract given prominence on the cover and the passages discussed here, there is a significant disjunction in their modes of address. From the playful rhythms of naming (recalling nursery rhymes) to an ironical sketch of the risks and regrets of casual sex, the age of an 'implied reader' lurches unpredictably between 'child' and 'adult'. The kinds of knowledge readers need to bring to the 'duck-hunting' episode to make sense of its gaps, silences and allusions – obviously specifically to sex – suggest an audience already somewhat familiar, if only through other representations, with the social world delineated here.[8]

Unlike those whose authorial identities are constructed in relation to a specified readership of either 'children' or 'young adults', Block has never explicitly positioned herself as writing for young people and makes no claim either to represent young people's experience or to know 'what they want'. Block's standpoint is autobiographical. Block (born in 1962) grew up in Los Angeles, and was connected to the Hollywood film scene through her father Irving Alexander Block (1910–86), an artist but also scriptwriter on *Forbidden Planet* and responsible for special effects in many other films. She repeatedly emphasises that in her own childhood she was given access to a great array of myth and fairy tale. She wrote *Weetzie Bat* in her twenties, while studying literature at the University of California at Berkeley. It is dedicated to her father. The novel is addressed to young readers in its publication *not in its writing*:

> I've spent a lot of time worrying about my books being in the YA category but I've decided to let someone else take on that cause. I didn't want to lead the way. I never planned to write for this audience and was published this way by chance. I am happy to have found so many wonderful young readers but luckily I have also reached the adults I intended to reach (Maughan 2000).

It may be that the early success of her writing with teenage girls lies precisely in its combination of disparate elements. The effect is to offer a process of learning where readers are offered both an array of familiar references and formulae (three wishes, for example) and incidents and encounters inviting (perhaps) puzzled curiosity. Though elements of children's stories – repetition, listing and word play – are prominent, they often point beyond childhood to more adult referents. As Jack Zipes suggested in a 1983 review of 'counter-cultural' fairy tales, there is a:

> 'Fusion of traditional configurations with contemporary references within settings and plotlines unfamiliar to readers yet designed to arouse their curiosity and interest. Fantastic projections are used here to demonstrate the changeability of contemporary social relations, and the fusion brings together all possible means for illuminating a concrete utopia' (Zipes 1991, 180).

Weetzie wishes for 'a Duck for Dirk, and My Secret Agent Lover Man for me, and a beautiful little house for us to live in happily ever after' and, once the genie has gone, remarks 'What a trip! I'd better call Dirk. I wonder if someone put something in my drink last night' (Block 1989, 24–5). The elements of traditional storytelling for children are thus somewhat parodied, read from within Weetzie's teenage scene as more likely drug induced than magical. But they are not thus dispelled. The authority of the 'omniscient narrator' calls readers to accept that these fantastic

---

8   See Trites (2004) for a reading of this episode as 'sending' a moral message about valid sexual behaviour. This seems to neglect the humour and irony of Block's writing.

or magical events belong to the real world inhabited by these characters – they are not delusional states (cf. Allende, 1985). The wishes, and their fulfilment, become founding moments in the elaboration of the larger narrative of the five novels. The generic characteristics of fairy tales are thus deployed in tension with those of realism. Rather than acquiescing in a notion of progression from fantasy to realism, as if readers 'grow' from one to the other, Block brings them together. The resources accumulated in her own 'literary' childhood are thus engaged in, and significantly strained by, an attempt to explore problems perhaps immediate to her own social world but not necessarily to that of younger teenage girls.

Dirk gets his lover, who turns out to be called Duck. Weetzie gets her man too, who turns out to be called My Secret Agent Lover Man.

> And so Weetzie and My Secret Agent Lover Man and Dirk and Duck and Slinkster Dog and Fifi's canaries lived happily ever after in their silly-sand-topped house in the land of skating hamburgers and flying toupees and Jah-Love blonde Indians (Block 1989, 38).

This fairy-tale ending arrives less than halfway through. Read as a story for children, it is 'too soon', 'in the wrong place'. Three major disruptions follow. First of all, Weetzie wants a child but My Secret Agent Lover Man, pessimistic about the state of the world, is unwilling. Secondly, Weetzie's father Charlie Bat dies on drugs in New York. Thirdly, Duck discovers that a friend is dying of AIDS and, dismayed by the contamination of sexual intimacy with disease and death, leaves Dirk and Hollywood.

Weetzie's determination to have a child is supported by her gay friends Dirk and Duck. Together, they resolve to go ahead and cleared by their HIV/STD test results, they embark on a celebratory meal at Noshi (Block 1989, 46), followed by what is, implicitly, a night of three-way sex:

> Weetzie changed into her lace negligee from Trashy Lingerie and went into Dirk and Duck's room and climbed into bed between Dirk and Duck … [dialogue omitted]. And that was how Weetzie and Dirk and Duck made the baby – well, at least that was how it began, and no one could be sure if that was really the night, but that comes later on (Block 1989, 46–7).

So Weetzie has sex with both Dirk and Duck and has had sex with My Secret Agent Lover Man before he goes away on a fishing trip. But this is not an uncomplicated fantasy magically satisfying Weetzie's desire. Told that Weetzie is pregnant and that either Duck or Dirk could be the father, My Secret Agent Lover Man leaves. Two girls are born out of this crisis, and become key figures in three of the subsequent novels. The first, Weetzie's child, is named Cherokee Bat, after her own father Charlie Bat. The second, Witch Baby, arises out of a brief encounter between My Secret Agent Lover Man and a Lanka witch, Vixanne Wigg, during the months of his estrangement from Weetzie. The reassurance of 'and lived happily ever after' is thus subject to considerable generic interference: though the household is reconstituted as a family, its composition and the fractured relations between its members continue to produce an unsettled harmony.

When Weetzie's father dies, the legacy of fairy tales is both rejected and rearticulated. Images of closure and comfort – 'happy endings' – associated with fairy tales are, again, undermined. And the more menacing aspects of fairy tales are invoked:

> Grief is not something you know if you grow up wearing feathers with a Charlie Chaplin boyfriend, a love-child papoose, a witch baby, a Dirk and a Duck, a Slinkster Dog, and a movie to dance in. You can feel sad and worse when your dad moves to another city, when an old lady dies, or when your boyfriend goes away. But grief is different. Weetzie's heart cringed in her like a dying animal. It was as if someone had stuck a needle full of poison into her heart. She moved like a sleepwalker. She was the girl in the fairy tale sleeping in a prison of thorns and roses. (Block 1989, 74–5)

The crisis between Dirk and Duck further erodes the scenario of 'wish fulfilment' – itself a fantasy of power and of closure. Their relationship is precarious too and has to be retrieved amidst the bleak circumstances of the AIDS epidemic on the West Coast in the later 1980s. Indeed, the narrative extends beyond Hollywood and Los Angeles, albeit briefly, to San Francisco, specifically to the gay scene there. Finding a bar called the Stud, filled with 'leathered, studded, moustached men in boots ... little surf boys with Lacoste shirts, Levi's, and Vans ... long-haired European-styled model types in black', Dirk gloomily reflects that love has become a 'dangerous angel'. But in this very bar, 'out of all the bars and all the nights and all the people and all the moments', Dirk finds Duck:

> Dirk went up to him and looked into his eyes. Duck dropped his cigarette and his eyes filled with tears. Then he fell against Dirk's shoulders while the lights fanned across the dark dance floor like a neon peacock spreading its tail (Block 1989, 84–5).

This romantic reunion is constructed around one of many allusions to Hollywood film, in this case *Casablanca*. Of course, the allusion is to a sombre and painful 'reunion' and not in fact to a 'happy ending'. The success of Dirk's search is, amidst the disco fantasy of a neon peacock spreading its tail, implicitly qualified. Moreover it's Dirk's grim reflection, that 'love is a dangerous angel', that provides the title for the five collected novels, foregrounding the ambivalence in discourses around sex in the 'post-AIDS' era (Weeks 1995; Richards 2004).

Trouble is provisionally overcome and conflict (almost) forgotten in the reconstitution of the household:

> When they got home, it was a purple, smoggy L.A. twilight. Weetzie and My Secret Agent Lover man and Cherokee and Witch Baby and Slinkster Dog and Go-Go Girl and the puppies Pee Wee, Wee Wee, Teenie Wee, Tiki Tee, and Tee Pee were waiting on the front porch drinking lemonade and listening to Iggy Pop's *Lust for Life* as the sky darkened and the barbecue summer smells filled the air (Block 1989, 87).

Once again the rhythms here (reminiscent perhaps of stories by John Burningham) and the playful names are suggestive of a story to be read aloud to children. In this respect such writing might seem distinctly uninviting to young people typically concerned to distance themselves from childhood. But, as I have argued, Block's standpoint is not that of a teenager anxious to move away from childhood associations or of a 'young adult' author seeking to move readers beyond fantasy to engage with realism. Intertextual reference is made across such boundaries, drawing on what, out of her childhood and youth, is 'to hand'. Myths, fairy tales, children's stories,[9] films and film stars (*Annie, Lost Horizon, Casablanca*, Monroe, Chaplin …), music (The Doors, Jimi Hendrix, Bob Marley, John Lennon, Iggy Pop, Dionne Warwick …), foods (Mexican, Italian, Pacific Rim …) and clothes (Vans, Levi's …) accumulate relentlessly. Is this just consumerist clutter?

In *Consuming Children* (2001), Kenway and Bullen comment:

> Style can also be understood as providing tools for 'constructing personhood', as a statement about who one is and wishes to be. Style allows people to imagine themselves differently; it provides an opportunity to define and redefine themselves; it can be an expression of fantasy – to quote Barthes (1983) 'a dream of identity', and even a 'dream of wholeness', in an age of fragmentation and alienation (Kenway and Bullen 2001, 19).

The argument can be pursued further. In Block's preoccupation with the interrelated matters of style, identity and consumption, there is also a concern with a 'life-politics' (see Giddens 1991; Kenway and Bullen 2001, 159). What Block's characters wear, what they eat and what they listen to seem to function as markers of a restless effort to enact identities (with others) – to hint at affiliations, perhaps even commitments, at odds with prescriptive traditions.

Since the 1998 publication of *Dangerous Angels*, Block's writing has continued both to reassert a central concern with the lives of characters who are teenaged or early twenties and also to pursue issues clearly unwelcome to the censorship lobby seeking to vet the circulation of 'bad books' in schools. Increasingly the age phase explored in her novels is comparable to that of recent, and very popular, TV shows such as *Buffy the Vampire Slayer* and *Dawson's Creek* (Nixon 2000). Thus *Echo* (2001) traces the late teenage, university and immediate post-university life of the eponymous character from a variety of viewpoints. *Nymph* (2000), a collection of interrelated short stories, offers moments of explicit, detailed sex more directly refusing the contract with schools implicit in the earlier formation of the 'young adult' market. *Wasteland* (2003) explores an incestuous brother–sister relationship. *Necklace of Kisses* (2005) revives Weetzie in middle-age, in a period of separation from My Secret Agent Lover Man. Of these, it seems highly unlikely that *Nymph* will ever appear in school libraries, but it is – through the internet – available to her existing readership and engages with issues of sexual identity and diversity inseparable from those addressed elsewhere in her writing.

Conclusion

The attention to and investment in the detail of daily life identified by Giddens in his account of 'lifestyles' might once have been seen as particular to youth and adolescence. But this preoccupation with detail, in combination with uncertainty

---

9   Perhaps, for example, Smith 1987: *The Witch Baby*.

about self-identity, in the Weetzie Bat novels, adds further to their amenability to the process of repositioning pursued by HarperCollins since 1998. And where the preoccupations and dilemmas of Block's characters seem particular to 'adolescence' these can be reframed – as they are on the back cover of *Dangerous Angels* – as enduring concerns almost irrespective of age. Thus 'adolescence', as Griffin (1993) suggests, is offered as salient to everyone for whom sexual identities and sexual relationships, and the futures they might entail, continue to be fluid and uncertain. The relaunching of Block's work in 1998 no doubt increased the sales of her novels and short stories and somewhat extended the range of her readers. But however profitable this strategy may have been, or successful in contributing to a generic shift in 'young adult' fiction, it is clear that the publication of *Dangerous Angels* also extended the audience for writing that, however bounded in its fictional milieu, directly questions many aspects of Christian conservatism.[10]

---

10 Zipes comments on a comparable instance of innovation in fairy tales in Germany in the late 1970s and early 1980s: 'Given the social import and the direct political tendency of the tales to contradict and criticise the dominant socialisation process in West Germany, these tales are not used widely in schools ... They have also been attacked by the conservative press because of their "falsifications" and alleged harmfulness to children. Nevertheless, the production of such tales has not abated in recent years, and such continuous publication may reflect ... the needs of young and adult readers to relate to fantastic projections which are connected more to the concrete conditions of their own reality' ('Who's Afraid of the Brothers Grimm? Socialization and Politicization through Fairy Tales', in Zipes 1991, 66–7).

Chapter 13

Images, Messages and the Paratext in Algerian Women's Writing

Pamela Pears
Washington College

As current events bring the world to focus more and more on Arab and Islamic cultures, popular fiction and non-fiction written by and about women from the Middle East and North Africa have seen a rise in publication.[1] Throughout the 1990s and into the early twenty-first century there has been a veritable boom in the publishing of Algerian writing in France. The cultural television programme, *Bouillon de Culture*, hosted by Bernard Pivot, aired on 18 April 1997 with the theme of Algerian resistance. The popular host's selected bibliography included works by Khalida Messaoudi, political and feminist activist, and Leïla Sebbar, a '*beur*'[2] fiction writer. In 1999 the large multimedia chain, FNAC, featured books by Algerian writers, CDs by various *beurs* and magazines focusing on contemporary Algeria. 2002 marked the 40th anniversary of the end of the Algerian war for independence from the French and also saw the release of numerous commemorative television programmes, special editions of magazines and memoirs. Thus, the North African country of Algeria has for the last two decades been a primary source for texts in France, and with subsequent translations, its presence has been pervasive on the international market. In spite of the numerous books treating the subject of Algerian women, the presentation of these women to the Western literary public remains a relatively complicated task. Undoubtedly many reasons exist that explain the difficulty of such a charge, but one particularly problematic element resides in the paratext of certain publications having Algerian women as their subject. Gérard Genette defines the paratext in the following manner:

> A literary work consists, entirely or essentially, of a text ... But this text is rarely presented in an unadorned state, unreinforced and unaccompanied by a certain number of verbal or other productions ... And although we do not always know whether these productions are to be regarded as belonging to the text, in any case they surround it and extend it, precisely in order to *present* it ... These accompanying productions, which vary in extent and appearance, constitute what I have called ... the work's *paratext* (Genette 1997, 11).

---

1   For example, a cursory glance at the WorldCat database (<http://www.worldcatlibraries. org>) shows a spike in publication numbers from 2001 to 2002. In 2001 the combined total of fiction and non-fiction works with North African or Arab women as their keyword subjects is 158. In 2002, however, it was 179. Since 2002, World Cat indicates that the numbers remain around 150.

2   *Beur* is the commonly used term referring to children of Maghrebian immigrants. They are, therefore, second generation and born in France.

In this discussion I will explore the paratextual elements, primarily the front covers of books, that are used as the immediate means of presenting Algerian women's writing to the Western literary market and examine the implications these marketing techniques have on the reception of the works. Specifically I have chosen four paperbacks that have experienced relative success in France and abroad, represent thematic trends in Algerian fictional writing and whose authors are either Algerian women or somehow directly tied to Algeria. Examining these particular four texts and their covers will ultimately lead to a broader analysis of the target audience and the way in which these books are received in relation to their covers.

The most prevalent image found on the front covers of these books depicts a nameless woman whose eyes are slightly blackened with kohl, a veil covering her forehead, reaching down to the eyebrows, and a scarf hiding the mouth and nose; she serves as a symbol for all Algerian women. This description no doubt reminds us of one of the postcards reproduced in Malek Alloula's 1981 study, *The Colonial Harem*. Alloula's work, which targets images from colonised Algeria of the nineteenth and early twentieth centuries, seeks to condemn the anonymous rendering of Algerian women through this iconography. Alloula specifically demonstrates how Algerian women are commodified and sold to the French and Western public at large in the form of these postcards. Anne McClintock further elucidates this problem by explaining how photography helps carry the colonial enterprise into Western consumer society:

> The colonial photograph (especially in its mass-produced form as postcard) is contradictory in effect. Promising to capture history at a glance and render the appearance of the world exactly as it is, the camera ironically proliferates the world. Instead of producing a finite catalogue of the real, photography expands the territory of surface reality to infinity. The camera thus lures imperial modernity deeper and deeper into consumerism. Hence the intense fetishistic value invested in the colonial photograph (Alloula 1981, 125).

In the twentieth and twenty-first centuries, this same desire to sell the Algerian woman as the exotic other translates into a regressively monolithic project. Marketing this particular fiction relies continually upon clichés or on audience expectations that can be traced back to the colonial era. This discussion examines the variance and contradiction between the interpellation made by book jackets and the content of four paperback editions of popular fictional texts about Algerian women. All of these authors are attempting to write about subjects which they feel are relevant to the contemporary era; therefore the broader discussion in this chapter considers whether the cover design relates to the authors' message or continues to reproduce the colonial images that have pervaded visual media representations of Algerian women.

All of the authors are women, and each has a tie to Algeria. In the case of Nina Bouraoui, whose 1991 edition of *La voyeuse interdite* we will examine, one parent, her mother, is French and her father is Algerian. Bouraoui's nationality is, however, French, and she was born in France.[3] The other two authors, Leïla Marouane and Malika Mokeddem, were born in Algeria but now make their homes in France. We will study Marouane's 2005 work, *La jeune fille et la mère*; and, finally, we will examine

---

3   McIlvanney points out that Bouraoui is a difficult writer to neatly categorise as *beur*, for example (2004, 105–6).

Mokeddem's 1993 novel, *L'interdite*, along with its subsequent American translation, *The Forbidden Woman* (1998). Paperbacks provide an interesting medium to analyse, because their covers often have images or even dust jackets with images. In addition, paperbacks target a wider audience than hardcover versions and appeal more readily to the mass market, because they are cheaper, less cumbersome and disposable.

According to Genette, the *peritext*, '... the cover, the title page, and their appendages ... present to the public at large and then to the reader many ... items of information ...' (Genette 1997, 23). The information shared on the book cover usually will include the author's name, the title of the work and the publisher's name. Occasionally there will be a generic indication, such as 'novel'. The cover image, however, juxtaposed with the book's title, tends to provide the reader with even more of an understanding of the book's content; or at least that is what readers have come to expect. When a potential reader browses in a bookstore, first they glance at the front cover. It is always the first part of the book to be recognised. If the cover does its job effectively, the potential reader will pick up the book and either look through the first few pages or turn the book over in order to glance at the back cover. Depending on the edition and the publishing house, covers may have a standard look and images are not always a part of that. For example, Leïla Marouane's paperback of *La jeune fille et la mère* is published by Seuil and has the standard Seuil cover with merely the author's name, the title of the novel and the indication *roman* (novel). On the very bottom of the front cover is the Seuil insignia. The paperback is nonetheless sold with a dust jacket that has an image on the front cover with a photograph and biographical information about the author on the inside flap. In this way the dust jacket conveys further information to the potential reader. They are drawn to the book because of this cover, which is more evocative of the novel's subject matter than the simple Seuil cover.

The covers of the four books I will discuss all present images of women on their front covers. In 1991 the French press, Gallimard, published Nina Bouraoui's novel, *La voyeuse interdite*, in a folio edition (Figure 13.1). The front cover suggests a veiled woman, although the image does not clearly indicate that she is wearing a veil. At the top of the page both the author's name and the title of the novel appear on a white background. There is a significant amount of white space left entirely blank before a band of orange.

Immediately below this band we meet a woman's gaze. We see nothing more than her brows and her eyes. The bridge of her nose is barely visible; another, wider band of orange quite literally masks the rest of the cover. Although there is no evidence of a veil, the illustration is clearly conveying this idea with the two bands of orange that give the appearance of covering the woman's face and hair. In the gaze there is a defiant stare. The model is looking directly at the reader and appears to have turned her head slightly in order to do so. According to Genette, the front cover may have any number of features, one of which is 'Likeness of the author or, for some biographical or critical studies, of whoever is the subject of the study' (Gennette 1997, 24). Although in this case we are dealing with a work of fiction, it seems likely that the reader is to assume that this young woman is the subject of the novel.

Figure 13.1 *La voyeuse interdite* paperback cover. Reproduced by permission of Editions Gallimard

As the novel begins, the narrator depicts the street that she sees through her window. Slowly we realise that the young woman, Fikria, who watches life on the street outside her window, is virtually imprisoned in her home. Since her active participation in the outside world is banned, her gaze brings it to her. We come to understand her world as one that is entirely located within the house. Throughout the text the most descriptive passages merely depict the interior of her house. She describes in great detail her room, where she spends days biding her time. Her glimpses into the outside world are only what she sees through her window, which she calls a '*hublot*' (Bouraoui 1991, 105). Translated into English, this could mean either a porthole or an aircraft window, both of which are characteristically small and provide only a limited view of the exterior. The cover illustration reflects this view. It is as if we are looking back through the porthole at her; thus, our view is restricted as well. Like the man who will choose Fikria as his wife, we see only a small portion of her face. The 'courtship' consists of his stopping in the street below her window. He never gets out of the car; hence, he glimpses her very narrowly from his car window through her tiny window in the house.

Appropriately the narrative ends after Fikria is betrothed to her suitor. 'With the advent of marriage, all remaining hope is banished' (McIlvanney 2004, 115). The marriage celebration takes place in her home, and we are witness to that in great detail again. However, once she is 'prepared' by the other women and being led down the stairs and out of her building, the narrative comes to an end. We no longer see her; nor will she have any further opportunity to see the outside world. She is about to embark upon her married life, and there is nothing in the text to make us think this newly acquired adult life will be any less confining than her adolescence; as a matter of fact, it appears to be quite the opposite. As Siobhan McIlvanney points out, 'Bouraoui's aim is not to provide an historically detailed representation of Algerian society, but to convey an impression of the isolation and sexually tense, repressive climate experienced by Algerian men and women living in a highly segregated society' (McIlvanney 2004, 106). Thus, Fikria's story gives the reader a mere glimpse into the hidden world of Algerian women. Again, this recalls the colonial postcard project, where French photographers sought to 'unveil' the secrets of the harem: 'Colonial photography ... promised to seek out the secret interiors of the feminised Orient and there capture as surface, in the image of the harem woman's body, the truth of the world' (McClintock 1995, 124). If we see the novel as a metaphoric postcard, then we, as readers, serve the role of voyeur.

The title of the book is *La voyeuse interdite*. A '*voyeuse*' is the feminine form of a '*voyeur*'. It is an interesting use of the term, because while she is in a sense a 'Peeping Tom', who surveys the street below from her small window, she is primarily an observer of the interior of her home and of her family. '... her acquisition of knowledge depends on her seeing without being seen' (McIlvanney 2004, 108). This is the impression we are also given by the front cover of the book. We get but a glimpse of her, and it reveals nothing to us. In reading the book, however, we become the voyeurs. We have an intimate understanding of this young woman's life by the end of the novel. Furthermore, the title's use of the participle '*interdite*' as an adjective also gives a double meaning. It could mean either disconcerted or bewildered, but it also comes from the verb '*interdire*', which means to forbid. The translated English title is *Forbidden Vision*, which takes the agency out of the title but highlights the importance of seeing. Here, we cannot help but understand the forbidden vision to be ours, not the protoganist's. After all, we are the intruders, seeing what is normally forbidden.

Bouraoui's novel was well received in France. She won the Prix Inter, which is a literary prize bestowed by the radio station, France Inter. Created by Paul-Louis Mignon in 1975, the prize is based on a book's popularity among average readers who listen to the radio station. Votes are compiled throughout the year, and in May or June of every year France Inter assembles a jury of 24 radio listeners, presided over by a writer, who then decide from among ten selected finalists. The success of Bouraoui's novel, 140,000 copies sold, came at a time when books by and about Algerian women were prevalent on France's literary scene. The text itself bears witness to the overwhelmingly desperate situation of one young, Algerian woman, but it also draws an implicit parallel between Fikria and Algerian women, in general. Bouraoui herself became something of a celebrity and appeared in magazines, on radio and television programmes.

Bouraoui's prose is unforgivingly violent, deeply visual and haunting, qualities she shares with one of her contemporaries, Leïla Marouane, whose 2005 novel *La jeune fille et la mère* recounts another cycle of hopelessness and violence. As the book opens, the narrator, a young Algerian girl named Djamila, relates her mother's story to us. Although her mother is a former resistance fighter in the Algerian war for independence, she, like many women who participated in the war, retained little freedom following her fight. Her ambitions of attending school and bettering herself through education following the war were swiftly swept aside by her family. When her dream did not become a reality, she patiently waited until she had her own daughter on to whom she could transfer this desire. She unrealistically expects Djamila to do well in school and pass a prestigious entrance exam that will allow her to attend a boarding school for young women. When she fails the exam, however, and loses her virginity before marriage, her mother is convinced that Djamila's life is over; thus, she resorts to inhumane treatment toward her daughter, who represents all of her own failures.

Due to Djamila's transgression of moral boundaries, her mother no longer wishes to protect her. She beats her, imprisons her in the back yard and treats her as a wild animal. Marouane demonstrates the resentment felt by Djamila's mother, who is the most violent aggressor in the book. Although Djamila's father is equally disappointed in his daughter and certainly does not show respect for her, he appears to be less physically violent than her mother. In the end, the young girl's brothers save her from certain death and help her escape; her mother goes crazy and is sent to an asylum.

The dust jacket reflects the dark, violent nature of the book. Without it we would merely see the traditional Seuil cover, which simply states the author's name, the title of the book, the indication *roman* and the publisher's insignia. The dust jacket gives all of this information, but does so with the backdrop of a woman's face. The face itself appears to be just out of our field of vision, because it is barely on the cover. It appears in the upper left-hand corner of the page. The rest of the cover is completely black. We only see half of the face: her one eye and part of her nose and just the very top of her mouth. The entire portrait is conveyed in a bluish colour with yellow splotches, giving the impression of a face covered in shadows and bruises. It is a very dark, foreboding image.

As in the case of *La voyeuse interdite* , the message of *La jeune fille et la mère* appears to be conveyed in part by way of the front cover. The covers of both books and the mysterious gazes of both women serve as powerful tools to sell these works. What is particularly interesting in the case of Marouane's book, however, is the inside front flap, which provides a striking visual contrast to the cover image. Here we find a black and white photo of the smiling author with a brief biographical blurb explaining that Marouane lived in Algeria until 1991. As Kate Douglas points out: 'Book jackets provide the glue binding author and text together; they are the site where the author's biography meets with marketing and criticism' (Douglas 2001, 807). The importance of Marouane's photo along with the biographical blurb lies in the fact that it is situated so closely to the front cover. The representation we have of a 'real' Algerian woman, Marouane, the author herself, is contradictory to both the front cover and the subject matter of the book. Additionally, on the back cover of *La jeune fille et la mère* there is a quotation from the book with a note at the bottom from the editor: '*Un été, dans une famille algérienne, une violence refoulée explose enfin: la haine des femmes, transmise ici de mère en fille*' [One summer, in an Algerian family, a repressed violence finally explodes: women's hatred, transmitted here from mother to daughter].[4] This notation from the editor, along with the selected quotation from the text, certainly reinforces the cover image and the theme of the book. Unlike the photograph on the front cover of Bouraoui's text, the one we have on Marouane's appears to be unambiguous. Bouraoui's cover, as I have discussed, coupled with the title and the theme of the book, creates a voyeuristic space for the reader. It seems to retain similar reader expectations from the early 1990s and carry them forward into the twenty-first century. However, Marouane's more recent novel bypasses the voyeuristic notion of unveiling what happens behind closed doors. Instead, her revelations are more centred on violent after-effects of a failed feminine revolutionary agenda. The disturbing photograph that appears on the dust jacket of her book directly communicates the sinister message of her book.

The case of Malika Mokeddem is slightly different. First, consider the '*Livre de poche*' edition of her novel, *L'interdite*. The narrative voice alternates between that of Sultana, an Algerian woman returning from France to attend a former lover's funeral, and that of Vincent, a French man who has recently undergone a kidney transplant and who learns that the organ donor who saved his life was an Algerian woman. Vincent travels to Algeria in order to make some sort of connection with the woman whose organ he received; whereas, Sultana's trip centres on her coming to terms with both her childhood and the contemporary situation of women in Algeria. Sultana struggles with the limitations that Algerian society has placed on women. When she attempts to run a health clinic in her native small town, Ain Nekhla, she is faced with a staggering number of problems. In order to do the work she would like to do, she must adapt to the restrictions placed on women in the town; and, this is something she refuses to do. Therefore, in spite of her good intentions, she realises that she does not want to stay in Algeria. Ultimately she leaves Algeria and its women behind. The title of the book, *L'interdite*, obviously refers to Sultana. She is both the forbidden one, meaning that she is not accepted by the patriarchal Algerian system, and the silent one, meaning that she is not capable of voicing her concerns. Although she is highly critical of the situation in Ain Nekhla, her outspoken criticism merely raises the ire of the locals.

The cover to Mokeddem's 1993 *Livre de poche* edition of *L'interdite*, unlike the other two book covers we have already examined, does not portray a woman with a defiant stare. The colour photograph that appears beneath the author's name and title of the novel shows a veiled woman from the left side. She is turned away from the camera lens; thus, we do not see any of her features, just the outline of her nose and a small indentation where we assume her left eye to be. In the background we see the veiled outline of what we presume to be another woman; however, none of her features are recognisable given the distance between the photographer's lens and her.

As in the other two novels we have already discussed, the solitary existence of an Algerian woman (here, Sultana) is at the centre of the entire story. In addition, it is Sultana's return from France and her Westernised dress and mannerisms that cause her to stand out even more in Algeria. The photo on the cover of this book seems to be conveying a much different image of Algerian women. The women who appear on the front cover are nameless, virtually faceless representations of Algeria. Unlike the other two covers we have seen, they present no individuality. While the other

---

4   My translation.

two are also nameless (*La voyeuse interdite* and *La jeune fille et la mère*), they do present individual characteristics and appear to evoke the character referenced in the title. Furthermore, on the back cover of this edition we find a black and white photograph of Mokeddem and a short summary of the book. In the photo the author is smiling slightly and looking directly at the camera lens. The final paragraph on the back cover states the following: '*C'est de sa vie et son expérience que Malika Mokeddem a tiré ce roman d'une société déchirée entre préjugés et progrès, religion et fanatisme*' [It is from her life and her experience that Malika Mokeddem has taken this novel about a society torn between prejudices and progress, religion and fanaticism].[5] The editors have, therefore, made a concerted effort to market this book as somewhat autobiographical. If this is indeed the case, the front cover does nothing to reflect the reality of Mokeddem's life or her appearance.

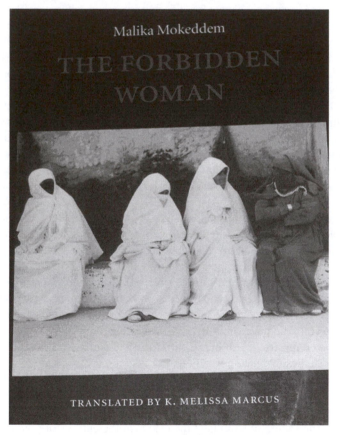

Figure 13.2 The front cover of *The Forbidden Woman* paperback cover reproduced by permission of the University of Nebraska Press. Photograph by Paul Strand: *Four Women*, Essaouira, Morocco, 1962 ©1971 Aperture Foundation Inc., Paul Strand Archive

---

5   My translation.

The English translation of *L'interdite*, *The Forbidden Woman*, similarly mistranslates the message of Mokeddem's book because, as we have seen, although the Algerian women in Ain Nekhla want Sultana to stay and help them in their fight against patriarchal oppression, she ultimately decides to return to her life in France. The photo gracing the cover of the English translation depicts four veiled women who are clearly having a conversation and are united in a community (Figure 13.2). Nothing of the solitary existence that is Sultana's appears on this front cover. In addition, the four women are entirely veiled, with only their eyes visible. As Richard Watts states: '… the photo of veiled women on the cover of Malika Mokeddem's *The Forbidden Woman* implies that the eponymous character is forbidden because veiled, when in fact just the opposite is true – she is forbidden because she does not wear the veil' (2005, 169). The cover stands therefore in direct opposition to Sultana's situation in the text.

Mokeddem's book garnered much success in both France and the United States. Published at around the same time as Bouraoui's *La voyeuse interdite*, Mokeddem's text invokes Western traditions as those which will liberate Algerian women. Her choice of France over Algeria would have played out well in the post-colonial atmosphere of France, especially in the 1990s, when reports of violent civil war in Algeria made daily headlines in French newspapers. *L'interdite* earned a special mention for the Prix Femina literary prize in France. The prize, created in 1904 under the direction of Anna de Noailles, is awarded annually by 22 contributors to the magazine *Femina*, and seeks to honour women writers who the contributors feel are often overlooked by the more established literary prizes. Mokeddem's book, thus, appealed strongly to a female audience who in all likelihood support a Western notion of women's freedom. In the end, then, the book and its popularity can be summed up by what was going on in both France and Algeria at the time.

In the United States, the marketing of Mokeddem's book would have been different. We can see this not only from the cover changes, but also from the preface accompanying the novel. Potential American readers would have perhaps had a more limited understanding or less familiarity with Algeria. Thus, although Mokeddem's account of a woman's return to her native Algeria remains fictitious, the American publishers chose to print the following on the back cover: 'Malika Mokeddem was born into an illiterate nomad family in Kenadsa, Algeria. She had the opportunity, rare for a Moslem female, to attend the university in Oran. Later, she completed her medical studies in Montpellier, France, where she currently practices medicine.' Mokeddem's biography serves as yet another vehicle to sell the book. As Douglas mentions: 'Author profiles are commonly preferred over book reviews or extracts for promoting books' (813). The fictitious story of Sultana is inextricably linked to Mokeddem's life, therefore allowing readers who are unfamiliar with Algerian texts and authors to contextualise the novel.

With all three novels in this study we see the importance of the front cover. Subsequent sales and popular literary prizes (in two cases) document the success of the marketing strategies chosen. In the first two examples (Bouraoui and Marouane) the cover photograph approximates the message of the text; however, for Bouraoui's novel, there remains the question of the regressive colonial project inherent in choosing a photograph that taps into the colonial history of voyeurism and fetishism.

In the case of Mokeddem the message of the text is not apparent thanks to the cover in either the French or the American versions. If anything, the back covers, especially that of the English translation marketed in the United States, contradict the author's message and the theme of the book. Watts explains: 'The covers to Mokeddem's translated works reduce them to a singular dimension through the exaggeration of a thematic element of her texts. The semiotics of the veiled Muslim woman suggest that by reading the novel, one has the opportunity to lift the veil and penetrate into a secret realm, as Delacroix once had' (Watts 2005, 169). This, in fact, takes us back to the problem we encountered with Bouraoui's novel; and we are stuck in the never-changing Occident–Orient battle over images. We run the risk of forever exoticising the Algerian woman and of reducing her to a monolith, in spite of authorial intentions.

Ultimately, a cover photograph carries with it a message, but it also remains open to interpretation. Often this interpretation comes thanks to the text which follows. Mary Vogl, in an analysis of *beur* author Leïla Sebbar's work on photographic images of Maghrebian men and women, explains that 'Sebbar often emphasises the ambivalent nature of a particular representation in order to underscore the idea that it is not the image itself that is positive or negative but rather the way it is viewed and used. Her work exhorts us against passively accepting images or voyeuristically consuming them' (2003, 144). In the cases of the four covers we have seen, it is the way the images are used that requires us to re-evaluate them. No image that appears on the front cover of a book should be ignored or passively accepted, because in every case someone has chosen this particular image in order to sell or market the text that follows. Each individual image, paired with its respective work of fiction, creates an expectation for the potential reader, one that is either mired in stereotypical representations dating back to the colonial era, or one that is directly relevant to the text at hand. It remains to be seen which direction future marketing strategies will take when it comes to selling Algerian women's fiction to a Western readership.

Bibliography

Addams, K., *Warped Desire* (New York: Beacon, 1960).

Agar, M.H., *The Professional Stranger: An Informal Introduction of Ethnography* (San Diego: American Press Inc. [1980] 1996).

Alberge, D., 'Booker Judges Attack "Pretension and Pomposity"', *The Times* (25 September 2002).

Aldiss, B.W. with Wingrove, D., *Trillion Year Spree: The History of Science Fiction* (London: Victor Gollancz, 1986).

Aldridge, A., 'Beatles Not All That Turned On', in Jonathan Eisen (ed.), *The Age of Rock: Sounds of the American Cultural Revolution* (New York: Vintage Books, 1969): 138–46.

Aldridge, A., *The Beatles' Illustrated Lyrics* (Boston/New York/London: Little, Brown, 1998).

Allende, I., *The House of the Spirits*, trans. Magda Bogin (London: Cape, 1985).

Alloula, M., *The Colonial Harem* (Geneva/Paris: Editions Slatkine, 1981).

Andrews, L., *The White Empress* (London: Corgi, 1989).

Andrews, L., *Mist Over the Mersey* (London: Corgi, 1994).

Atwood, M., *The Blind Assassin* (London: Bloomsbury, 2000).

———, 'A Tasty Slice of Pi and Chips', *Sunday Times* (5 May 2002).

Aynsley, J., 'Fifty Years of Penguin Design', in L. Lloyd Jones and J. Aynsley (eds), *Fifty Penguin Years* (London: Penguin, 1985): 107–33.

Bainbridge, W.S., *Dimensions of Science Fiction* (Cambridge MA: Harvard University Press, 1986).

Bainbridge, W.S. and Murray, D., 'The Shape of Science Fiction', *Science Fiction Studies* (5 July 1978): 165–71.

Baines, P., *Penguin by Design: A Cover Story 1935–2005* (London: Allen Lane, 2005).

Ball, S.J., Maguire, M. and Macrae, S., *Choice, Pathways and Transitions Post-16: New Youth, New Economies in the Global City* (London: Routledge/Falmer, 2000).

Ballard, J.G., *The Drowned World* (Harmondsworth: Penguin, 1965).

———, *The Wind from Nowhere* (Harmondsworth: Penguin, 1967).

———, *A User's Guide to the Millennium: Essays and Reviews* (London: HarperCollins, 1996).

Bannon, A., [Ann Thayer/Weldy], *Beebo Brinker* (New York: Fawcett, 1962).

———, *Beebo Brinker* (Tallahassee: Naiad, 1983).

———, *Beebo Brinker* (San Francisco: Cleis, 2001).

———, 'Foreword', in J. Zimet, *Strange Sisters: The Art of Lesbian Pulp Fiction* (Toronto: Penguin Books Canada Ltd, 1999): 1–15.

———, *I am a Woman* (New York: Fawcett, 1959).

———, *I am a Woman* (Tallahassee: Naiad, 1983).

———, *I am a Woman* (San Francisco: Cleis, 2002).

————, *Journey to a Woman* (New York: Fawcett, 1960).

————, *Journey to a Woman* (Tallahassee: Naiad, 1983).

————, *Journey to a Woman* (San Francisco: Cleis, 2003).

————, *Odd Girl Out* (New York: Fawcett, 1957).

————, *Odd Girl Out* (2nd edn, New York: Fawcett, 1957).

————, *Odd Girl Out* (Tallahassee: Naiad, 1983).

————, *Odd Girl Out* (San Francisco: Cleis, 2001).

————, *The Marriage* (New York: Fawcett, 1960)

————, *Women in the Shadows* (New York: Fawcett, 1959).

————, *Women in the Shadows* (Tallahassee: Naiad, 1983).

————, *Women in the Shadows* (San Francisco: Cleis, 2002).

Bannon, A. and Davis, L. E., *Beebo Brinker's Greenwich Village Walking Tour*, Pink Ink Literary Festival. The Publishing Triangle. New York, 12 June 2004.

Bannon, A. and Meaker, M., 'Doyennes of Desire: A Conversation with Two Legendary Writers of Pulp Fiction', Pink Ink Literary Festival. The Publishing Triangle. Lesbian, Gay, Bisexual and Transgender Community Centre, New York, 12 June 2004.

Banville. J., *The Sea* (London: Picador 2005).

Barale, M.A., 'Queer Urbanities: A Walk on the Wild Side', in Cindy Patton and Benigno Sanchez-Eppler (eds), *Queer Diasporas* (Durham NC: Duke University Press, 2000).

Barnicoat, J., *A Concise History of Posters* (London: Thames & Hudson, 1972).

Barthes, R., *The Fashion System*, trans. M. Ward and R. Howard (New York: Hill and Wang, 1983).

————, *Image Music Text* (New York: Hill and Wang, 1977).

Batts, J., 'American Humor: The Mark of Twain on Jerome K. Jerome', in J. Wagner-Lawlor, *The Victorian Comic Spirit: New Perspectives* (Aldershot: Ashgate, 2000).

Baverstock, A., *Are Books Different?* (London: Kogan Page, 1993).

————, *How to Market Books* (3rd edn, London: Kogan Page, 2000).

Baxter, A. 'Market Opens New Chapter for Covers', *Financial Times* (13 September 2005): 10.

Bell, B., Bevan, Jonquil and Bennett, P. (eds), *Across Borders: The Book in Culture and Commerce* (Winchester: St Paul's Biblios, 2000).

Bernard Martin, R., *The Triumph of Wit: A Study of Victorian Comic Theory* (Oxford: Clarendon, 1974).

Blackstock, Colin, 'Booker Winner in Plagiarism Row', *The Guardian* (8 November 2002).

Blake, C., *From Pitch to Publication: Everything You Need to Know to Get Your Novel Published* (London: Macmillan, 1999).

Block, F.L., *Baby Be-Bop* (New York: Joanna Cotler/HarperCollins, 1995).

————, *Baby Be-Bop* (New York: Harper Trophy, 1997).

————, *Cherokee Bat and the Goat Guys* (New York: Charlotte Zolotow/HarperCollins, 1992).

————, *Cherokee Bat and the Goat Guys* (New York: Harper Trophy, 1993).

————, *Dangerous Angels: The Weetzie Bat Books* (New York: HarperCollins, 1998).

————, *Echo* (New York: Joanna Cotler Books/HarperCollins, 2001).

————, *Ecstasia* (New York: Firebird [1993] 2004).

————, *Girl Goddess #9* (New York: Joanna Cotler Books/HarperCollins, 1996).

————, *Girl Goddess #9* (New York: Harper Trophy, 1998).

————, *Guarding the Moon: A Mother's First Year* (New York: Harper Resource/HarperCollins, 2003).

————, *I was a Teenage Fairy* (New York: Joanna Cotler Books/HarperCollins, 1998).

————, *Missing Angel Juan* (New York: HarperCollins, 1993).

————, *Missing Angel Juan* (New York: Harper Trophy, 1995).

————, *Necklace of Kisses* (New York: HarperCollins, 2005).

————, *Nymph* (Cambridge: Circlet Press, 2000, 2003).

————, *Primavera* (New York: Firebird, [1994] 2004).

————, *The Hanged Man* (New York: HarperCollins, 1994).

————, *The Rose and the Beast: Fairy Tales Retold* (New York: Joanna Cotler Books/HarperCollins, 2000).

————, *Violet and Claire* (New York: Joanna Cotler Books/HarperCollins, 1999).

————, *Wasteland* (New York: Joanna Cotler Books/HarperCollins, 2003).

————, *Weetzie Bat* (London: Collins Teen Tracks, 1989).

————, *Weetzie Bat* (New York: Charlotte Zolotow/Harper and Row Junior Books, 1989).

————, *Weetzie Bat* (New York: HarperCollins Juvenile Books, 1991).

————, *Weetzie Bat* (New York: HarperCollins/Joanna Cotler, 1999).

————, *Witch Baby* (New York: Charlotte Zolotow/HarperCollins, 1991).

————, *Witch Baby* (New York: Harper Trophy 1992).

Block, F.L. and Carlip, H., *Zine Scene: The do it yourself guide to zines* (Girl Press, 1998).

Bloom, C., *Bestsellers: Popular Fiction since 1900* (London: Palgrave/Macmillan, 2002).

Bluestone, G., *Novels into Film* (Berkeley: University of California Press, 1966).

Bolonik, K., 'Page to Screen and Back', *Publishers Weekly* 248(40) (October 2001): 17.

Bolter, J.D., MacIntyre, B., Gandy, M. and Schweitzer, P., 'New Media and the Permanent Crisis of Aura', *Convergence: The journal of research into new media technologies* 12(1) (2006): 21.

Book Facts, *Book Facts 2001: An Annual Compendium* (London: Book Marketing Ltd, 2001).

Book Sales Yearbook, *Book Sales Yearbook 2001 An Analysis of Retail Book Sales in the UK during 2000* (London: Bookseller Publications, 2001).

————, *Book Sales Yearbook 2004 Book 1 The Year in Focus: Publishers, Sectors, Trends* (London: Bookseller Information Group, 2004).

Booker 30: A Celebration of 30 Years of The Booker Prize for Fiction 1969–1998 (London: Booker plc, 1998).

Booker, Christopher, *The Neophiliacs: A Study of the Revolution in English Life in the Fifties and Sixties* (London: Collins, 1969).

The Bookseller, 8 April 1936.

————, Front cover, 20 May 1936.

————, 'Christmas in the Bookshops' (7 January 1978): 28–35.

———— (2002a), 'Canongate Sights Booker Uplift' (25 October): 5.

———— (2002b), 'Hallowe'en Bewitches the Charts' (1 November): 11.

——— (2002c), 'Christmas Number One – The Field is Still Wide Open' (8 November): 13.

Borchardt, D.H. and Kirsop, W. (eds), *The Book in Australia: Essays Towards a Cultural & Social History* (Melbourne: Australian Reference Publications, 1988).

Bouraoui, N., *La voyeuse interdite* (Paris: Editions Gallimard, 1991).

Bourdieu, P., *The Field of Cultural Production: Essays on Art and Literature*, trans. Randal Johnson (Cambridge: Polity Press, 1993).

Bradbury, M., *The Social Context of Modern English Literature* (Oxford: Basil Blackwell, 1971).

Bradbury, M. and Wilson, B., 'Introduction', in Robert Escarpit, *Sociology of Literature*, trans. Ernest Pick (London: Frank Cass, [1965] 1971): 7.

British Library Integrated Catalogue online at http://blpc.bl.uk (accessed 16 November 2005).

Brockes, E., '14th Time Lucky', *The Guardian* (12 October 2005).

Brown, C., *Contacts* (London: Cassell, 1935).

Brown, P., 'The Great Thing About …', *The Sun* (25 October 2002).

Buckingham, D., *After the Death of Childhood: Growing Up in the Age of Electronic Media* (Cambridge: Polity Press, 2000).

Burroughs, W., *Nova Express* (London: Panther, 1968).

Bury, L. (2005a), *Expanding the Book Market* (London: Bookseller Publications).

———, 'Yesterday's Novel Format', *The Bookseller* (20 May 2005): 26–7.

Calder, A., *The People's War: Britain 1939–1945* (London: Jonathan Cape Ltd/ Cambridge University Press, 1969).

Carey, J., *The Intellectuals and the Masses: Pride and Prejudice among the Literary Intelligentsia 1880–1939* (London: Faber & Faber, 1992).

———, 'Unconditional Generosity', *London Review of Books* (18 December 2003): 4.

———, *True History of the Kelly Gang* (New York: Knopf, 2000).

———, *True History of the Kelly Gang* (Booker Prize hardback) (St Lucia: Qld: University of Queensland Press, 2000).

———, *True History of the Kelly Gang* (limited edition hardback) (St Lucia: Qld: University of Queensland Press, 2000).

———, *True History of the Kelly Gang* (trade paperback) (St Lucia: Qld: University of Queensland Press, 2000).

———, *True History of the Kelly Gang* (new edition, paperback) (St Lucia: Qld: University of Queensland Press, 2000).

———, *True History of the Kelly Gang* (London: Faber & Faber, 2001).

———, *True History of the Kelly Gang* (New York: Vintage Books, 2001).

———, *True History of the Kelly Gang* (paperback) (St Lucia: Qld: University of Queensland Press, 2001).

Carlip, H., *Girl Power: Young Women Speak Out! Personal Writings from Teenage Girls* (New York: Warner Books, 1995).

Cassell, J. and Jenkins, H., *From Barbie to Mortal Kombat: Gender and Computer Games* (Cambridge: MIT Press, 2000).

Chatman, S., 'What Novels Can Do That Films Can't (And Vice Versa)', in L. Braudy and M. Cohen (eds), *Film Theory and Criticism* (New York: Oxford University Press, 1999): 435–51.

Chevalier, J. and Gheerbrant, A., *The Penguin Dictionary of Symbols*, trans. John Buchanan-Brown (New York: Penguin, 1996).

'Clays', in *Booker 30: A Celebration of 30 Years of The Booker Prize for Fiction 1969–1998* (London: Booker plc): 58.

Clee, N., 'Where the Heart Is', *The Bookseller* (19 December 2003): 26.

Cleis Press, <http://www.cleispress.com/> (19 November 2005).

Clymer, P., Interviewed by the author [Angus Phillips], Chorion offices, London (12 December 2005).

Cohn, N., *Awopbopallbopalopbamboom: Pop From the Beginning* (St Albans: Paladin Collier Books, 1970).

Collin, D., 'Bookmaking: publishers' readers and the physical book', *Publishing History* 44 (1998): 59–76.

Compaine, B. and Gomery, D., *Who Owns the Media? Competition and Concentration in the Mass Media Industry* (Mahway, NJ: Lawrence Erlbaum Associates, 2000).

Confidential memo dated 1934, *The Bodley Head Papers*, University of Reading Library [uncatalogued].

Connolly, J., *Jerome K. Jerome: A Critical Biography* (London: Orbis, 1982).

Connor, S., *The English Novel in History: 1950–1995* (London: Routledge, 1996).

Cook, V.J. Jr and Mindak, W.A., 'Search for Constants: The "Heavy User" Revisited', *Journal of Consumer Marketing* 1(4) (1984): 79–81.

Corrigan, T., *Film and Literature* (Upper Saddle River, NJ: Prentice Hall, 1998).

Corso, G., Ferlinghetti, G. and Ginsberg, A., *Penguin Modern Poets 5* (Harmondsworth: Penguin, 1963).

Coser, L., Kadushin, C. and Powell, W., *Books: The Culture and Commerce of Publishing* (New York: Basic Books, 1982).

Cosgrove, P., 'The Cinema of Attractions and the Novel in Barry Lyndon and Tom Jones', in R. Mayer (ed.), *Eighteenth-Century Fiction on Screen* (Cambridge: Cambridge University Press, 2002).

Crider, B., 'Some Notes on Movie Editions', *Paperback Quarterly* 2(1) (Spring 1979): 32–4.

Currie, E., *She's Leaving Home* (London: Warner Books [1997] 1998).

Curtis, G., *Visual Words: Art and the Material Book in Victorian England* (Aldershot: Ashgate, 2002).

Dalley, J., 'The Future may not be Orange', *Independent on Sunday* (23 February 1997): 4–5.

Damisch, H., 'La culture de poche', in *Mercure de France* 1213 (Paris, 1964).

Darnton, R., 'What is the history of books?', in R. Darnton, *The Kiss of Lamourette: Reflections in Cultural History* (New York: W.W. Norton and Co., 1990): 107–36.

Davis, M., *City of Quartz: Excavating the Future in Los Angeles* (London: Verso, 1990).

Davis, Percy J. to Allen Lane, 6 July 1936; H.L. Mason to E.R. Bennett, 3 December 1936: DM1819, folder 5d, Penguin Archive, Bristol University Library.

de Bellaigue, E., *British Book Publishing as a Business Since the 1960s: Selected Essays* (London: The British Library, 2004).

Dean, J., 'That Special Something', *The Bookseller* (8 July 2005): 26–7.

Di Fate, V., *Infinite Worlds: The Fantastic Visions of Science Fiction Art* (New York: Penguin Studio, 1997).

di Marzo, C., 'Harper Introduces Francesca Lia Block to a Wider Audience', *Publishers Weekly* (18 May 1998): <http://www.publishersweekly.com/article/CA165635.html>, accessed 17 April 2004.

Dietz, H., *Gone with the Wind Souvenir Program* (New York: Greenstone Press, 1939).

Douglas, K., 'Blurbing Biographical: Authorship and Autobiography', *Biography: An Interdisciplinary Quarterly* 24(4) (2001): 806–27.

Drew, N. and Sternberger, P., *By Its Cover: Modern American Book Cover Design* (Princeton NJ: Princeton Architectural Press, 2005).

Dyckhoff, T., 'They've Got it Covered', *The Guardian* (15 September 2001).

Eco, U., *Faith in Fakes* (London: Secker and Warberg, 1986).

Edwards, M., 'SF Publishing: The Economics', in D. Wingrove (ed.), *The Science Fiction Sourcebook* (Harlow: Longman, 1984).

Ellis, H., 'Sexual Inversion', in H. Ellis, *Studies in the Psychology of Sex* 1(1901) (New York: Random House, 1936): 1–384.

English, J.F., 'Winning the Culture Game: Prizes, Awards, and the Rules of Art', *New Literary History* 33(1) (2002): 109–35.

———, *The Economy of Prestige: Prizes, Awards, and the Circulation of Cultural Value* (Cambridge MA: Harvard University Press, 2005).

Escarpit, R., *The Sociology of Literature*, trans. E. Pick (London: Frank Cass, 1971).

Ezard, J., 'Irish Stylist Springs Booker Surprise', *The Guardian* (11 October 2005).

Faurot, R., *Jerome K. Jerome* (New York: Twayne, 1974).

Fay, L., 'Wexford's Winner', *Sunday Times* (16 October 2005).

Feather, J., 'Book Publishing in Britain: An Overview', *Media Culture and Society* 15(2) (April 1993): 167–82.

Feather, J. and Reid, M., 'Bestsellers and the British Book Industry', *Publishing Research Quarterly* 11(1) (1995): 57–75.

Featherstone, M., *Consumer Culture and Postmodernism* (London: Sage Publications, 1991).

Feldman, B., 'Covers that catch the eye: a look at how book jackets influence prospective young readers', *Publishers Weekly* 238(48) (November 1991): 46–8.

Fenwick, G., 'Alan Powers. Front Cover: Great Book Jacket and Cover Design', *Papers of the Bibliographical Society of Canada* 40(2) (Fall 2002): 107–10.

Fetterman, D.M., *Ethnography Step By Step* (London: Sage Publications, 1989).

Filmer, K. (ed.), *Twentieth Century Fantasists: Essays on Culture, Society and Belief in Twentieth Century Mythopoeic Literature* (London: Palgrave, 1992).

Findlater, R., *The Book Writers: Who Are They?* (London: Society of Authors, 1996).

Fischer, T., 'Worthy but Forgettable', *The Guardian* (11 October 2005).

Fish, S., 'Literature in the Reader: Affective Stylistics', *New Literary History* 2 (1) (Autumn 1970): 123–62.

Flanagan R., *Gould's Book of Fish* (London: Atlantic Books, 2002).

———, *Gould's Book of Fish: A Novel in Twelve Fish* (Sydney: Pan Macmillan, 2001).

———, *Gould's Book of Fish* (New York: Grove Press, 2001, 2003).

———, *Gould's Book of Fish* (Sydney: Picador, 2002).

Flynn, K., *A Liverpool Lass* (London: Heinemann, 1993).

———, *Rainbow's End* (London: Heinemann, 1997).

Forrester, H., *Twopence to Cross the Mersey* (London: Jonathan Cape, [1974] 1995).

———, *Three Women of Liverpool* (London: HarperCollins, [1984] 1994).

Fowler, B., *The Alienated Reader: Women and Popular Romantic Literature in the Twentieth Century* (London: Harvester Wheatsheaf, 1991).

Francis, J., *A Sparrow Doesn't Fall* (London: Piatkus, 1990).

———, *Going Home To Liverpool* (London: Piatkus, 1996).

Fredericks, C., *The Future of Eternity: Mythologies of Science Fiction and Fantasy* (Bloomington: Indiana University Press, 1982).

Frith, S., *Sound Effects: Youth, Leisure and the Politics of Rock* (London: Constable, 1983).

———, 'Towards an Aesthetic of Popular Music', in R. Leppert and S. McClary, *Music and Society: The Politics of Composition, Performance and Reception* (Cambridge: Cambridge University Press, 1987).

Frith, S. and Horne, H., *Art into Pop* (London: Methuen, 1987).

Garcia Marquez, G., *One Hundred Years of Solitude*, trans. Gregory Rabassa (London: Cape, 1970).

Gardiner, J., *All on A Summer's Day* (London: Arrow, [1991] 1992).

Geering, K. (ed.), *It's World That Makes the Love Go Round: Modern Poetry Selected from 'Breakthru'* (London: Corgi, 1968).

Genette, G., *Narrative Discourse: An Essay in Method*, trans. J.E. Lewin (Oxford: Blackwell, 1980).

———, *Figures of Literary Discourse*, trans. A. Sheridan (Oxford: Blackwell, 1982).

———, *Paratexts: Thresholds of Interpretation*, trans. J.E. Lewin and R. Mackay (Cambridge: Cambridge University Press, [1987] 1997).

———, 'Les livres vus de dos', *Lire Magazine* (September 2002): 30–40.

Giddens, A., *Modernity and Self-Identity: Self and Society in the Late Modern Age* (Cambridge: Polity Press, 1991).

Giddings, R. and Sheen, E. (eds), *The Classic Novel From Page to Screen* (Manchester: Manchester University Press, 2000).

Giddings, R., Selby, K. and Wensley, C. (eds), *Screening the Novel: The Theory and Practice of Literary Dramatization* (New York: St. Martin's Press, 1991).

Glasgow University Archive Services, UGD243, Wm Collins, Son & Co., Publishers, 1/6/22 Mardersteig 1934 Report.

Goff, M., 'Unconditional Generosity', *London Review of Books* (18 December 2003): 4.

Going, C., 'Writing Sagas for Headline Books', course notes: SAMWAW Weekend, May 1994.

Goldstein, R. (ed.), *The Poetry of Rock* (New York: Bantam, 1969).

Green, E., *Penguin Books: The Pictorial Cover 1960–1980* (Manchester: Manchester Polytechnic Library, 1981).

Green, J., *All Dressed Up: The Sixties and the Counter-Culture* (London: Pimlico, 1998).

Griffin, C., *Representations of Youth: the Study of Youth and Adolescence in Britain and America* (Cambridge: Polity Press, 1993).

———, 'Imagining New Narratives of Youth: Youth research, the 'new Europe' and global youth culture', *Childhood* (8)2 (2001):147–66.

Groves, J., 'Judging literary books by their covers: house styles, ticknor and fields, and literary promotion', in M. Moylan and L. Stiles (eds), *Reading Books: Essays on the Material Text and Literature in America* (Amherst: University of Massachusetts Press, 1996): 75–100.

Hagestadt, E., 'Bridges Over Troubled Waters', *The Independent* (23 April 2004).

Hamblett, C., and Deverson, J., *Generation X* (London: Tandem Books, 1964).

Hamer, D., 'I am a Woman': Ann Bannon and the Writing of Lesbian Identity in the 1950s', in M. Lilly (ed.), *Lesbian and Gay Writing: An Anthology of Critical Essays* (Philadelphia: Temple University Press, 1990): 47–75.

Hamilton, A., 'Clogs By The Aga: The fastsellers of 1993', *The Guardian* (11 January 1994).

———, 'Alex Hamilton's paperback fastsellers of 1999', *The Bookseller* (7 January 2000): 20–23.

Hamilton, D., 'Introduction', in S. Thorgerson and R. Dean (eds), *Album Cover Album* (Limpsfield: Dragon's World, 1977).

Hamilton, R., *Collected Words: 1953–1982* (London: Thames & Hudson, 1982).

Hare, S. (ed.), *Penguin Portrait: Allen Lane and the Penguin Editors 1935–1970* (Harmondsworth: Penguin, 1995).

Harkin, P., 'The Reception of Reader-Response Theory' *College Composition and Communication* 56 (3) (February 2005): 410–25.

Hartley, J., 'The Way We Read Now', *The Bookseller* (1 April 2003): 27–9.

Harvey, D., *The Condition of Postmodernity* (Oxford: Blackwell: 1989).

Heller, S., and Chwast, S., *Jackets Required: An Illustrated History of American Book Jacket Design, 1920–1950* (San Francisco: Chronicle Books, 1995).

Henri, A. McGough, R. and Patten, B., *Penguin Modern Poets 10: The Mersey Sound* (Harmondsworth: Penguin, 1967).

Hewison, R., *Too Much: Art and Society in the Sixties 1960–75* (London: Methuen, 1986).

Hocking, S.K., *Her Benny* (Liverpool: The Gallery Press, [1876] 1968).

Hoggart, R., *The Uses of Literacy* (Harmondsworth: Penguin, 1958 [1957]).

Holland, S., *The Mushroom Jungle: A History of Postwar Paperback Publishing* (Westbury: Zeon Books, 1993).

Hooper, C., *A Child's Book of True Crime* (London: Jonathan Cape, 2002).

———, *A Child's Book of True Crime* (New York: Scribner, 2002).

———, *A Child's Book of True Crime* (Sydney: Vintage, 2002).

———, *A Child's Book of True Crime* (Sydney: Knopf, 2002).

———, *A Child's Book of True Crime* (New York: Scribner, 2003).

Horak, T., 'Film tie-ins can boost audiobook sales', *Billboard* 108(20) (May 1996): 49–50.

Horovitz, M. (ed), *Children of Albion: Poetry of the 'Underground' in Britain* (Harmondsworth: Penguin, 1969).

Howard, A., *All The Dear Faces* (London: Hodder & Stoughton, 1992).

———, *There Is No Parting* (London: Hodder & Stoughton, [1992] 1993).

http://www.goodreports.net.

http://www.u-grenoble3.fr/les_enjeux/2000/Legendre/Legendre.pdf.

Huggan, G., *The Postcolonial Exotic: Marketing the Margins* (London: Routledge, 2001).

Hulme, K., *The Bone People* (London: Hodder & Stoughton, 1985).

Husserl, E., *General Introduction to Pure Phenomenology* (New York: Collier Books, 1962).

Huxley, A., *The Doors of Perception and Heaven and Hell* (Harmondsworth: Penguin, [1954, 1956] 1969).

Hyde, S. (ed.), *Selling the Book: A Bookshop Promotion Manual* (London: Clive Bingley, 1977).

Hyland, A., 'By the Book', *Design Week* (6 October 2005): 14.

Inglis, I., 'Men of Ideas? Music, Anti-Intellectualism and the Beatles', in I. Inglis (ed.), *The Beatles, Popular Music and Society: A Thousand Voices* (Basingstoke/London: Macmillan, 2000): 1–22.

Jakubowski, M. and Edwards, M., *The Complete Book of Science Fiction and Fantasy Lists* (London: Granada, 1983).

Jameson, F., *The Political Unconscious: Narrative as a Socially Symbolic Act* (London: Methuen, 1981).

———, *Postmodernism, or, The Cultural Logic of Late Capitalism* (London: Verso, [1991] 1999).

———, 'Radical Fantasy', *Historical Materialism* 10(4) (2002): 273–80.

Jeffries, S., 'Make Way for Noddy in China', *The Guardian* (22 March 2004).

Jerome, J.K., *My Life and Times* (New York/London: Harper and Brothers, 1926).

———, *Trois Hommes dans un Bateau*, trans. Déodat Serval, (ed.) André Topia (Paris: Flammarion, 1990).

———, *Three Men in a Boat* (Harmondsworth: Penguin, 1994).

Johanson, G., *A Study of Colonial Editions in Australia 1843–1972* (Wellington, New Zealand: Elibank, 2000).

Johnson-Woods, T., *Pulp: A Collector's book of Australian Pulp Fiction Covers* (Sydney: National Library of Australia, 2004).

Jonker, J., *When One Door Closes* (Liverpool: Print Origination (NW), 1991).

———, *Taking A Chance On Love* (London: Headline, 2001).

Jordan, J., 'Animal Magnetism', *The Guardian* (25 May 2002).

Jorgensen, D.L., *Participant Observation: A Methodology for Human Studies* (London: Sage Publications, 1989).

Kästner, H., 75 Jahre Insel-Bücherei 1912–1987: Eine Bibliographie (Leipzig: Insel, 1987).

Katz, E. and Liebes, T., *The Export of Meaning: Cross-Cultural Readings of 'Dallas'* (London: Polity Press, [1993] 2004).

Kean, D. (2005a), 'How to Sell it like Sarah Jessica', *Independent on Sunday* (15 May): 28–9.

——— (2005b), 'The Sassy New Romantics', *The Bookseller* (1 April): 22–3.

Kenway, J. and Bullen, E., *Consuming Children: Education-Entertainment-Advertising* (Buckingham: Open University Press, 2001).

Kerton, P., *The Freelance Writer's Handbook* (London: Ebury Press, 1986).

Kidd, C., Run with the dwarves and win: adventures in the book trade, *Print* 49 (3) (May–June 1995): 21–6.

Koenig-Woodyard, C., 'Gérard Genette, Paratexts: Thresholds of Interpretation.' *Romanticism On the Net* (13, February 1999), http://www.erudit.org/revue/ron/1999/v/n13/005838ar.html, accessed 12 February 2005 and 1 November 2005.

Kotler, P. and Armstrong, G., *Principles of Marketing* (New Jersey: Prentice Hall, 2001).

Kotler, P., Armstrong, G., Saunders, J. and Wong, V., *Principles of Marketing* (Harlow: FT Prentice Hall, 2004).

Lacy, D., 'From Family Enterprise to Global Conglomerate', in E.E. Dennis, E.C Pease and C. LaMay (eds), *Publishing Books* (New Brunswick: Transaction Publishers, 1997): 3–12.

Laczynska, L., 'Do judge a book by its cover', *The Bookseller* (14 March 1997): 49–54.

Laing, S., 'The Politics of Culture: Institutional Change', in Bart Moore-Gilbert and John Seed (eds), *Cultural Revolution? The Challenge of the Arts in the 1960s* (London: Routledge, 1992): 72–95.

Lamb, L., 'Penguin Books: Style and Mass Production' *Penrose Annual* (46) (1952): 39–42.

Lane, A., 'All about the Penguin Books' *The Bookseller* (22 May 1935): 497.

———, 'Penguins and Pelicans', *The Penrose Annual* (40) (1938): 40–42.

Langford, D., *Josh Kirby: A Cosmic Cornucopia* (London: Paper Tiger, 1999).

Larson, R., *Films into Books: An Analytical Bibliography of Film Novelizations, Movie, and TV Tie-ins* (Metuchen NJ: Scarecrow Press, 1995).

Laurel, B., *Computers as Theatre* (Boston: Addison Wesley, 1993).

——— (ed.), *The Art of Human–Computer Interface Design* (Boston: Addison Wesley, 1990).

Le Naire, O., 'A fond les poches', *L'Express* [Paris] (2 January 2003).

Leavis, Q.D., *Fiction and the Reading Public* (London: Bellew, [1932] 1990).

Lee, M., *Lights Out Liverpool* (London: Orion, 1995).

Leitch, T., 'Twelve Fallacies in Contemporary Adaptation Theory', *Criticism* 45 (2) (Spring 2003): 149–71.

'Les livres de poche', *Les Temps Modernes* (227) (April 1965).

Lewis, J., *The Twentieth Century Book: Its Illustration and Design* (London: Studio Vista, 1967).

Livres Hebdo, 'Comment les Français lisent-ils', (506) (21 March 2003): 108–42.

Lloyd-Jones, L., 'Fifty Years of Penguin Books', in *Fifty Penguin Years* (Harmondsworth: Penguin, 1985): 13–103.

London, J., *Gilgamesh* (Sydney: Pan Macmillan, 2001).

———, *Gilgamesh* (New York: Grove Press, 2003).

Loog Oldham, A., 'Six Hip Malchicks', in H. Kureishi and J. Savage (eds), *The Faber Book of Pop* (London: Faber & Faber, [1964] 1995): 216–19.

Lorimer, R. and Scannell, P., 'Editorial', *Media Culture and Society* (15) (1993): 163–6.

Luey, B., 'The 'Book' on Books – Mammon and the Muses', in E.E. Dennis, E.C. Pease and C. LaMay (eds), *Publishing Books* (New Brunswick: Transaction Publishers, 1997): 141–50.

Lundwall, S.J., *Science Fiction: An Illustrated History* (New York: Grosset and Dunlop Inc., 1977).

Lupoff, R.A., *The Great American Paperback: An Illustrated Tribute to Legends of the Book* (Portland: The Collector's Press, 2001).

Lynch, K., *The Image of the City* (Cambridge MA: MIT Press, [1960] 1998).

Lyons, Martin, 'Britain's Largest Export Market', in M. Lyons and J. Arnold (eds), *A History of the Book in Australia 1891–1945: A National Culture in a Colonised Market* (St Lucia: University of Queensland Press, 2001): 21–40.

McAleer, Joseph, *Popular Reading and Publishing in Britain 1914–1950* (Oxford: Clarendon Press, 1992).

McCleery, A., 'The Return of the Publisher to Book History: The Case of Allen Lane', *Book History* (5) (2002): 161–85.

———, 'The 1969 Edition of Ulysses: The Making of a Penguin Classic', *James Joyce Quarterly* (2008).

McClintock, A., *Imperial Leather: Race, Gender and Sexuality in the Colonial Context* (New York: Routledge, 1995).

McCormick, A., 'HC Feeds on the Fear Factor', *The Bookseller* (10 June 2005): 28–9.

McCrum, R., 'Comment: I Want to Tell You a Story', *The Observer* (29 September 2002).

McEvoy, D. and Maryles, D., 'Numbers up; fiction dominates: make way for veterans, movie tie-ins and more novels in all editions', *Publishers Weekly* 251(12) (22 March 2004): 29–35.

McFarlane, B., *Novel to Film: An Introduction to the Theory of Adaptation* (Oxford: Clarendon Press, 1996).

McIlvanney, S., 'Double Vision: The Role of the Visual and the Visionary in Nina Bouraoui's La Voyeuse Interdite (Forbidden Vision)', *Research in African Literatures* 35(4) (2004): 105–20.

McLuhan, M., *Understanding Media: The Extensions of Man* (London: Sphere Books, [1964] 1967).

———, *Counterblast* (New York: Harcourt and Brace, 1969).

Malik, R., 'The Difficult Place of Endnotes in Classics Publishing', *Interfaces: Image, Texte, Langage* 15 (1999).

Malinowski, Bronislaw, 'Subject, Method and Scope', in S. Rapport and H. Wright (eds), *Anthropology* (New York: New York University Press, 1967).

The Man Booker Prize for Fiction (2005a), <http://www.themanbookerprize.com>, accessed 22 November 2005.

——— (2005b), 'Rules and Entry Form', <http://www.themanbookerprize.com/about/2005_rules.pdf>, accessed 8 November 2005.

——— (2005c), 'Public Libraries & The Man Booker Prize: Displays', <http://www.themanbookerprize.com/librarians/displays.php>, accessed 8 November 2005.

Manlove, C.N., *Modern Fantasy: Five Studies* (Cambridge, Cambridge University Press, 1975).

————, *The Impulse of Fantasy* (London: Macmillan, 1987).

Mansfield, J., *Book/Cover* (unpublished masters thesis, Monash University, Australia, 2003).

Marler, R., 'About Cleis: An Interview with Cleis Publishers Felice Newman and Frederique Delacoste', Cleis Press, 19 November 2005, <http://www.cleispress.com/about.html>.

Marouane, L., *La jeune fille et la mère* (Paris: Editions du Seuil, 2005).

Martel, Y., *The Facts Behind the Helsinki Roccamatios and Other Stories* (London: Faber & Faber, 1993).

————, *Self* (London: Faber & Faber, 1996).

————, *Life of Pi* (Edinburgh: Canongate, 2002).

————, 'The Silence and the Fury: Winning the 2002 Man Booker Prize', in *The Man Booker Prize: 35 Years of the Best in Contemporary Fiction 1969–2003* (London: The Booker Prize Foundation, 2003): 31–3.

————, *The Facts Behind the Helsinki Roccamatios and Other Stories* (Edinburgh: Canongate, 2004).

Maryles, D., 'Dead Author's Society', *Publishers Weekly* 243 (3) (15 January 1996): 322.

————, 'Read the Book First', *Publishers Weekly* 248(32) (6 August 2001): 19.

Massie, A., 'In Pi's Magic Circle', *The Scotsman* (11 May 2002).

Matthews, N., 'Collins and the Commonwealth: Publishers' Publicity and the Twentieth Century Circulation of Popular Fiction Titles', in H. Hinks and C. Armstrong (eds), *Worlds of Print* (New Castle DE: Oak Knoll Press/British Library, 2006).

Maughan, S., 'Making the Teen Scene', *Publishers Weekly* (18 October 1999): <http://www.publishersweekly.com/article/CA167490.html>; accessed 17 April 2004.

————, 'Writing with Magic: Interview with Francesca Lia Block', Teenreads.com (10 March 2000): <http://www.teenreads.com/authors/au-block-francesca.asp>, accessed 28 September 2003.

Mayer, R. (ed), *Eighteenth-Century Fiction on Screen* (Cambridge: Cambridge University Press, 2002).

Mayne, R., 'Love in a Hot Climate', *Sight and Sound* 55(2) (Spring 1986): 134.

Mellor, D., *The Sixties Art Scene in London* (London: Phaidon, 1993).

Melly, G., *Revolt Into Style: The Pop Arts in Britain* (Harmondsworth, Penguin, [1970] 1972).

Merril, J., 'What Do You Mean: Science? Fiction?', in T.D. Clareson (ed.), *SF: The Other Side of Realism* (Bowling Green OH: Bowling Green University Press, 1971).

Miles, B., *Paul McCartney: Many Years From Now* (London: Secker & Warburg, 1997).

————, *In the Sixties* (London: Pimlico, 2003).

Miller, L.J., *Reluctant Capitalists: Bookselling and the Culture of Consumption* (Chicago: University of Chicago Press, 2006).

Mintel, 'Books, UK, June 2005 Market Research Report', <http://reports.mintel.com/>.

Mistry, R., *Family Matters* (London: Faber & Faber, 2002).

Mokeddem, M., *L'interdite* (Paris: Editions Grasset & Fasquelle, 1993).

———, *The Forbidden Woman*, trans. K.M. Marcus (Lincoln: University of Nebraska Press, 1998).

Molesworth, M. and Dengeri-Knott, J., 'The pleasures and practices of virtualised consumption in digital spaces', *Digital Games Research Conference 2005: Changing Views: Worlds in Play* (Vancouver, 16–20 June 2005).

Moody, N., 'Maeve and Guinevere: Women's Fantasy Writing in the Science Fiction Market Place', in L. Armitt (ed.), *Where No Man Has Gone Before: Women and Science Fiction* (London: Routledge, 1991).

———, 'The Leaving of Liverpool: Popular Fiction in Context', in G. Norquay and G. Smyth, *Space and Place: The Geographies of Literature* (Liverpool: Liverpool John Moores University Press, 1997): 309–20.

———, 'Are Books Still Different?', *Association for Research in Popular Fictions Newsletter* (16 September 2006).

Moran, J., 'The Role of Multimedia Conglomerates in American Trade Book Publishing', *Media, Culture and Society* 19(3) (July 1997): 441–55.

Morris, M. and Ashton, J., *The Pool of Life: A Public Health Walk in Liverpool* (Liverpool: Maggi Morris/Department of Public Health, 1997).

Moylan, M. and Stiles, L., *Reading Books: Essays on the Material Text and Literature in America* (Amherst: University of Massachusetts Press, 1996).

Mullan, J., 'When It's Acceptable to Judge a Book by Its Cover', *The Guardian* (18 October 2003): 12.

Murphy, E., *The Land is Bright* (London: Headline, 1989).

———, *There is a Season* (London: Headline, 1991).

———, *A Wise Child* (London: Headline, 1994).

———, *Honour Thy Father* (London: Headline, 1996).

Murray, J., *Hamlet on the Holodeck: The Future of Narrative in Cyberspace* (Cambridge MA: MIT Press, 1998).

Naremore, J., *Film Adaptation* (New Brunswick: Rutgers University Press, 2000).

Nile, R. and Walker, D., 'The Mystery of the Missing Bestseller', in M. Lyons and M. Arnold (eds), *A History of the Book in Australia, 1891–1945: A National Culture in a Colonised Market* (St Lucia: University of Queensland Press, 2001).

Niven, A., 'A Common Wealth of Talent', in *Booker 30: A Celebration of 30 Years of The Booker Prize for Fiction 1969–1998* (London: Booker plc, 1998): 40–42.

Nixon, H., 'Dawson's Creek: Sex and Scheduling in a Global Phenomenon', *The English and Media Magazine* 42(3) (November 2000): 25–9.

Noiville, F., 'Angleterre, le Roi Poche', *Le Monde* (6 January 1995).

Nolan, P., 'Re: Movie tie-in inquiry', email to R. Mitchell (10 October 2004).

Oder, N., '"Sense"-ible tie-ins', *Publishers Weekly* 243(1) (1 January 1996): 36.

The Officina Bodoni, *The operation of a Hand-press during the first six years of its work* (Paris/New York: Editiones Officinae Bodoni At the Sign of the Pegasus, 1929).

Ogle, R., Interviewed with O'Neill, G. and Nightingale, J, by the author [Angus Phillips], Random House offices, London, 28 November 2005.

Orange, 'Orange Prize for Fiction Research 2000', <http://www.orangeprize.co.uk>, accessed 21 November 2005.

Orr, J., and Nicholson, C. (eds), *Cinema and Fiction: New Modes of Adapting, 1950–1990* (Edinburgh: Edinburgh University Press, 1992).

Owen, T., and Dickson, D., *High Art: A History of the Psychedelic Poster* (London: Sanctuary Publishing, 1999).

Packer, V., [Marijane Meaker], *Spring Fire* (New York: Fawcett, 1952).

Palacios, J., *Lost in the Woods: Syd Barrett and the Pink Floyd* (London: Boxtree, 1998).

Paperback Writers, 'Towards the Millenium: The Sixties', BBC Radio 3, 18 March 1997 (presented by Andy Martin).

Pauli, M., 'The Middle Way', *The Guardian* (3 May 2005).

Peary, G. and Shatzkin, R. (eds), *The Classic American Novel and the Movies* (New York: Frederick Ungar, 1977).

Pedersen, M., 'To tie in or not to tie in; booksellers dispute the effect of movie edition cover art', *Publishers Weekly* (240) (30 July 1993): 24–6.

Perry, G. and Aldridge, A., *The Penguin Book of Comics* (Harmondsworth: Penguin, 1967).

Petroski, H., *The Book on the Bookshelf* (New York: Knopf, 1999).

Pierre, D.B.C., *Vernon God Little* (London: Faber & Faber, 2003).

Platt, C., 'The Vanishing Midlist', *Interzone* (May–June 1989): 49–50, 72.

Powers, A., *Front Cover: Great Book Jacket and Cover Design* (London: Mitchell Beazley, 2001).

Pressler, K.H., 'Tauchnitz und Albatross: Zur Geschichte des Taschenbuchs', *Börsenblatt für den Deutschen Buchhandel* (8) (29 January 1985): A1–A5.

Pryce-Jones, A., 'The Visual Impact of Books', *Penrose Annual* (46) (1952): 15–18.

Public Lending Right annual 'top 100' most borrowed books at TRENDS, <http://www.plr.uk.com/enhancedindex.htm>, accessed 16 November 2005.

Queer Covers Lesbian Survival Literature Exhibit, curated by Morgan Gwenwald and Micki Trager (New York: Lesbian Herstory Archives, 1993).

Radway, J., *Reading the Romance: Women, Patriarchy and Popular Literature* (Chapel Hill: University of North Carolina Press, 1984).

———, 'Identifying Ideological Seams: Mass Culture, Analytical Method and Political Practice', *Communication* 9 (1986), quoted by A. Ruddock, *Diegesis* (2) (1998): 51.

———, 'The Institutional Matrix of Romance', in S. During, *The Cultural Studies Reader* (London: Routledge ([1993] 2000): 564–76).

———, *A Feeling for Books: the Book-of-the-month club, literary taste, and middle-class desire* (Chapel Hill: University of North Carolina Press, 1997).

Raugust, K., 'Film Tie-ins: A Risky Business', *Publishers Weekly* 248 (20) (14 May 2001): 34.

Rawlinson, N., 'Why Not Judge a Book by its Cover?', *Publishers Weekly* 247 (6) (February 2000): 6.

Ray, A., 'The author-brand identity', *The Bookseller* (22 April 2005): 24–5.

Raymond, H., Harold Raymond to Ralph Pinker, 8 October 1935, MS2444/149, Chatto and Windus letterbook, University of Reading Library.

————, *Publishing and Bookselling: A Survey of Post-war Developments and Present-day Problems* (London: Dent, 1938).

Reid, Suzanne and Hutchinson, Brad, 'Lanky Lizards! Francesca Lia Block Is Fun To Read But … Reading Multicultural Literature in Public Schools', *The Assembly on Literature for Adolescents at the National Council of Teachers of English (ALAN) Review* 21(3) (Spring 1994).

Report on the Canadian Book Trade 1944, 'Printed for the Members and for confidential circulation', Coll. G 2046, London School of Economics Library.

Reynolds, N., 'Now Let's Have Fun, Say Booker Judges', *Daily Telegraph* (25 September 2002).

Rich, A., 'Compulsory Heterosexuality and Lesbian Existence', in A. Jaggar and P. Rothenberg (eds), *Feminist Frameworks* (Toronto: McGraw-Hill, 1984: 416–19.

Richards, C., 'What are we? Adolescence, sex and intimacy in Buffy the Vampire Slayer', *Continuum: Journal of Media and Cultural Studies* 18 (1) (March 2004): 121–37.

Ries, A. and Trout, J., *Positioning: The Battle for Your Mind* (New York, McGraw-Hill, 2001).

Robinson, F.M., *Science Fiction of the Twentieth Century: An Illustrated History* (Portland OR: The Collectors Press, 1999).

Roche, P. (ed.), *Love, Love, Love: The New Love Poetry* (London: Corgi, 1967).

Rose, J., *The Case of Peter Pan or The Impossibility of Children's Fiction* (London: Macmillan, 1984).

Ryan, M.L., *Narrative as Virtual Reality: Immersion and Interactivity in Literature and Electronic Media* (Baltimore/London: Johns Hopkins University Press, 2001).

————, 'Beyond Myth and Metaphor: The Case of Narrative in Digital Media', *Game Studies* (1): 1.

Rylance, R., 'Reading with a Mission: The Public Sphere of Penguin Books', *Critical Quarterly* 47(4) (2005): 48–66.

Sarkowski, H., *Der Insel-Verlag: Eine Bibliographie 1899–1969* (Frankfurt am Main: Insel, 1970).

Schmoller, H., 'The Paperback Revolution', in A. Briggs (ed.), *Essays in the history of publishing in celebration of the 250th anniversary of the House of Longman, 1724–1974* (London: Longman, 1974).

————, 'Reprints: Aldine and After', *Penrose Annual* (47) (1953): 35–8.

Scholes, R. and Rabkin, E.S., *Science Fiction: History Science Vision* (New York: Oxford University Press, 1977).

Schreuders, P., *The Book of Paperbacks: A Visual History of the Paperback Book* (London: Virgin, 1981).

Scliar, M., *Max and the Cats*, trans. Eloah F. Giacomelli (New York: Plume, [1981] 2003).

Sexton, D., 'You can't judge a book by its publisher', *Evening Standard* (19 August 2002): 41.

Shaughnessy, A., 'Balance the Books', *Design Week* (15 April 2004): 18–19.

Shields, C., *Unless* (London: Fourth Estate, 2002).

Shields, S.A., 'When a book cover speaks volumes', *The Chronicle of Higher Education* 49 (39) (6 June 2003): B5.

Silverman, R., 'Judging a book by its cover', unpublished paper from the Mountain Plains Library Association Conference, 1999.

Skeggs, B., *Class, Self, Culture* (London: Routledge, 2004).

Smith, W., *The Witch Baby* (Harmondsworth: Puffin, 1987).

Sontag, S., 'Notes "On Camp": Against Interpretation and Other Essays' (New York: Dell, 1966).

———, *On Photography* (New York: Anchor Books, 1989).

Stam, R., *Literature through Film: Realism, Magic, and the Art of Adaptation* (Oxford: Blackwell, 2005).

Stam, R. and Raegno, A. (eds), *Literature and Film: A Guide to the Theory and Practice of Adaptation* (Oxford: Blackwell, 2005).

Steinberg, S.H., *Five Hundred Years of Printing* (Harmondsworth: Penguin, 1955).

Stover, L., 'Science Fiction, The Research Revolution and John Campbell', *Extrapolation* 14 (2) (May 1973): 129–48.

Strongman, L., *The Booker Prize and the Legacy of Empire* (Amsterdam: Rodopi, 2002).

Stryker, S., *Queer Pulp: Perverted Passions from the Golden Age of the Paperback* (San Francisco: Chronicle Books, 2001).

Sturt-Penrose, B., *The Art Scene* (London/New York: Paul Hamlyn, 1969).

Susina, J., 'The Rebirth of the Postmodern Flaneur: Notes on the Postmodern Landscape of Francesca Lia Block's Weetzie Bat', *Marvels and Tales: Journal of Fairy-Tale Studies* 16 (2) (2002): 188–200.

Sutherland, J., *Bestsellers, Popular Fiction of the 1970s* (London: Routledge and Kegan P., 1981).

———, 'Fiction and the Erotic Cover', *Critical Quarterly* 33 (2) (Summer 1991): 3–18.

———, 'The Judge's Tale', *The Guardian* (12 October 2005).

Svensson, M., Laaksolahti, J., Waern, A. and Höök, K., 'A recipe based online food store', <http://www.sics.se/~martins/publications/chi99.pdf> (2000).

Tanselle, G.T., 'Book Jackets, Blurbs and Bibliographers', *The Library* XXI (2) (1971): 91–123.

Tauchnitz Edition 1931 (Hamburg: Tauchnitz, 1932).

Taylor, D., *It Was Twenty Years Ago Today* (New York and London: Bantam Press, 1987).

Thévenin, P., 'Un faux bon-march', *Les Temps Modernes* 227 (April 1965): 1748–52.

Thorpe, V., 'Booker Covered in Glory', *The Observer* (14 August 2005).

Todd, R., *Consuming Fictions: The Booker Prize and Fiction in Britain Today* (London: Bloomsbury, 1996).

Todd, W.B., 'A New Measure of Literary Excellence: The Tauchnitz International Editions 1841–1943', *Papers of the Bibliographical Society of America* 78 (1984): 333–402.

Tonkin, B., 'The Wrong Choice in a List Packed with Delights', *The Independent* (11 October 2005).

Torres, T., *Women's Barracks* (New York: Fawcett, 1950).

Trevor, W., *The Story of Lucy Gault* (London: Viking, 2002).

Trites, R.S., *Disturbing the Universe: Power and Repression in Adolescent Literature* (Iowa City: University of Iowa Press, 2004).

United States Congress, House Report of the Select Committee on Current Pornographic Materials. 82nd Cong, 2nd sess. House Report 2510 (Washington DC: Government Printing Office, 1952).

Unwin, P.S., 'A New Reading Public?', *The Bookseller* (5 April 1934): 184.

Updike, J., 'Deceptively conceptual: Books and their covers', *The New Yorker* (17 October 2005).

Urry, J., *Consuming Places* (London: Routledge, 1995).

Villanova, R., *Her Woman* (New York: Beacon, 1962).

Villarejo, A., 'Forbidden Love: Pulp as Lesbian History', in E. Hanson (ed.), *Out Takes: Essays on Queer Theory and Film* (Durham NC: Duke University Press, 1999).

Vogl, M., *Picturing the Maghreb: Literature, Photography, (Re)Presentation* (Lanham MD: Rowman & Littlefield, 2003).

Wagner, G., *The Novel and the Cinema* (Madison NJ: Fairleigh University Press, 1975).

Walker, J.A., *Cross-Overs: Art into Pop/Pop into Art* (London: Comedia, 1987).

Warhol, R., *Having A Good Cry* (Columbus: Ohio State University Press, 2003).

Waters, S., *Fingersmith* (London: Virago, 2002).

Watts, R., *Packaging Post/Coloniality: The Manufacture of Literary Identity in the Francophone World* (Lanham MD: Lexington Books, 2005).

Webby, E., 'Introduction', in Franklin, M., *My Brilliant Career* (Sydney: Harper Perennial, 2004).

Weeks, J., *Invented Moralities: Sexual Values in an Age of Uncertainty* (Cambridge: Polity Press, 1995).

Weidemann, K. (ed.), *Book Jackets and Record Covers – An International Survey* (New York: Frederick A. Praeger, 1969).

Weir, A. and Wilson, E., 'The Greyhound Bus Station in the Evolution of Lesbian Popular Culture', in Sally Munt (ed.), *New Lesbian Criticism: Literary and Cultural Readings* (New York: Columbia University Press, 1992): 95–113.

Whitehead, P. (director), *Tonite Let's All Make Love in London* (1967).

Williams, S., 'The Mystery of the Declining Sales', *Survey* 6(2) (Summer 1989): 2–6.

Williams, W.E., *The Penguin Story* (Harmondsworth: Penguin, 1956).

Williamson, V. (2000a), 'Consuming Poverty: Saga Fiction in the Nineties', in N. Moody and J. Hallam (eds), *Consuming for Pleasure: Selected Essays in Popular Fiction* (Liverpool: Association for Research into Popular Fiction/ Liverpool John Moores University Press,): 268–86.

——— (2000b), 'The Role of the Librarian in the Reconfiguration of Gender and Class in Relation to Professional Authorship', in E. Kerslake and N. Moody (eds), *Gendering Library History* (Liverpool: Association for Research into Popular Fiction/Liverpool John Moores University Press, 2000): 163–78.

———, 'Regional Identity – a Gendered Heritage? Reading Women in Nineties Fiction', in S. Caunce, E. Mazierska, S. Sydney-Smith and J.K. Walton (eds), *Relocating Britishness* (Manchester: Manchester University Press, 2004): 183–95.

Wilson, A., *The Design of Books* (New York: Reinhold Publishing Company, 1967).

Winton, T., *Dirt Music* (Sydney: Picador, 2001, 2002).

————, *Dirt Music* (London: Picador, 2002, 2003).

————, *Dirt Music* (New York: Scribner, 2002, 2003).

Wood, J. (2003a), 'The Lie-World', *London Review of Books* (20 November): 25.

———— (2003b), 'Unconditional Generosity', *London Review of Books* (18 December): 4.

Woolf, V., 'Movies and Reality', *The New Republic* XLVII (2 August 1926).

Worpole, K., *Dockers and Detectives: Popular Reading: Popular Writing* (London: Verso, 1983).

————, *Reading by Numbers: Contemporary Publishing & Popular Fiction* (London: Comedia, 1984).

———— (1992a), *Towns for People: Transforming Urban life* (Buckingham: Open University Press).

———— (1992b), 'Lost Cities: Civic & Urban Renewal in Britain Today', The Institute for Cultural Policy Studies, Griffith University, Australia, <http://www. gu.edu.au/centre/cmp/Worpole.html>, accessed 3 January 2003. [Now defunct: activate this link, then try Griffiths University search to find cached version.]

Wyatt, J., *High Concept: Movies and Marketing in Hollywood* (Austin: Texas University Press, 1994).

Wyndham Lewis to Stuart Gilbert, 19 June 1934, Stuart Gilbert Papers 2.3, Harry Ransom Humanities Research Center, University of Texas, Austin.

Young, E., 'The Early Days of Penguins', *The Book Collector* 1(4) (Winter 1952): 210–16.

Zimet, J., *Strange Sisters: The Art of Lesbian Pulp Fiction 1949–1969* (Toronto: Penguin, 1999).

Zipes, J., *Fairy Tales and the Art of Subversion: The Classical Genre for Children and the Process of Civilization* (New York: Routledge. 1991).

————, *Happily Ever After: Fairy Tales, Children, and the Culture Industry* (New York: Routledge, 1997).

————, *Sticks and Stones: The Troublesome Success of Children's Literature from 'Slovenly Peter' to 'Harry Potter'* (London: Routledge, 2002).

Index